DAO Object Model

The Definitive Reference

DAO Object Model
The Definitive Reference

Helen Feddema

O'REILLY®

Beijing · Cambridge · Farnham · Köln · Paris · Sebastopol · Taipei · Tokyo

DAO Object Model: The Definitive Reference
by Helen Feddema

Published by O'Reilly & Associates, Inc., 101 Morris Street, Sebastopol, CA 95472.

Editor: Ron Petrusha

Production Editor: Clairemarie Fisher O'Leary

Cover Designer: Edie Freedman

Printing History:

> January 2000:   First Edition.

ISBN: 1-56592-435-5   [7/00]
[M]

Table of Contents

Preface

Access has an object model, but that isn't where its data is kept. I can recall the first time I tried to work with Access data, from Word VBA code. I set up a reference to the Access type library, then opened the Object Browser with the Access library selected, and looked for objects representing the Access tables and fields that I could use to get at the data I wanted to import into a Word document. I couldn't find anything! There were only a few major components in the Access object model, and none of them had anything to do with data. After some research, I found that what I needed was another object model entirely—DAO (Data Access Objects). Until recently, if you wanted to work with the data stored in Access tables, you had to use DAO. Now there is another object model that can be used to get at data in Access tables—ADO (ActiveX Data Objects)—but DAO is still the primary object model used for manipulating Access data.

What This Book Is About

This book explains all the objects in the DAO object model, down to the fields that contain the data, including their methods and properties. I will let you know where a property or method doesn't work the way Help says it should. Since you might be working with DAO from a variety of applications, I don't just cover using it in Access and Excel VBA, like the examples in Help; my examples include Access, Word, Outlook, Excel VBA, Outlook VBS (used for code behind Outlook forms), and even a few WSH (Windows Scripting Host) examples, so you can see the syntax needed to work with DAO in these dialects of VB (sometimes it is surprisingly different).

What This Book Covers

This book covers the DAO object model that represents Access data; it applies to DAO versions 3.5 to 3.6 (Access 97 to Access 2000), since there are minimal differences between these versions. Basically, DAO 3.6 added support for Jet 4.0 and made some changes in the way non-Access data is handled.

Who This Book Is For

If you need to work with data stored in Access tables from another Office application, in VBA or VBS, this book is for you. Even if you work with DAO exclusively within Access, you will find it handy, especially if you are working with Access 2000, because of a very unfortunate change in the way Help is handled between Access 97 and Access 2000.

Why Not Just Use Online Help?

In Access 97, when you are working with code in a module and you open Help, there is a DAO book in the Help Contents tab. In addition, DAO objects, methods, and properties are listed in the Help index, so you can open these while working in Access VBA code, which is where you need information on these objects.

In Access 2000, however, opening Help from a code module will get you Microsoft Visual Basic Help, which has lots of well-organized information about VBA (as you would expect), but DAO is a different matter. There is no Help book for DAO in the Help index, but there is some DAO information buried in Help, along with information related to the new ADO object model, some of whose objects have the same name as objects in the DAO object model, to make it even more confusing! As is the case with HTML Help in general, if you follow the links from topic to topic, you will find yourself viewing topics belonging to many different applications, since there is no structure in HTML Help to ensure that you remain in a thread of topics appropriate for the language or object model with which you are working.

For example, if you look up "recordset" in the Help index, you will get a list of topics, some of which apply to DAO and some to ADO, and it isn't always easy to tell which object model a topic belongs to. There is no way of examining DAO objects in an organized manner because of the lack of a DAO Help book in the Contents list. HTML Help suffers from the same deficiency as many web search engines, which blindly pull up all topics containing a particular word, regardless of whether they are relevant or not.

To get at the DAO Help topics in Access 2000, you have to open Help from the main Access window and open the DAO book. If you then switch from Help back to Access, open a module, and select Help from the VBE menu, you will get an "Unable to display Help" error message, and Help will switch to the VB Help topics, with a "The page cannot be displayed" message where the Help topic should be. Since Access Help is now less helpful than ever, a DAO reference work which is available when you are working in Access code is essential. Word is, Microsoft is working on an improved interface for Access 2000 Help, but for the time being, Help is more of a hindrance than a useful tool.

How This Book Is Organized

Each chapter in this book covers a DAO collection together with its singular object (or an individual object) and provides a complete reference to that object and its properties and methods. (There are no events in the DAO object model.) The treatment of each collection or object follows a standard format. The collection (or object) is described, summary tables list its properties and methods, and (where appropriate) code samples are given. In addition, the end of the section containing the general description of the collection or object includes an "Access" section that provides you with the following items of information:

- Whether the object is creatable. That is, whether a new instance of a class can be instantiated in VBA by using the New keyword or the *CreateObject* function, or in a scripted environment by using the VBScript *CreateObject* function or an object creation method provided by the scripted environment's object model (such as Server.CreateObject in ASP, for instance). To retrieve a reference to an object that is not creatable (such as a Recordset object), you must either navigate to it, access it through another object's property, or handle it as the return value of another object's method.

- The properties and methods of particular objects that return that type of collection or object.

Each object in the DAO object model is covered, with the exception of the Connection object, which is used only with ODBCDirect.

The treatment of collection and object properties also follows a standardized format, which consists of the following:

- An icon that indicates whether a property is read-only—that is, that a property's value can be retrieved but cannot be set. All other properties are either read-write (which is true of the vast majority of properties) or have an unusual behavior that is explained in the property description.

- The syntax needed to set to retrieve a property for those cases, such as collections and property arrays, where simple assignment does not work.

- The property's data type.

- A description of the property

- Where they are appropriate, tips and suggestions for using the property effectively or for avoiding some pitfall associated with the property.

- Where relevant, a code fragment that uses the property either in VBA code, in VBScript code, or in both.

Collection and object methods also are treated consistently throughout the book. Each entry for the method of a DAO collection or a DAO object includes the following:

- The method's syntax

- A description of the method's parameters

- A general description of the method

- Where they are appropriate, tips and suggestions for using the method effectively or for avoiding some pitfall associated with the method

- Where relevant, a code fragment that uses the method either in VBA code, in VBScript code, or in both

About the CD-ROM

The CD-ROM accompanying *DAO Object Model:The Definitive Reference* includes all the sample code from the book, along with the Object Model Browser, an enhanced object browser for DAO. Unlike the Object Browser, which offers a flat, one-dimensional view of an object browser, Object Model Browser graphically depicts an object model hierarchically, so that you can easily determine how to navigate the object hierarchy or what methods and/or properties return objects of a particular type. For documentation on the Object Model Browser, see the appendixes.

For details on the organization of the CD-ROM as well as any other last-minute changes, see the *ReadMe.txt* file in the root directory of the CD-ROM.

Conventions in This Book

Throughout this book, we've used the following typographic conventions:

`Constant width`
> Constant width in body text indicates a language construct such as a VBA statement (like `For` or `Set`), an intrinsic or user-defined constant, a user-

defined type, or an expression (like `DBEngine.Workspaces.Count - 1`). Code fragments and code examples appear exclusively in constant width text. In syntax statements and prototypes, text in constant width indicates such language elements as the function, procedure, or method's name and any other invariable elements required by the syntax.

`Constant width italic`

Constant width italic in body text indicates argument and variable names. In syntax statements or prototypes, it indicates replaceable parameters.

Italic

Italicized words in the text indicate intrinsic or user-defined functions and procedure names. Many system elements like paths and filenames are also italicized, as are new items.

This symbol indicates a tip.

This symbol indicates a warning

`RO`

Indicates a property that is read-only at runtime. If neither the `RO` nor the `WO` (write-only) icon appears beside a property name, that property is either read-write or its precise read-write status is explained in the description.

How to Contact Us

We have tested and verified all the information in this book to the best of our ability, but you may find that features have changed (or even that we have made mistakes). Please let us know about any errors you find, as well as your suggestions for future editions, by writing to:

O'Reilly & Associates, Inc.
101 Morris Street
Sebastopol, CA 95472
1-800-998-9938 (in the U.S. or Canada)
1-707-829-0515 (international/local)
1-707-829-0104 (fax)

You can also send messages electronically. To be put on our mailing list or to request a catalog, send email to:

info@oreilly.com

To ask technical questions or comment on the book, send email to:

bookquestions@oreilly.com

For our Visual Basic-related web site that includes a discussion forum and featured articles on assorted programming topics, see:

http://vb.oreilly.com

Call for Additions and Amendments

I would be the first to acknowledge that I don't know everything about every component of the DAO object model. If you know how to do something that I said can't be done or have some tips or warnings that might be useful to others, please submit them on the discussion forum at our web site, *http://forums.oreilly. com/~vb/*.

Acknowledgments

My editor at O'Reilly, Ron Petrusha, has been of great help to me in guiding this book through a long process. Originally, the book was to cover both the Access and DAO object models, but when we saw that the number of major objects in the Access 2000 object model had jumped from 6 to 21, we realized that the book couldn't do justice to the Access object model without growing to enormous size. So we decided to split it into two books: the present book on the DAO object model and an upcoming book on the Access object model.

In addition to Ron, Katie Gardner, Tara McGoldrick, and Cheryl Smith at O'Reilly have assisted ably during the process of putting the book together. My thanks also go to my agent, Claire Horne, who was the one who first put together the book project. Thanks to tech editor Russ Darroch for many helpful suggestions, and to Matt Childs for carefully testing the code. Many people associated with *Woody's Office Watch* have been helpful in answering questions and prying information out of Microsoft, particularly Woody Leonhard and Peter Deegan. The readers of *Woody's Access Watch* (I am the editor of this e-zine) have also been helpful in suggesting workarounds for various Access and Office programming problems.

1

Introduction

As Windows versions have progressed, the techniques available for transferring data among Windows applications have improved, from the simple cut and paste available through the Windows 3.0 clipboard, to Dynamic Data Exchange (DDE) and Open Database Connectivity (ODBC), to the presently dominant technique, currently called Automation (it was originally called Object Linking and Embedding, then OLE Automation). With Automation code you can work directly with the components and functionality of applications that support Automation, using their object models.

OLE Servers and Clients

Microsoft used to make a distinction between applications that were OLE servers, which exposed their objects for manipulation by code running from other applications, and OLE clients, which hosted a VB dialect with functions and methods used to manipulate objects in OLE server applications' object models.

In previous versions of Office, some applications were OLE servers only, some were OLE clients only, and some were both OLE clients and servers. With Office 2000, however, all the major Office applications (Access, Word, Excel, Outlook, and PowerPoint) support Automation both as clients and servers, so Microsoft has stopped making this distinction and simply notes that an application supports Automation.

An object model represents the components of an application (or a subset of its components) as a set of objects (usually arranged hierarchically), each of which has properties, methods, and events (though not necessarily all three) that developers can reference in code. Theoretically, any language can access the DAO object model (for example, JScript or Perl running in IIS/ASP, or C/C++). But in real life, Visual Basic for Applications (VBA) or VBScript (VBS) are the most common languages used to work with object models, probably by several orders of magnitude. An *object* generally represents something you work with in the application's interface—for example, Access tables, forms, and reports; Word documents, tables, and words; Excel worksheets, charts, and ranges; and so forth. Additionally, some of the objects in an object model may be collections of other objects, such as the Reports collection in Access (which is a collection of all open Report objects) or the Worksheets collection in Excel (which is a collection of all the Worksheet objects in a particular workbook).

When you write code in a dialect of Visual Basic to work with other applications that support Automation, you need to understand the server application's object model, so that you will be able to reference the appropriate application components as represented in its object model, and use their methods and properties to achieve the desired results. While the names of objects in an object model may be familiar to you from working with the corresponding objects in the interface (for example, Access tables, forms, and reports), in other cases the object names may not be familiar from working in the application's interface (such as the Access Screen and DoCmd objects, the DAO Container objects, the Outlook NameSpace, Explorer and Inspector objects, or the Word Range object.)

 An application's object model may not represent all of the application's functionality. For example, the Outlook object model omits Views, and the Access object model omits Import/Export specifications. The DAO object model avoids such discrepancies, as it has no interface.

Early and Late Binding

Visual Basic for Applications allows you to access an object model using either *early binding* or *late binding*. In contrast, VBScript, because its code is interpreted rather than compiled and because it supports only the Variant data type and does not allow strong typing, supports only late binding.

Late binding means that references to objects in the object model are resolved at runtime; this is because those references cannot be resolved at design time either because precise object types are unknown or because the language does not support early resolution of object references. Typically, in VBA, which supports explicit data typing, this means that object variables are declared to be of the generic Object data type, rather than of more specific object types (like a Database object, a TableDef object, or a Workspace object, for instance).

The VBA code shown in Example 1-1 uses late binding to display the number of records in the Customers table of the Northwind database. The equivalent VBScript code (which is nearly identical) is shown in Example 1-2. Note the use of a named constant for the recordset type argument in the VBA code, while the VBS code uses its numeric equivalent.

 The code in Example 1-1 can use a String variable because String is not a component of an object model. This is possible in VBA code, but not in VBS code, which doesn't permit data typing of any variables.

Example 1-1. VBA Code Using Late Binding

```
Private Sub cmdRecordCountLB_Click()

    Dim objDBEng As Object
    Dim objRS As Object
    Dim objDB As Object
    Dim strDBName As String

    strDBName = "D:\Documents\Northwind.mdb"
    'Use DBEngine.35 for Access 97, DBEngine.36 for Access 2000.
    Set objDBEng = CreateObject("DAO.DBEngine.35")
    Set objDB = objDBEng.OpenDatabase(strDBName)
    Set objRS = objDB.OpenRecordset("Customers", dbOpenTable)

    Debug.Print objRS.RecordCount & " records in Customers table"

    objRS.Close
    objDB.Close

End Sub
```

Example 1-2. VBScript Code Using Late Binding

```
Sub cmdRecordCount_Click()

    Dim dbe
    Dim wks
    Dim dbs
    Dim rst
    Dim strDBName
    strDBName = "D:\Documents\Northwind.mdb"

    Set dbe = Application.CreateObject("DAO.DBEngine.35")
    Set wks = dbe.Workspaces(0)
```

Example 1-2. VBScript Code Using Late Binding (continued)

```
Set dbs = wks.OpenDatabase(strDBName)
Set rst = dbs.OpenRecordset("Customers", 1)
Msgbox rst.RecordCount & " records in Customers"
rst.Close
dbs.Close

End Sub
```

Early binding, on the other hand, involves accessing an automation object's type library (a library that contains information about an object model) to resolve references at design time rather than at runtime. This in turn requires that the development environment produce compiled code; hence, scripting languages such as VBScript cannot support early binding. Taking advantage of early binding requires exact typing of object variables; variables can't be declared as generic objects of the Object data type, but must instead be declared as specific objects defined by the object model.

The VBA code in Example 1-3 is the equivalent of that in Example 1-1, except that it uses early binding. Note that, rather than declaring generic object variables of type Object, the code declares specific object types (the DBEngine, Recordset, and Database objects) defined by the DAO object model. Also note that the code takes advantage of a symbolic constant, **dbOpenTable**, that is defined in the type library.

Example 1-3. VBA Code Using Early Binding

```
Private Sub cmdRecordCountEB_Click()

    Dim dbe As DAO.DBEngine
    Dim dbs As DAO.Database
    Dim rst As DAO.Recordset
    Dim strDBName As String

    strDBName = "D:\Documents\Northwind.mdb"
    'Use DBEngine.35 for Access 97, DBEngine.36 for Access 2000.
    Set dbe = CreateObject("DAO.DBEngine.35")
    Set dbs = dbe.OpenDatabase(strDBName)
    Set rst = dbs.OpenRecordset("Customers", dbOpenTable)

    Debug.Print rst.RecordCount & " records in Customers table"

    rst.Close
    dbs.Close

End Sub
```

Late binding is vastly inferior to early binding in two major respects:

Performance

> Because all object references must be resolved at runtime rather than at design time, in most cases late binding involves an enormous performance penalty. It is not uncommon for a particular operation in late-bound code to consume anywhere from 25% to 1000% more time than the same operation in early-bound code.

Assistance when coding

> Both the Visual Basic and VBA development environments (though not the VBS Script Editor) offer a feature called Auto List Members that allows you to select an item that completes an expression from a popup list box. For example, Figure 1-1 shows the list box that appears when you type *dbs* (the name of a Database object variable) followed by a period, indicating that you want to use a method or property of a Database object. Support for auto list members is not available for late-bound objects.

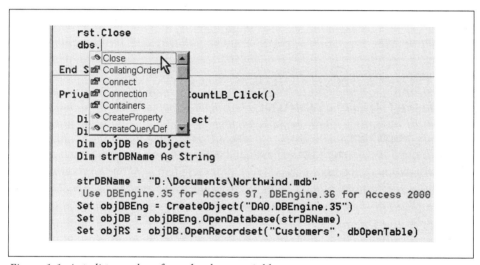

Figure 1-1. Auto list members for a database variable

In other words, unless there's a compelling reason to do otherwise, it's best to take advantage of early-bound object references.

Typically, early binding to a particular object model is made available to VB or VBA by adding a reference to the object library to a project. In VB this is done by selecting the References option from the Project menu; in hosted VBA environments, by selecting the References option from the Tools menu. The result is the References dialog, shown in Figure 1-2, which allows you to select object model references from a list box.

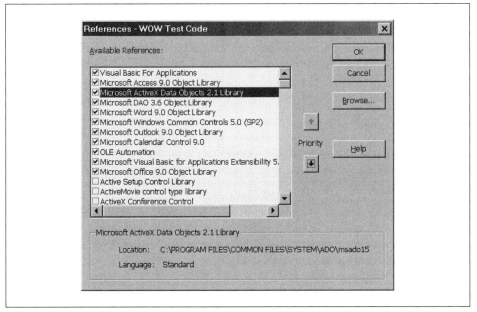

Figure 1-2. The References dialog with references set to the ADO and DAO object libraries

The Object Models for Working with Access

While most applications have only one object model, Access has three: one for the interface, one for data stored in Access databases, and one for data stored in either Access databases or external data sources. (One of them—ADO—is a recent addition to Microsoft's stable of data access technologies and new to Access 2000.)

The Access Object Model

The Access object model (shown in Figure 1-3) represents the Access interface elements (forms, reports, and modules) and a good deal of the application's functionality via the Screen and DoCmd objects. Although there is some overlap of functionality between the Access and DAO object models (via the DBEngine object, located under the Application object), the Access object model is primarily used to work with Access objects, such as forms and reports.

The DAO Object Model

The DAO (Data Access Objects) object model represents the data stored in Access tables. You need to work with the DAO object model both within Access VBA and when working with data stored in Access databases from other applications, using

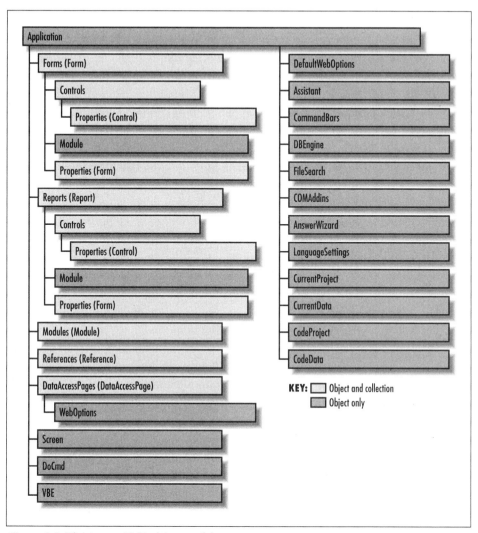

Figure 1-3. The Access 2000 object model

VBA and VBS. The DAO object model is available to anyone who has the Jet engine library installed (this library is fairly easy to redistribute), while in order to use the Access object model, the user must have Access installed on his machine. There are two versions of the DAO object model: one for Jet workspaces (shown in Figure 1-4) and one for ODBCDirect workspaces (shown in Figure 1-5).

When you write code to work with Access, you need the DAO object model to retrieve data from tables, append records to tables, or update data in tables, and you need the Access object model to display forms, print reports, or run macros. Often you will need to use both the Access and DAO object models in the same

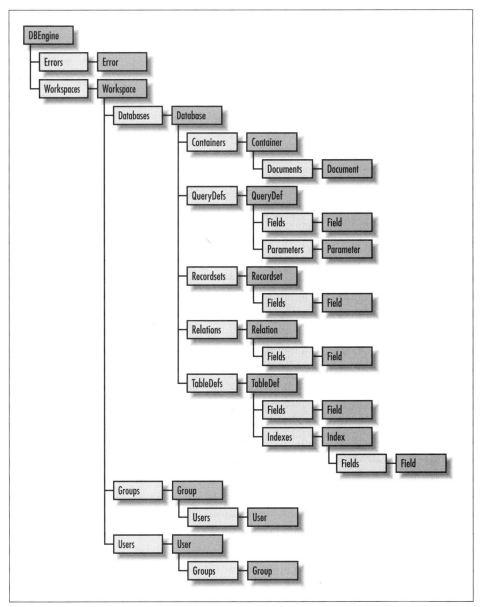

Figure 1-4. The DAO object model for Jet workspaces

procedure. The DAO object model (primarily the more extensive Jet version) is covered in this book; an upcoming book will cover the Access 2000 object model.

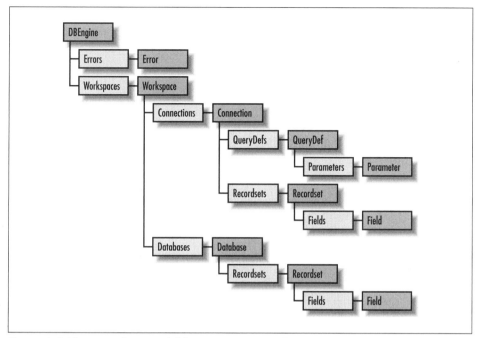

Figure 1-5. The DAO object model for ODBCDirect workspaces

ActiveX Data Objects

The ADO (ActiveX Data Objects, with a silent "X") object model (shown in Figure 1-6) can represent data in Access tables, but it is also used to work with data in external (non-Access) data sources. As a rule of thumb, if you are working exclusively with Access data, you can stick with the DAO object model; if you need to work with data in non-Access data sources, you need the ADO object model. However, ADO is a new (think version 1.0) technology, which many developers consider to be lacking in robustness; many are waiting until the next version to rely on ADO for real-world applications.

Each of the Connection, Command, Recordset, and Field objects also has its own Properties collection, as shown in Figure 1-7.

 See the forthcoming *ActiveX Data Objects: The Definitive Guide*, written by Jason T. Roff and published by O'Reilly & Associates, for more details on the ADO object model.

However, despite concerns about ADO's reliability, there are some circumstances in which ADO code is more efficient for working with Access data, such as using

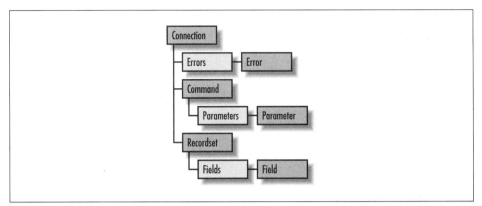

Figure 1-6. The ADO object model

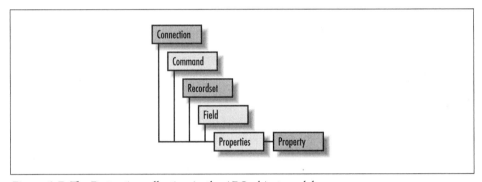

Figure 1-7. The Properties collection in the ADO object model

an ADO recordset to fill the drop-down list of a combo box in place of a cumbersome fill function, or saving a recordset to a file on your computer, which is possible with ADO recordsets but not with DAO recordsets.

If you need to use both the DAO and ADO objects models in your code, bear in mind that they have some identically named objects, recordsets in particular. Even though an object name may be the same in both object models, its functionality may differ in ADO and DAO, which can result in strange bugs in your code. If you have references set to both the DAO and ADO object models (see Figure 1-2) and you don't use prefixes in your code to indicate which object model your database variables belong to, when the code is compiled, variables for objects such as recordsets will be assumed to belong to whichever object model is highest in the list of available object libraries, possibly with unfortunate results. By default, new Access 2000 databases have a reference set to the ADO object library, but not to the DAO object library, while converted databases will usually have a reference set to the DAO object library.

If you get compile errors after converting an Access 97 database to Access 2000, this may be because the ADO reference is located above the DAO reference in the References list. If you don't anticipate using ADO in the database, just uncheck its reference; otherwise, move the DAO reference above the ADO reference in the list, so any ambiguous objects will be interpreted as belonging to the DAO object model.

To prevent confusion (particularly likely with recordsets, which are the most commonly used objects in both object models), use the prefix DAO when declaring a DAO database or recordset and the prefix ADODB when declaring a recordset, as in the following code samples (and Example 1-3):

```
Dim dbs as DAO.Database
Dim rst as DAO.Recordset
Dim rst as ADODB.Recordset
```

(You have to work down to recordsets from databases in DAO, while in ADO you can create a recordset variable directly.)

If you only need to work with a single object model (DAO or ADO) in your code, you can eliminate the need to use prefixes by checking only the appropriate library in the References dialog so as to remove ambiguity in your code. However, it may be prudent to use prefixes even in that case, as you may need to use the other object model at a later time. If you use prefixes right from the start, you won't have to rewrite your code later on when you add the second reference.

The Visual Basic Dialects

You can work with object models in any programming language that supports Automation. For working with Office applications using their object models, generally you will use a dialect of Visual Basic—either Visual Basic (VB) itself, Visual Basic for Applications (VBA), or Visual Basic Scripting Edition (VBS). VBA is well documented in the Help files provided with Office, but VBS is another matter. The documentation for the dialect of VBS used in Outlook is quite inadequate: covering only properties, methods, and events, and omitting functions, operators, keywords, and other language components. Microsoft provides online documentation for VBS at *http://msdn.microsoft.com/scripting/default.htm* (and you can download the documentation to your computer for offline access).

To work with object models representing other applications, you can use the *CreateObject* and *GetObject* functions (or, in some dialects, methods). In some cases, the New keyword can be used when declaring an object using early bind-ing, thus avoiding the need to use *CreateObject* or *GetObject*:

```
Dim appWord As New Word.Application
```

However, different dialects of VB and different Office applications are inconsistent in their support of these features, so you may need to experiment with the New keyword, *CreateObject*, and *GetObject* in a particular procedure to see which is most reliable. Depending on the dialect of VB you are using and the object model you are manipulating, you may get different results. In Outlook VBS, for example, *GetObject* doesn't work at all, while when working with the Outlook object model from another application, there appears to be no difference between using the New keyword and the *CreateObject* method to create an instance of Outlook.

In my experience, sometimes *GetObject* works with Excel worksheets, and some-times it doesn't. When you use the New keyword to create an instance of Word 2000, you can create multiple Word instances by repeated use of the keyword (with different application variables). When you try the same thing with Outlook 2000, however, you won't get any extra instances of Outlook. These differences depend on whether the target application is an SDI (Single Document Interface) application (like Word 2000) or an MDI (Multiple Document Interface) application (like Excel 2000) and perhaps other factors as well.

While working with various dialects of VBA and VBS on several Office applica-tions, I have found the *CreateObject* method to be the most reliable way of creat-ing an instance of an application; it works with all dialects and all target applications. The New keyword works in many cases, and the *GetObject* method works in some cases. Regardless, once you have created an instance of an applica-tion, you can always work down through its object model to the particular compo-nent you need to work with. So *GetObject* is not needed, though if it works in a particular case, it can be a handy shortcut.

 There is a difference between Access and other hosted apps (as well as VB). Since the database engine is always active in Access, you don't have to instantiate a new DBEngine object; with VB and hosted VBA in Word, etc., you do.

VBA and VBS have been upgraded a number of times since their introduction; the VBA versions are listed in Table 1-1, and VBS versions are listed in Table 1-2.

Table 1-1. VBA Versions

Product	VBA Version	Year
Excel 5.0	1.0	1993
Project 4.0	1.0	1994
Excel 95	1.0	1995
Visual Basic 4.0	2.0	1994
Access 95	2.0	1995
Office 97	5.0	1997
Office 2000	6.0	1999

Table 1-2. VBS Versions

Product	VBS Version	Year
Internet Explorer 3.0	1.0	1996
Internet Information Server 3.0	2.0	1997
Internet Explorer 4.0	3.0	1998
Windows Scripting Host 1.0	3.0	1998
Outlook 98	3.0	1998
Visual Studio 6.0	4.0	1998
Internet Explorer 5.0	5.0	early 1999
Internet Information Server 5.0	5.0	early 1999
Preliminary releases of Windows 2000	5.1	late 1999

The main differences between VB, VBA, and VBS are listed in Table 1-3.

Table 1-3. The Visual Basic Dialects

VB	VBA	VBS
Allows you to create a standalone executable	Doesn't support creating a standalone executable; runs from a module or macro	Doesn't support creating a standalone executable; runs from code attached to a form (Outlook), a web page (IE), or a standalone script (WSH)
Must be purchased separately	Included with most Office and other Microsoft applications (substantially the same dialect) and many third-party applications (e.g., AutoCAD)	Included with Internet Explorer, Outlook, and Windows 98 (significantly different dialects)
Has a rich developer's environment	Has a rich developer's environment	Has a limited developer's environment
Has powerful debugging tools	Has powerful debugging tools	Has limited or nonexistent debugging tools
Has a full-featured Object Browser	Has a full-featured Object Browser	Has a limited Object Browser

Table 1-3. The Visual Basic Dialects (continued)

VB	VBA	VBS
Supports data typing of variables	Supports data typing of variables	Does not support data typing of variables (all variables are Variants)
Supports named constants and arguments	Supports named constants and arguments	Offers very limited support for named constants (developers must use numeric values or declare their own constants) and no support for named arguments
Produces compiled code stored in the "document"	Produces compiled code stored in the "document"	Runs from script that is interpreted by Outlook, IE, IIE, or WSH

Given a choice, VBA is generally preferable since it is provided with most Microsoft Office applications. With Office 2000, Outlook finally hosts VBA as well as VBS. In Office 97, Word, Access, Excel, and PowerPoint host VBA, while Outlook only hosts VBS. Internet Explorer 4.x and 5.x host VBS, and Windows 98 includes VBS as well in the form of the Windows Script Host. Additionally, some non-Office Microsoft applications (such as Project) host VBA, as do some non-Microsoft applications, such as Visio (which was recently purchased by Microsoft). VBA also provides the developer with a sophisticated work environment (VBE), unlike VBS with its Notepad-like Script Editor.

If you need to run a procedure directly from an Outlook form, from an IE web page, from an Active Server page or from the Windows command line, you need to write the code in VBS; if the code can be run from Access, Word, Excel, Outlook 2000 (for application-wide code), or PowerPoint, you can use the more powerful VBA dialect. On the other hand, if you need to create a standalone application, you must use VB.

The samples in Example 1-4 and Example 1-5 perform the same actions (running a make-table query and then listing the TableDefs in the Northwind database) in Access VBA and Outlook VBS code.

Example 1-4. Access VBA Code

```
Private Sub cmdExecute_Click()

    Dim wks As Workspace
    Dim dbs As Database
    Dim qdf As QueryDef
    Dim strSQL As String
    Dim tdf As TableDef

    Set wks = Workspaces(0)
    Set dbs = wks.OpenDatabase("D:\Documents\Northwind.mdb")
```

Example 1-4. Access VBA Code (continued)

```
strSQL = _
   "SELECT Orders.*, * INTO tmakNewOrders FROM Orders WHERE OrderDate>#1/6/96#;"
Set qdf = dbs.CreateQueryDef("qmakTestQuery", strSQL)

'Execute a make-table query to produce the tmakRecentOrders table.
qdf.Execute

For Each tdf In dbs.TableDefs
   Debug.Print "Table Name: " & tdf.Name & vbTab & vbTab & _
      "Attributes: " & tdf.Attributes
Next tdf
dbs.Close

End Sub
```

Example 1-5. VBScript Code

```
Sub cmdExecuteQDF_Click()

   Dim dao
   Dim wks
   Dim dbs
   Dim strSQL
   Dim qdf

   Set dao = Application.CreateObject("DAO.DBEngine.35")
   Set wks = dao.Workspaces(0)
   Set dbs = wks.OpenDatabase("D:\Documents\Northwind.mdb")
   Set qdf = dbs.QueryDefs("qmakRecentOrders")

   'Execute a SQL statement to produce the tmakRecentOrders table.
   qdf.Execute

   For Each tdf In dbs.TableDefs
      MsgBox "Table Name: " & tdf.Name
   Next
   dbs.Close

End Sub
```

 Since VBA has a richer developer's environment than Outlook VBS, it is often easier to write and debug a procedure in VBA, then convert it to Outlook VBS.

The following syntactical differences between the VBA and VBS code are typical of the changes you need to make when converting code from VBA to VBS. This would be necessary, for example, if you need to retrieve Access data using the DAO object model for display on an Outlook form:

- There are no data types in VBS, so you can't declare variables as any specific data type.

- In VBA, the bang (!) operator is used to indicate a member of a collection, such as a field in a recordset, while the dot (.) operator is used to indicate methods or properties. In VBS, you must use the dot operator both for members of collections and for properties and methods.

- In VBA, you can use named constants (such as **dbHiddenObject**) as function arguments or as free-standing expression components (such as **vbTab**). In VBS (with a very few exceptions, such as **True** and **False**), you must use the argument's numeric value or define the constant yourself using the **Const** keyword.

- VBS lacks the Debug window, so you need to replace **Debug.Print** calls with *MsgBox* functions.

- The **With...End With** statement is not supported by VBS, so you have to use the full syntax every time you reference a variable.

- When using a looping code structure (such as **For Each...Next**), you can't specify the looping variable—just use **Next** instead of **Next tdf**.

- When you call an object model method from VBA, you have a choice between using positional arguments or named arguments. For example, some developers prefer to write code like the following:

```
Set rst = qdf.OpenRecordset(dbOpenForwardOnly)
```

in which the meaning of an argument is determined by its function call. Others find it easier to write code like the following:

```
Set rst = qdf.OpenRecordset(Type:=dbOpenForwardOnly)
```

in which arguments are identified by their names. In VBScript, you don't have this choice, since VBScript supports only positional arguments.

The following chapters will contain code samples for Access VBA and (where appropriate) one of the other Office VBA dialects, Outlook VBS or WSH (Windows Script Host) VBS, as well, so you can see the syntactical differences in usage between VBA and VBS code.

2

DBEngine Object

The DBEngine object is the highest-level object in the Jet/DAO object model, representing the entire hierarchy of data objects you can manipulate from code. There is only one DBEngine object, and you can't create additional ones. This object corresponds to the Application object that is at the top of most of the Microsoft Office object hierarchies.

DAO has two flavors: Jet and ODBCDirect. The Jet version of DAO lets you access data in Jet databases (basically, Access databases or *.mdb* databases used by other Microsoft applications), Jet-connected ODBC databases, and installable ISAM data sources such as Paradox or Lotus (although ISAM data sources have become much less important in Office 2000). The object model for the Jet version of DAO is shown in Figure 2-1.

The ODBCDirect version of DAO is used to access data sources through ODBC without use of the Jet engine. Its object model is shown in Figure 2-2. This object model lacks some of the components that are needed for working with data in Jet databases. This chapter will cover the more extensive Jet version of the DAO object model.

The DBEngine object contains two collections, Errors and Workspaces, which will be discussed in the next two chapters. The VBA code behind an Access form, shown in Example 2-1, lists the DBEngine object's properties if Access has been started by the user, rather than through automation. The resulting message box is shown in Figure 2-3.

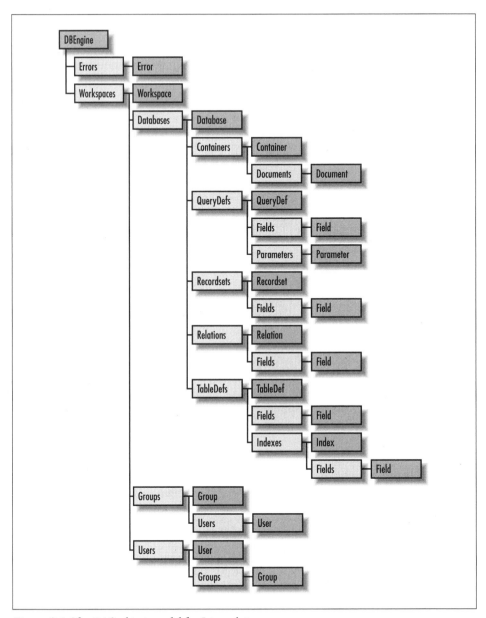

Figure 2-1. The DAO object model for Jet workspaces

Example 2-1. Access Code to Display DBEngine Properties

```
Private Sub cmdDBEngine_Click()

    Call AppProperties(Me)

End Sub
```

Example 2-1. Access Code to Display DBEngine Properties (continued)

```
Private Function AppProperties(obj As Object) As Integer

    Dim objAccess As Access.Application
    Dim i As Integer
    Dim strProperties As String

    On Error Resume Next
    Set objAccess = obj.Application

    If objAccess.UserControl = True Then
        For i = 0 To objAccess.DBEngine.Properties.Count - 1
            strProperties = strProperties & _
                objAccess.DBEngine.Properties(i).Name & vbCrLf
        Next i
    End If

    MsgBox left(strProperties, Len(strProperties) - 2), _
        vbOKCancel, "DBEngine properties"

End Function
```

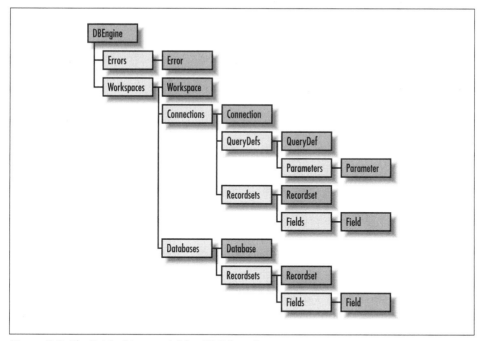

Figure 2-2. The DAO object model for ODBC workspaces

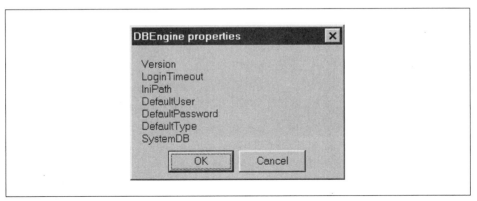

Figure 2-3. DBEngine object properties when Access is started by the user

Although the example in Access Help implies that you will get a different set of properties when Access is started from Automation code rather than by the user, the code in Example 2-2, an Excel VBA function that opens Access using automation code, produces the same listing of properties.

Example 2-2. Excel VBA Code to Display DBEngine Properties

```
Function ListDBEngineProps()

    Dim objAccess As New Access.Application
    Dim i As Integer
    Dim strProperties As String

    If objAccess.UserControl = False Then
        For i = 0 To objAccess.DBEngine.Properties.Count - 1
            strProperties = strProperties & _
                objAccess.DBEngine.Properties(i).Name & vbCrLf
        Next i
    End If

    MsgBox Left(strProperties, Len(strProperties) - 2), _
        vbOKCancel, "DBEngine properties"

End Function
```

Since it is more than likely that there will be several different versions of DAO on any computer (installed by various versions of Microsoft applications), in order to avoid an "ActiveX component can't create object" error, you should append the version number after the DBEngine object reference in your call to the *CreateObject* function, as shown in the following Word VBA and Outlook VBScript code samples. For Access 97, the DAO version ranges from 3.0 (referenced in code as 30) to 3.51 (referenced as 35) depending on whether you have the original release, SR-1, or SR-2; for Access 2000, it is 3.6 (referenced as 36).

The first parameter passed to the VBA *CreateObject* function is a programmatic identifier. When it includes only an object reference (as in DAO.DBEngine), it is a version-independent programmatic identifier. When it includes a version in the object reference (as in DAO.DBEngine.36), it is a version-dependent programmatic identifier. Typically, version-independent programmatic identifiers in the registry are updated to include information about the most recent installed version of that object. DAO, however, does not appear to do this, making it more important that a version-dependent programmatic identifier be used when calling the *CreateObject* function.

In order to use the DAO object model from other applications, such as Word or Outlook, you need to first define a reference to the DBEngine object. Example 2-3 and Example 2-4, both of which use the *CreateObject* function to create an instance of the DBEngine object, show how to do this using VBA for Word and VBScript for Outlook, respectively. The Word VBA code in Example 2-3 imports three fields from the sample Northwind Products table into a Word table that's also created from code (see Table 2-1 for a portion of the table of imported data). The Outlook VBScript code in Example 2-4 imports three fields of data from the Northwind Customers table into a list box on an Outlook form. The Word VBA code in Example 2-3 uses early binding (after setting references to the Access and DAO object libraries) and declares its variables as specific data types; the Outlook VBScript code in Example 2-4 uses late binding and no data types because VBScript does not support early binding or data typing.

Table 2-1. Data Imported into a Word Table from the Northwind Products Table

ID	Product Name	Units in Stock
1	Chai	39
2	Chang	17
3	Aniseed Syrup	13
4	Chef Anton's Cajun Seasoning	53
5	Chef Anton's Gumbo Mix	0
6	Grandma's Boysenberry Spread	120
7	Uncle Bob's Organic Dried Pears	15
8	Northwoods Cranberry Sauce	6
9	Mishi Kobe Niku	29
10	Ikura	31

Example 2-3. Word VBA Code to Access the DBEngine Object

```
Sub FillTableFromAccess()

    Dim dao As DAO.DBEngine
    Dim wks As Workspace
    Dim dbs As Database
    Dim rst As Recordset
    Dim strAccessDir As String
    Dim strDBName As String
    Dim objAccess As New Access.Application

    'Get path to Access database directory from Access SysCmd function.
    Set objAccess = CreateObject("Access.Application")
    strAccessDir = objAccess.SysCmd(9)
    strDBName = strAccessDir & "Samples\Northwind.mdb"
    Debug.Print "DBName: " & strDBName
    objAccess.Quit

    'Set up reference to Access database.
    Set dao = CreateObject("DAO.DBEngine.35")
    Set wks = dao.Workspaces(0)
    Set dbs = wks.OpenDatabase(strDBName)

    'Set reference to Products table.
    Set rst = dbs.OpenRecordset("Products")

    'Create 3-column Word table to fill with Access data.
    ActiveDocument.Tables.Add Range:=Selection.Range, _
        NumRows:=2, NumColumns:=3
    With Selection
        .TypeText Text:="ID"
        .MoveRight Unit:=wdCell
        .TypeText Text:="Product Name"
        .MoveRight Unit:=wdCell
        .TypeText Text:="Units in Stock"
        .MoveRight Unit:=wdCell
    End With

    'Write info from a record in Products to a row of the Word table;
    'loop through recordset until all data has been written to the table.
    Do Until rst.EOF
        With Selection
            .TypeText Text:=rst![ProductID]
            .MoveRight Unit:=wdCell
            .TypeText Text:=rst![ProductName]
            .MoveRight Unit:=wdCell
            .TypeText Text:=rst![UnitsInStock]
            .MoveRight Unit:=wdCell
        End With
        rst.MoveNext
    Loop

End Sub
```

Example 2-4. VBS Outlook Code to Import Data into a Listbox on an Outlook Form

```
Function FillListBox()

    Dim rst
    Dim dao
    Dim wks
    Dim dbs
    Dim ctl
    Dim strAccessDir
    Dim objAccess
    Dim CustomerArray(99, 2)

    'Get path to Access database directory from Access SysCmd function.
    Set objAccess = Item.Application.CreateObject("Access.Application")
    strAccessDir = objAccess.SysCmd(9)
    strDBName = strAccessDir & "Samples\Northwind.mdb"
    'MsgBox "DBName: " & strDBName
    objAccess.Quit

    'Set up reference to Access database.
    Set dao = Application.CreateObject("DAO.DBEngine.35")
    Set wks = dao.Workspaces(0)
    Set dbs = wks.OpenDatabase(strDBName)

    'Retrieve Customer info from table.
    Set rst = dbs.OpenRecordset("Customers")
    Set ctl = Item.GetInspector.ModifiedFormPages( _
            "Filling Combo & List Boxes").Controls("lstCustomers")

    ctl.ColumnCount = 3
    ctl.ColumnWidths = "50; 150 pt; 75 pt"

    'Assign Access data to an array of 3 columns and 100 rows.
    CategoryArray(99, 2) = rst.GetRows(100)

    'Display array data in list box.
    ctl.Column() = CategoryArray(99, 2)

End Function
```

In addition to the 2 collections we've briefly discussed (the Errors and Work-spaces collections), the DBEngine object supports 8 properties (shown in Table 2-2) and 12 methods (shown in Table 2-3).

Table 2-2. DBEngine Properties

Property	Description
DefaultPassword	Defines the type of the next Workspace object to be created
DefaultUser	Defines the user name used to create the default workspace whenever it is initialized
DefaultType	Defines the password used to create the default workspace whenever it is initialized

Table 2-2. DBEngine Properties (continued)

Property	Description
IniPath	Indicates the registry key containing information about Jet engine settings
LoginTimeout	Determines the number of seconds to wait before an attempt to log onto an ODBC database is considered unsuccessful
Properties	Returns a reference to the DBEngine object's Properties collection
SystemDB	Defines the Jet engine's workgroup information file
Version	Indicates the version of the Jet engine

Table 2-3. DBEngine Methods

Method	Description
BeginTrans	Begins a new transaction
CommitTrans	Ends a transaction and saves the changes
CompactDatabase	Compacts a closed database
CreateDatabase	Creates a new database
CreateWorkspace	Creates a Workspace object
Idle	Suspends processing to allow the database engine to complete any pending tasks
OpenConnection	Opens a database connection
OpenDatabase	Opens a database
RegisterDatabase	Stores connection information for an ODBC data source in the system registry
RepairDatabase	Repairs a corrupted database
Rollback	Ends a transaction and discards its changes
SetOption	Temporarily overrides default configuration settings

It's worth emphasizing that all of the members of the DBEngine object are globally available to any VB or VBA application (although not to VBS host applications) that has a reference to the DAO object library. In other words, although you can reference each member of the DBEngine object by explicitly including a reference to the DBEngine object, you can also reference the member without referencing the DBEngine object. For example, the following two statements are identical:

```
Set db = DBEngine.Workspaces(0).Databases(0)
Set db = Workspaces(0).Databases(0)
```

Similarly, the following two method calls are identical:

```
Set db = DBEngine.OpenDatabase(NORTHWIND)
Set db = OpenDatabase(NORTHWIND)
```

The global members of the DBEngine Object are listed in Table 2-4.

Table 2-4. Global Members of the DBEngine Object

DBEngine Member	Type	Global Availability
BeginTrans	Method	Yes
CommitTrans	Method	Yes
CompactDatabase	Method	Yes
CreateDatabase	Method	Yes
CreateWorkspace	Method	Yes
DefaultPassword	Property	Yes
DefaultType	Property	Yes
DefaultUser	Property	Yes
Errors	Property/Collection	Yes
Idle	Method	Yes
IniPath	Property	Yes
LoginTimeout	Property	Yes
OpenConnection	Method	Yes
OpenDatabase	Method	Yes
Properties	Property/Collection	Yes
RegisterDatabase	Method	Yes
RepairDatabase	Method	Yes
Rollback	Method	Yes
SetOption	Method	Yes
SystemDB	Property	Yes
Version	Property	Yes
Workspaces	Property/Collection	Yes

The following sections document the DBEngine object's methods and properties, with the exception of the three properties (Errors, Properties, and Workspaces) that return collections.

Access to the DBEngine Object

Creatable

> Yes

Returned by

> The DBEngine object is the top-level object in the DAO object model.

DBEngine Properties

DefaultPassword `WO`

Data Type

String

Description

When it is initialized, uses a case-sensitive string to set the password used to create the default workspace. The password string can be 1–20 characters in length for Jet workspaces or any length for ODBCDirect workspaces. Any character is permitted except ASCII 0. By default, DefaultPassword is a zero-length string, which means that the database is not password protected. DefaultPassword must be set before the default workspace is used in order to have any effect. Use this method if you want to assign a certain password to all new databases. See the DefaultUser entry for a code sample using this method.

DefaultType `WO`

Data Type

Long

Description

Sets or returns a value dictating what type of workspace (Jet or ODBCDirect) the next Workspace object created will be. The property can be set to the values listed in Table 2-5.

Table 2-5. The Values of the DefaultType Property

Named Constant	Value	Description
dbUseJet	2	Creates Workspace objects connected to the Jet engine
dbUseODBC	1	Creates Workspace objects connected to an ODBC data source

DefaultUser

Data Type

String

Description

When it is initialized uses a string 1–20 characters in length to set the user name used to create the default workspace. Alphabetic characters, accented characters, numbers, spaces, and symbols are permitted, except for the characters listed in Table 2-6, leading spaces, and control characters (ASCII 00 to ASCII 31). By default, DefaultUser is set to "admin."

Normally, user names aren't case sensitive, except when you are recreating a user account created or deleted in another workgroup. In that case, the user name must be a case-sensitive match to the original name.

Table 2-6. Characters Not Permitted in DefaultUser Strings

Character	ASCII Number	Description
"	34	Double quotes
/	47	Forward slash
\	92	Backslash
[	91	Left bracket
]	93	Right bracket
:	58	Colon
		124	Pipe
<	60	Less than
>	62	Greater than
+	43	Plus
=	61	Equal sign
;	59	Semicolon
,	44	Comma
?	63	Question mark
*	42	Asterisk

IniPath

Data Type

String

Description

Sets or returns a value indicating the Windows Registry key containing information about Microsoft Jet database engine settings or parameters needed for installable ISAM (Indexed Sequential Access Method) databases such as Excel, dBASE, and Paradox. This property must be set *before* invoking any other DAO code, or the change has no effect.

You can use either the HKEY_LOCAL_MACHINE or the HKEY_LOCAL_USER key (as a String) with this property. If you don't supply a root key, HKEY_LOCAL_MACHINE will be used as the default. When setting the property, note that the DAO engine does not test for the existence of the registry key; it simply assigns the string you specify to the IniPath property.

The code sample from Access 97 and Access 2000 Help does not work if run from Microsoft Access, presumably because of some "under the hood" initialization of DAO by Access itself. (Recall that the IniPath property must be set before any other DAO code is invoked.) It does work properly if run from Visual Basic or any other VBA-hosted environment.

Word VBA Code

This example shows how to use the IniPath property to retrieve and set the value of the registry key containing information about the Jet database engine or install-able ISAM driver settings, as shown in Figure 2-4.

```
Private Sub cmdIniPath_Click()

On Error GoTo cmdIniPath_ClickError

    Debug.Print "Original IniPath setting = " & _
        IIf(DBEngine.IniPath = "", "[Empty]", DBEngine.IniPath)
        DBEngine.IniPath = _
        "HKEY_LOCAL_MACHINE\SOFTWARE\Microsoft\" & _
        "Jet\3.5\ISAM Formats\Excel 3.0"
    Debug.Print "New IniPath setting = " & _
        IIf(DBEngine.IniPath = "", "[Empty]", _
            DBEngine.IniPath)

cmdIniPath_ClickExit:
    Exit Sub

cmdIniPath_ClickError:
    MsgBox "Error No: " & Err.Number & "; Description: " & Err.Description
    Resume cmdIniPath_ClickExit
End Sub
```

LoginTimeout

Data Type

Integer

Description

Sets or returns the number of seconds allowed before an error occurs when you try to log on to an ODBC database. The default value is 20 seconds. If LoginTime-out is set to 0, no timeout will occur.

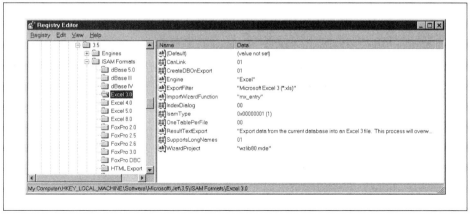

Figure 2-4. The Windows 98 Registry Editor, showing Excel ISAM formats

SystemDB

Data Type

String

Description

Sets or returns the workgroup information file (typically *System.mdw*) for Microsoft Jet workspaces. In the interface, you can change to a different workgroup file by using the Workgroup Administrator applet (*Wrkgadm.exe*), usually found in the Windows system folder for Access 97, and the Office folder for Office 2000. Typically, you need to change to a different workgroup information file in order to log on to a secured database.

Version   `RO`

Data Type

String

Description

Returns a string representing the version of DAO currently in use. Table 2-7 shows how Jet versions map with various Microsoft application versions.

Table 2-7. Jet Engine and Application Versions

Jet Version and Year	Access	Visual Basic	Excel	Visual C++
1.0 (1992)	1.0	N/A	N/A	N/A
1.1 (1993)	1.1	3.0	N/A	N/A

Table 2-7. Jet Engine and Application Versions (continued)

Jet Version and Year	Access	Visual Basic	Excel	Visual C++
2.0 (1994)	2.0	N/A	N/A	N/A
2.5 (1995)	N/A	4.0 (16-bit)	N/A	N/A
3.0 (1995)	95 (7.0)	4.0 (32-bit)	95 (7.0)	4.x
3.5 (1996)	97 (8.0)	5.0	97 (8.0)	5.0
3.6 (1999)	2000 (9.0)	N/A	N/A	N/A

VBA Code

This example reports on the Jet version currently in use in the running database:

```
Private Sub cmdVersion_Click()

    MsgBox "Currently using Jet, v. " & DBEngine.Version

End Sub
```

DBEngine Methods

BeginTrans

```
DBEnginw.BeginTrans()
```

The BeginTrans method is listed in Access 97 Help as a method of the DBEngine object. Actually, it is a method of the Workspace object, one of the members of the Workspaces collection under the DBEngine object, so it will be discussed in Chapter 4, *Workspaces Collection and Workspace Object*. This error has been corrected in Access 2000 Help.

CommitTrans

```
DBEngine.CommitTrans()
```

As with BeginTrans, this method is actually a method of the Workspace object and will be discussed in Chapter 4.

CompactDatabase

```
DBEngine.CompactDatabase srcname, dstname, [dstlocale], [options], [srclocale]
```

Argument	Data Type	Description
srcname	String	The filename (including extension) of a closed database. May include full path and can be in UNC convention (*server1*\ *share1**dir1**db1.mdb*). If *srcname* is currently open, DAO generates runtime error 3049 ("Can't open database…") or 3356 ("You attempted to open a database that is already opened exclusively…").

Argument	Data Type	Description
dstname	String	The filename and path of the new, compacted database. Must be different from *srcname*. If *dstname* already exists, runtime error 3204, "Database already exists," is generated.
dstlocale	Variant	(Optional) Sets the collating order for creating *dstname*. If omitted, the locale is the same as that of *srcname*. See Table 2-8 for a list of constants that can be used for this argument and their values. Help says that you can create a password for *dstname* by concatenating the password string (starting with ";pwd=") with a constant in the *dstlocale* argument to save having to specify two parameters. If *dstname* is to be a password-protected database that uses the same locale as *srcname*, you can omit the *dstlocale* constant and supply just the password preceded by the string ";pwd=".
options	Integer	(Optional) Defines the format (version and encryption) of the database. See Table 2-9 for a list of constants that can be used for this argument, and their integer values. If omitted, the encryption and version of *dstname* is the same as that of *srcname*. If supplied, the version constant must represent the same or a later version than that of *srcname*.
srclocale	Variant	(Optional) For password-protected databases, a Variant containing a String expression. The string ";pwd=" must precede the password. This setting is ignored if you include a password setting in the *dstlocale* argument.

This method must have been changed at the last moment before the release of Office 97, because Access 97 Help incorrectly lists the parameters as *olddb*, *newdb*, *locale*, *options*, and *password*. The correct parameter names are listed in the IntelliSense popup. These incorrect parameter names are still listed in Access 2000 Help.

Table 2-8. The dstlocale Named Constants

Named Constant	Value	Description
dbLangGeneral	";LANGID=0x0409;CP=1252;COUNTRY=0"	English, German, French, Portuguese, Italian, and Modern Spanish
dbLangArabic	";LANGID=0x0401;CP=1256;COUNTRY=0"	Arabic
dbLangChineseSimplified	";LANGID=0x0804;CP=936;COUNTRY=0"	Simplified Chinese
dbLangChineseTraditional	";LANGID=0x0404;CP=950;COUNTRY=0"	Traditional Chinese
dbLangCyrillic	";LANGID=0x0419;CP=1251;COUNTRY=0"	Russian
dbLangCzech	";LANGID=0x0405;CP=1250;COUNTRY=0"	Czech

Table 2-8. The dstlocale Named Constants (continued)

Named Constant	Value	Description
dbLangDutch	";LANGID=0x0413;CP=1252;COUNTRY=0"	Dutch
dbLangGreek	";LANGID=0x0408;CP=1253;COUNTRY=0"	Greek
dbLangHebrew	";LANGID=0x040D;CP=1255;COUNTRY=0"	Hebrew
dbLangHungarian	";LANGID=0x040E;CP=1250;COUNTRY=0"	Hungarian
dbLangIcelandic	";LANGID=0x040F;CP=1252;COUNTRY=0"	Icelandic
dbLangJapanese	";LANGID=0x0411;CP=932;COUNTRY=0"	Japanese
dbLangKorean	";LANGID=0x0412;CP=949;COUNTRY=0"	Korean
dbLangNordic	";LANGID=0x041D;CP=1252;COUNTRY=0"	Nordic languages (Microsoft Jet database engine version 1.0 only)
dbLangNorwDan	";LANGID=0x0414;CP=1252;COUNTRY=0"	Norwegian and Danish
dbLangPolish	";LANGID=0x0415;CP=1250;COUNTRY=0"	Polish
dbLangSlovenian	";LANGID=0x0424;CP=1250;COUNTRY=0"	Slovenian
dbLangSpanish	";LANGID=0x040A;CP=1252;COUNTRY=0"	Traditional Spanish
dbLangSwedFin	";LANGID=0x040B;CP=1252;COUNTRY=0"	Swedish and Finnish
dbLangThai	";LANGID=0x041E;CP=874;COUNTRY=0"	Thai
dbLangTurkish	";LANGID=0x041F;CP=1254;COUNTRY=0"	Turkish

Table 2-9. The Options Named Constants

Named Constant	Value	Description
dbEncrypt	2	Encrypts the database while compacting
dbDecrypt	4	Decrypts the database while compacting
dbVersion10	1	Creates a database that uses the Microsoft Jet database engine version 1.0 file format while compacting
dbVersion11	8	Creates a database that uses the Microsoft Jet database engine version 1.1 file format while compacting
dbVersion20	16	Creates a database that uses the Microsoft Jet database engine version 2.0 file format while compacting

Table 2-9. The Options Named Constants (continued)

Named Constant	Value	Description
dbVersion30	32	Creates a database that uses the Microsoft Jet database engine version 3.0 file format (compatible with version 3.5) while compacting

The CompactDatabase method copies and then compacts a closed database, with options for changing the database's DAO version, collating order, and encryption. The basic functionality of the CompactDatabase method in Access 97 is somewhat different than compacting in the Access 97 interface, where you can use the new compact-in-place functionality, eliminating the need to compact to another database (as in earlier versions of Access). Access 2000 combines Compact and Repair into a single command in the interface, also as an in-place option. The Compact-Database method also offers a few extra choices not available in the interface.

Specifying a different **dbVersion** constant for the compacted database doesn't convert the compacted database to another version of Access—only the data format is affected (for purposes of DAO access). Microsoft Access objects, such as forms and reports, are not affected. To convert a database to another version of Access, you need to select Tools → Database Utilities → Convert Database in the Access interface. The only supported conversion on this menu is from Access 2000 to Access 97.

VBA Code

This code compacts a copy of an Access 97 database with DAO 3.51 code to a database with DAO 2.0 code. The **On Error Resume Next** statement is used before the **Kill** statement so that the **Kill** statement does not generate an error if the *Northwind20.mdb* database does not exist:

```
Private Sub cmdCompact_Click()

    Dim strAccessDir As String
    Dim strDBName35 As String
    Dim strDBName20 As String

    'Get default Access directory from SysCmd function.
    strAccessDir = SysCmd(9)
    strAccessDir = strAccessDir & "Samples\"
    strDBName35 = strAccessDir & "Northwind35.mdb"
    strDBName20 = strAccessDir & "Northwind20.mdb"

    On Error Resume Next
    Kill strDBName20
    DBEngine.CompactDatabase srcname:=strDBName35, _
```

```
        dstname:=strDBName20, _
        Options:=dbEncrypt + dbVersion20

    End Sub
```

 In my experience, using the *dstlocale* parameter to set a new password, with or without a new locale, does not work; the following two code samples (without any error messages) do not create new databases. The third code sample, using the *srclocale* parameter, does create a new database with the new password.

The following three code examples attempt to define a password for the database produced by calling the CompactDatabase method. The first provides a locale (dblangSpanish) and a password in the argument passed to *dstlocale*. The second provides only a password in the *dstlocale* argument. Neither of these procedures successfully compacts the database. The final example, which passes the password in the *srclocale* argument, does work as expected:

```
    Private Sub cmdCompactPW1_Click()

        Dim strAccessDir As String
        Dim strOldDBName As String
        Dim strNewDBName As String

        'Get default Access directory from SysCmd function.
        strAccessDir = SysCmd(9) & "Samples\"
        strOldDBName = strAccessDir & "Northwind.mdb"
        strNewDBName = strAccessDir & "New Northwind 1.mdb"

        On Error Resume Next
        Kill strNewDBName
        DBEngine.CompactDatabase srcname:=strOldDBName, _
            dstname:=strNewDBName, dstlocale:="dblangSpanish;pwd=Mortimer"

    End Sub

    Private Sub cmdCompactPW2_Click()

        Dim strAccessDir As String
        Dim strOldDBName As String
        Dim strNewDBName As String

        'Get default Access directory from SysCmd function.
        strAccessDir = SysCmd(9) & "Samples\"
        strOldDBName = strAccessDir & "Northwind.mdb"
        strNewDBName = strAccessDir & "New Northwind 2.mdb"

        On Error Resume Next
        Kill strNewDBName
```

```
    DBEngine.CompactDatabase srcname:=strOldDBName, _
        dstname:=strNewDBName, dstlocale:=";pwd=Mortimer"

End Sub

Private Sub cmdCompactSetPW3_Click()

    Dim strAccessDir As String
    Dim strOldDBName As String
    Dim strNewDBName As String

    'Get default Access directory from SysCmd function.
    strAccessDir = SysCmd(9) & "Samples\"
    strOldDBName = strAccessDir & "Northwind.mdb"
    strNewDBName = strAccessDir & "New Northwind 3.mdb"

    On Error Resume Next
    Kill strNewDBName
    DBEngine.CompactDatabase srcname:=strOldDBName, _
        dstname:=strNewDBName, srclocale:=";pwd=Mortimer"

End Sub
```

CreateDatabase

The CreateDatabase method is listed in Help as a method of the DBEngine object, but actually it is a method of a Workspace object in the Workspaces collection under the DBEngine object, so it will be discussed in Chapter 4. This error remains in Access 2000 Help.

CreateWorkspace

```
Set workspace = CreateWorkspace(name, username, password, [usetype])
```

Argument	Data Type	Description
workspace	Workspace object	The Workspace object you are creating.
name	String	The name of the new Workspace object. Must be unique.
username	String	The new Workspace's owner.
password	String	The new Workspace's password. Can be up to 14 characters long and can include any characters except ASCII Character 0 (Null).
usetype	Integer	(Optional) A named constant or Integer value indicating the workspace type (see Table 2-10).

Creates a second workspace within the DBEngine object. The first (default) workspace is created automatically, so you need to use this method only in the rare cases in which you need to work with two or more workspaces simultaneously.

Workspaces aren't permanent and can't be saved to disk. Once created, only the Workspace object's Name property can be altered, and that property can only be altered before appending the new Workspace to the Workspaces collection.

When calling CreateWorkspace, it is not necessary to specify DBEngine before the method call.

Table 2-10. The Type Intrinsic Constants

Named Constant	Value	Description
dbUseJet	2	Creates a Jet workspace
dbUseODBC	1	Creates an ODBCDirect workspace

Idle

```
DBEngine.Idle[dbRefreshCache]
```

This method suspends data processing so the Jet database engine can complete any pending tasks, such as memory optimization or page timeouts. The optional **dbRefreshCache** argument forces any pending writes to *.mdb* files and refreshes memory with current data from the *.mdb* file.

There is no point in using this method in single-user environments, unless you are running multiple instances of an application. In multi-user situations, it may improve performance since it forces the database engine to write data to the disk, releasing memory locks.

VBA Code

This example uses the Idle method (run from a function called from the procedure) to ensure that an output procedure uses the most current data available from the database:

```
Private Sub cmdIdle_Click()

On Error GoTo cmdIdle_ClickError

    Dim strAccessDir As String
    Dim strDBName As String
    Dim dbs As Database
    Dim strCountry As String
    Dim strSQL As String
    Dim rstOrders As Recordset
```

```
      strAccessDir = SysCmd(9)
      strAccessDir = strAccessDir & "Samples\"
      strDBName = strAccessDir & "Northwind.mdb"
      Set dbs = OpenDatabase(strDBName)

      'Get name of country from user and build SQL statement with it.
      strCountry = Trim(InputBox("Enter country:"))
      strSQL = "SELECT * FROM Orders WHERE ShipCountry = '" & _
         strCountry & "' ORDER BY OrderID"

      'Open Recordset object with SQL statement.
      Set rstOrders = dbs.OpenRecordset(strSQL)

      'Display contents of Recordset object.
      IdleOutput rstOrders, strCountry

      rstOrders.Close
      dbs.Close

   cmdIdle_ClickExit:
      Exit Sub

   cmdIdle_ClickError:
      MsgBox "Error No: " & Err.Number & "; Description: " & Err.Description
      Resume cmdIdle_ClickExit

   End Sub

   Sub IdleOutput(rstTemp As Recordset, strTemp As String)

      'Call the Idle method to release unneeded locks, force
      'pending writes, and refresh the memory with the current
      'data in the .mdb file.
      DBEngine.Idle dbRefreshCache

      'Enumerate the Recordset object.
      With rstTemp
         Debug.Print "Orders from " & strTemp & ":"
         Debug.Print , "OrderID", "CustomerID", "OrderDate"
         Do While Not .EOF
            Debug.Print , !OrderID, !CustomerID, !OrderDate
            .MoveNext
         Loop
      End With

   End Sub
```

OpenDatabase

This method is listed in Help as a method of the DBEngine object, but actually it is a method of a Workspace object in the Workspaces collection under the DBEngine object, so it will be discussed in Chapter 4.

RegisterDatabase

```
DBEngine.RegisterDatabase dsn, driver, silent, attributes
```

Argument	Data Type	Description
dsn	String	The name used in the OpenDatabase method, referring to a block of descriptive information about the data source.
driver	String	The name of the ODBC driver.
silent	Boolean	Set to True (-1) to hide the ODBC driver dialog boxes prompting for driver-specific information or False (0) to display the dialogs. If *silent* is True, *attributes* must contain all the necessary driver-specific information; otherwise, the dialogs will be displayed.
attributes	String	A list of keywords to be added to the Windows Registry in the form of a carriage-return-delimited string.

Enters connection information for an ODBC data source in the Windows Registry. This information is needed by the ODBC driver when the ODBC data source is opened during an ODBC session.

 If you have access to the system on which the code will run, it is a lot easier to use the ODBC Data Source Administrator applet in the Control Panel to add new data sources or edit existing ones than to use the RegisterDatabase method.

VBA Code

This example registers a SQL Server data source named *Publishers in the Windows Registry*.

```
Private Sub cmdRegister_Click()

Dim dbsRegister As Database
    Dim strDescription As String
    Dim strAttributes As String
    Dim errLoop As Error

    'Build keywords string.
    strDescription = InputBox("Enter a description " & _
       "for the database to be registered.")
    strAttributes = "Database=pubs" & _
       vbCr & "Description=" & strDescription & _
       vbCr & "OemToAnsi=No" & _
       vbCr & "Server=Server1"

    'Update Windows Registry.
    On Error GoTo Err_Register
```

```
DBEngine.RegisterDatabase "Publishers", "SQL Server", _
    True, strAttributes
On Error GoTo 0

MsgBox "Use regedit.exe to view changes: " & _
    "HKEY_CURRENT_USER\" & _
    "Software\ODBC\ODBC.INI"

Exit Sub

Err_Register:

    'Notify user of any errors that result from
    'the invalid data.
    If DBEngine.Errors.Count > 0 Then
        For Each errLoop In DBEngine.Errors
            MsgBox "Error number: " & errLoop.Number & _
                vbCr & errLoop.Description

Next errLoop
    End If

    Resume Next

End Sub
```

RepairDatabase

```
DBEngine.RepairDatabase name
```

Argument	Data Type	Description
name	String	The path and filename of an existing Jet database file. If your system supports UNC naming, you can specify a network path as *server1**share1**dir1**db1.mdb*.

This method attempts to repair a closed database. If you run it on an open database, an error occurs. In Access 2000, Compact and Repair are combined into a single command in the interface, but they remain separate methods in code.

 Before repairing, it is a good idea to back up your database for safety. After repairing a database, it is a good idea to compact it.

VBA Code

This procedure repairs and compacts the Northwind sample database:

```
Private Sub cmdRepair_Click()
```

```
Dim strAccessDir As String
Dim strDBName As String
Dim strCDBName As String

'Get default Access directory from SysCmd function.
strAccessDir = SysCmd(9)
strDBName = strAccessDir & "Samples\Northwind35.mdb"
strCDBName = strAccessDir & "Samples\Compacted Northwind.mdb"

DBEngine.RepairDatabase strDBName
DBEngine.CompactDatabase srcname:=strDBName, dstname:=strCDBName

End Sub
```

Rollback

Rollback is a method of both the DBEngine object and a Workspace object in the Workspaces collection. The method is generally used with a workspace, so it will be discussed in Chapter 4.

SetOption

DBEngine.SetOption *option, value*

Argument	Data Type	Description
option	Long	The value whose default setting (as defined in the registry) is to be changed (see Table 2-11)
value	Variant	Value to set *value* to

Temporarily overrides registry values at run time. The values supplied as *option* arguments all represent value entries of the registry key HKEY_LOCAL_MACHINE\ Software\Microsoft\Jet*x.x*\Engines\Jet *x.x*, where *x.x* is the version of the Jet engine. The changes remain in effect until either SetOption is used again to change them or the DBEngine object is closed. This is in contrast to the Save-Setting statement in the Access object model, where the changes to the registry are preserved after the Access object is closed. (However, SaveSetting can only be used for changes to the settings for custom applications you create.)

Table 2-11. The Parameter Intrinsic Constants

Named Constant	Value	Description
dbExclusiveAsyncDelay	60	The ExclusiveAsyncDelay value
dbFlushTransactionTimeout	66	The FlushTransactionTimeout value
dbImplicitCommitSync	59	The ImplicitCommitSync value
dbLockDelay	63	The LockDelay value
dbLockRetry	57	The LockRetry value

Table 2-11. The Parameter Intrinsic Constants (continued)

Named Constant	Value	Description
dbMaxBufferSize	8	The MaxBufferSize value
dbMaxLocksPerFile	62	The MaxLocksPerFile value
dbPageTimeout	6	The PageTimeout value
dbRecycleLVs	65	The RecycleLVs value
dbSharedAsyncDelay	61	The SharedAsyncDelay value
dbUserCommitSync	58	The UserCommitSync value

 Don't confuse this method with the SetOption method in the Access object model, which refers to options in the Access Tools → Options dialog.

VBA Code

This example lets the user temporarily change the maximum buffer size while a procedure is running. Note that the SetOption method is qualified as belonging to the DAO.DBEngine object to avoid an ambiguous reference, since SetOption is also a method of the Access Application object:

```
Private Sub cmdSetOption_Click()

    Dim intMaxBuffer As Integer

    'Ask user for new value for MaxBufferSize.
    intMaxBuffer = Val(InputBox("Enter the Maximum Buffer Size"))
    If intMaxBuffer > 0 Then
        DAO.DBEngine.SetOption dbMaxBufferSize, intMaxBuffer
        MsgBox "Maxmum buffer size set to " & intMaxBuffer & _
            " for the duration of the procedure"
    Else
        MsgBox "Maximum buffer size not changed"
    End If

End Sub
```

3

Errors Collection and Error Object

The Errors collection is one of two collections located directly under the DBEngine object in the DAO object model, as shown in Figure 3-1. The Errors collection contains all the stored Error objects for a single DAO operation. Any time you run code involving DAO objects, there is a possibility of errors. Any time an error occurs, an Error object is placed in the Errors collection for that operation. When another DAO operation generates an error, the previous Errors collection is cleared and a new Errors collection is started for the new operation.

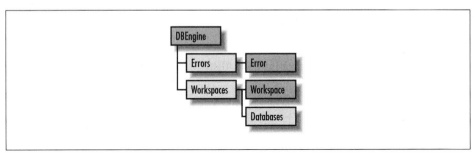

Figure 3-1. The Errors collection and Error object in the DAO object model

 The highest-numbered object in the Errors collection (`DBEngine.Errors.Count - 1`) is the error reported by the VBA Err object.

The Errors collection has only three members: two properties, Count and Item (shown in Table 3-1) and a single method, Refresh (shown in Table 3-2).

Table 3-1. Errors Collection Properties

Property	Description
Count	Indicates the total number of items in the Errors collection
Item	Returns a reference to an Error object within the Errors collection; Item is a hidden property in the Object Browser

Table 3-2. Errors Object Method

Method	Description
Refresh	Updates the objects in the Errors collection

The Error objects in a specific Errors collection for a DAO operation are arranged hierarchically. The first Error object represents the lowest-level error, the second represents the next higher level, and so on, depending on the type of operation involved. The Error object itself has four properties, as shown in Table 3-3.

 Error objects are added to the Errors collection automatically, so the Errors collection doesn't support the usual Append and Delete methods for collections.

Table 3-3. Error Object Properties

Properties	Description
Description	A textual description of the error
HelpContext	The identifier that points to the location in the Help file that contains information about the error
HelpFile	The path and filename containing additional information about the error
Number	A number that identifies the error
Source	The object or application that generated the error

Access to the Error Object

Creatable

No

Returned by

The Errors property of the DBEngine object

Errors Collection Properties

Count   `RO`

Type

Integer

Description

Returns the number of Error objects in the Errors collection. Collection numbering is zero-based (the first member is numbered 0), so if you loop through the Errors collection, you should start with 0 and end with Count −1. The Count property is never **Null**; instead, if there are no errors, its value is 0, indicating that there is no collection to count.

 With previous versions of Access, the Count property was needed to loop through this collection. Since Access 95, it is no longer needed for this purpose; you can use the more efficient **For Each...Next** construct instead.

Item   `RO`

DBEngine.Errors.Item(*Index*)

Type

Error object

Description

Returns the Error object found at the *Index* ordinal position in the Errors collection. Since Item is the default member of the Errors collection, the Item property need not be explicitly referenced in code. For example, the following two statements each retrieve the last Error object from the Errors collection:

```
DBEngine.Errors.Item(DBEngine.Errors.Count - 1)
DBEngine.Errors(DBEngine.Errors.Count - 1)
```

Note that it is far more efficient to iterate the Errors collection using the **For Each...Next** construct than to use the **For...Next** construct with the Count property.

Errors Collection Methods

Refresh

```
Errors.Refresh
```

Updates the objects in the Errors collection so that the Number property of the last member of the Errors collection matches the value of the VBA Err object. This is necessary if you are going to use a `Select Case` statement to identify the particular DAO error or errors that occurred, for example, in an error-handling construct.

Error Object Properties

Description   [RO]

Type

String

Description

Describes the error. You can use this string in standard error-handling code when you don't want (or need) to write your own custom error messages, as in the following code sample.

VBA Code

Figure 3-2 shows the dialog box generated by the code in this example, which lists all of the Error object's properties:

```
Public Function ErrorProps()

On Error GoTo ErrorPropsError

    Dim dbs As Database
    Dim strError As String
    Dim err As Error

    'Try to set dbs to a nonexistent database to
    'generate a DAO error.
    Set dbs = OpenDatabase("None.mdb")

ErrorPropsExit:
    Exit Function

ErrorPropsError:

    For Each err In Errors
        With err
            strError = "Error#: " & .Number & vbCr
```

```
            strError = strError & vbTab & .Description & vbCr
            strError = strError & vbTab & "(Source: " & .Source & ")" & vbCr
            strError = strError & "Press F1 to see topic " & .HelpContext _
                    & vbCr
            strError = strError & vbTab & "in the file " & .HelpFile & "."
        End With
        MsgBox strError
    Next

    Resume Next

End Function
```

Figure 3-2. A message box displaying error properties

HelpContext   `RO`

Data Type

Long

Description

References a Help topic. Used together with the HelpFile property, it can be used to display the Help file it identifies, as in the VBA code in the Description section. Note that in the DAO 3.6 object library, the HelpContext property is hidden.

HelpFile   `RO`

Data Type

String

Description

The fully qualified path to a Help file. You can use it together with the Help-Context property to display the Help file it identifies, as in the VBA code in the

Description section. Note that in the DAO 3.6 object library, the HelpFile property is hidden.

Number RO

Data Type

Long

Description

An error number, which can be used to determine which error occurred. See the VBA code sample in the Description section for an example of using this property.

Source RO

Data Type

String

Description

The class name or other identifier for the object or application that generated the error. Used together with other Error properties, it can provide information about an error to the user, as in the VBA code sample in the Description section.

Using **On Error Resume Next** instead of **On Error GoTo** when handling errors guarantees that the Error.Number property and the Error.Source property refer to the same error.

4

Workspaces Collection and Workspace Object

The Workspaces collection is the second collection located directly under the DBEngine object in the DAO object model, as shown in Figure 4-1. It is a collection of all the Workspace objects under the DBEngine object, excluding those that are inactive or hidden. Normally, when you are using Access, you only have a single workspace, but it is possible to create multiple workspaces using the Create-Workspace method of the DBEngine object. This can be a handy technique when you need to roll back transactions, as illustrated in the code sample for the Begin-Trans section.

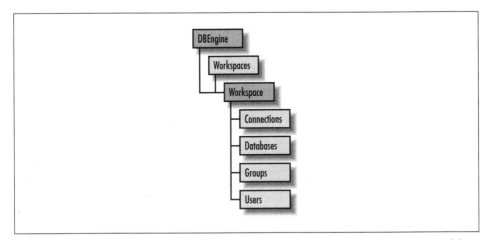

Figure 4-1. The Workspaces collection and the Workspace object in the DAO object model

The Workspaces object itself has only three methods (of which only one is functional), which are shown in Table 4-2, and two properties, which are listed in Table 4-1.

Table 4-1. Workspaces Collection Properties

Property	Description
Count	Indicates the total number of Workspace objects in the Workspaces collection.
Item	Returns a particular member of the Workspaces collection. Although hidden in the DAO type library, it is the default member of the Workspaces collection.

Table 4-2. Workspaces Collection Methods

Method	Description
Append	Adds a Workspace object to the collection
Delete	Not functional
Refresh	Not functional

Both the Object Browser and Help (Access 97 and Access 2000) list Delete and Refresh as methods of the Workspaces collection. However, both of these methods apply only to *persistent* objects—that is, to objects physically stored in the database, rather than to objects (such as workspaces) created in memory. Calls to the Delete method produce runtime error 3273, "Method not applicable for this object." But that doesn't mean you can't "delete" a workspace—just use the Close method of the Workspace object.

A Workspace object is used to manage the current session—the Jet engine database operations performed from user logon to logoff. Typically, multiple workspaces (sessions) are needed when working with transactions, and they may be needed for other purposes too, such as running multiple transactions for SQL Server connections (see the IsolateODBCTrans section for an example of this).

The first time you reference a Workspace object, you create the default Workspace, `DBEngine.Workspaces(0)`, with a UserName property of `Admin` (unless security is enabled, in which case the UserName property is set to the name of the logged-on user) and a Name property of `"#Default Workspace#"`. See the VBA code in the Append section for an example of opening the default workspace and one other workspace.

A Workspace object can be referenced by any of the following syntax variants:

```
DBEngine.Workspaces(0)
DBEngine.Workspaces("name")
DBEngine.Workspaces![name]
```

The Workspace object contains six properties shown in Table 4-3. It also supports the five collections shown in Table 4-4 and the nine methods, shown in Table 4-5.

Table 4-3. Workspace Object Properties

Property	Description
DefaultCursorDriver	Defines the cursor driver used on a connection created by the OpenConnection or OpenDatabase methods
IsolateODBCTrans	Indicates whether multiple transactions that involve the same Microsoft Jet-connected ODBC data source are isolated
LoginTimeout	Defines the number of seconds that the Jet engine attempts to connect to an ODBC data source before an error is raised
Name	The name of the workspace
Type	The workspace type
UserName	The owner of the Workspace object

Table 4-4. Workspace Object Collections

Collection	Description
Connections	Returns a collection of Connection objects for the workspace.
Databases	Returns a collection of Database objects representing databases opened in the workspace. The Databases collection and the Database object are documented in Chapter 5, *Databases Collection and Database Object*.
Groups	Returns a collection of Group objects. The Groups collection is documented in Chapter 11, *Groups Collection and Group Object*.
Properties	Returns a collection of Property objects.
Users	Returns a collection of User objects. The Users collection and the User object are documented in Chapter 12, *Users Collection and User Object*.

Table 4-5. Workspace Object Methods

Method	Description
BeginTrans	Begins a transaction
Close	Closes the Workspace object
CommitTrans	Ends a transaction and saves changes
CreateDatabase	Creates a new database
CreateGroup	Creates a new Group object
CreateUser	Creates a new User object
OpenConnection	Opens a connection in the workspace
OpenDatabase	Opens a database in the workspace
Rollback	Ends a transaction and discards changes

Access to the Workspace Object

Creatable

No

Returned by

The CreateWorkspace method of the DBEngine object

The Workspaces property of the DBEngine object

Workspaces Collection Properties

Count   RO

Data Type

Integer

Description

Gives the number of objects in the Workspaces collection. In previous versions of Access, Count was useful for setting up loops to process all objects in a collection, as in the following code example. However, the `For Each...Next` loop is a more efficient way of iterating through the members of a collection (see the Append section for an example of using `For Each...Next` to process all members of the Workspaces collection).

VBA Code

```
Private Sub cmdCount_Click()

    Dim wks As Workspace
    Dim wks1 As Workspace
    Dim wks2 As Workspace
    Dim wks3 As Workspace
    Dim wks4 As Workspace
    Dim prp As Property
    Dim intCount As Integer
    Dim wksCount As Integer

    Set wks1 = Workspaces(0)
    Set wks2 = CreateWorkspace("Workspace1", "Admin", _
        "", dbUseJet)
    Workspaces.Append wks2
    Set wks3 = CreateWorkspace("Workspace2", "Admin", _
        "", dbUseJet)
    Workspaces.Append wks3
    Set wks4 = CreateWorkspace("Workspace3", "Admin", _
        "", dbUseJet)
    Workspaces.Append wks4
    wksCount = Workspaces.Count
```

```
'Iterate through Workspaces collection and list names.
    For intCount = 0 To wksCount - 1
        Debug.Print "Workspace " & intCount & vbTab & _
                    Workspaces(intCount).Name
    Next intCount

wks1.Close
wks2.Close
wks3.Close
wks4.Close

End Sub
```

Item   RO

```
Workspaces.Item(Index)
```

Argument	Data Type	Description
Index	Integer	Represents either the ordinal position of the Workspace object in the Workspaces collection or a string containing the name of the Workspace object to be retrieved from the Workspaces collection

Data Type

Workspace object

Description

Retrieves a particular Workspace object from the Workspaces collection. A Workspace object can be retrieved either based on its ordinal position in the Workspace collection or based on its name. Since Workspaces is a zero-based collection, the following code fragment returns the first (default) workspace:

```
Dim wks As Workspace
Set wks = DBEngine.Workspaces.Item(0)
```

You can also retrieve a particular Workspace object by name. Typically, a Workspace object's name is assigned in the call to the DBEngine object's CreateWorkspace method. An exception is the default workspace, whose name is `"#Default Workspace#"`. The following code fragment, for instance, retrieves the default workspace object:

```
Dim wks As Workspace
Set wks = DBEngine.Workspaces.Item("#Default Workspace#")
```

Note that, since the Item property is the default member of the Workspaces collection, it does not need to be explicitly specified when retrieving a particular Workspace object. In other words, the following two statements are equivalent; both retrieve the first (or default) workspace:

```
Set wks = DBEngine.Workspaces.Item(0)
Set wks = DBEngine.Workspaces(0)
```

Similarly, the following two statements are equivalent; both retrieve the default workspace by name:

```
Set wks = DBEngine.Workspaces.Item("#Default Workspace#")
Set wks = DBEngine.Workspaces("#Default Workspace#")
```

Workspaces Collection Methods

Append

```
Workspaces.Append object
```

Description

Adds a newly created Workspace object to the Workspaces collection, as in the example code.

VBA Code

The CreateWorkspace method of the DBEngine object is used to return a reference to *object*, which is then added to the Workspaces collection by using its Append method. Note that there is no need to explicitly create the default workspace, or `Workspaces(0)`, so when you explicitly create a workspace, it is the second (or higher) workspace in the Workspaces collection:

```
Private Sub cmdAppend_Click()

    Dim wks As Workspace
    Dim wks2 As Workspace
    Dim prp As Property

    Set wks2 = CreateWorkspace("Workspace1", "Admin", _
        "", dbUseJet)
    wks2.Name = "Workspace 2"
    Workspaces.Append wks2

    'List Workspace properties.
        For Each wks In Workspaces
            With wks
                Debug.Print .Name & " properties:"
                For Each prp In .Properties
                    On Error Resume Next
                    If prp <> "" Then Debug.Print vbTab & _
                        prp.Name & " = " & prp
                    On Error GoTo 0
                Next prp
            End With
        Next wks
```

```
    wks2.Close

  End Sub
```

Delete

Although Delete is listed as a method of the Workspaces collection, it will cause an error if you try to use it. Just use the Close method of the Workspace object to remove a workspace you have created, as in the preceding code sample.

Refresh

Much like the Delete method, although Refresh is listed as a method of the Workspaces collection, it is nonfunctional for the Workspaces collection. However, a call to the Refresh method generates neither a compile-time nor a runtime error; it simply has no effect.

Workspace Object Properties

DefaultCursorDriver

Data Type

Long

Description

Sets or returns the cursor driver type used on a connection created by the OpenConnection or OpenDatabase methods for ODBCDirect workspaces. Possible values are shown in Table 4-6.

Table 4-6. The DefaultCursorDriver Intrinsic Constants

Named Constant	Value	Description
dbUseDefaultCursor	-1	(Default) Uses server-side cursors if the server supports them; otherwise uses the ODBC Cursor Library.
dbUseODBCCursor	1	Always uses the ODBC Cursor Library. This option provides better performance for small result sets, but degrades quickly for larger result sets.
dbUseServerCursor	2	Always uses server-side cursors. For most large operations this option provides better performance, but might cause more network traffic.
dbUseClientBatchCursor	3	Always uses the client batch cursor library. This option is required for batch updates.

Table 4-6. The DefaultCursorDriver Intrinsic Constants (continued)

Named Constant	Value	Description
dbUseNoCursor	4	Opens all cursors (that is, Recordset objects) as forward-only type, read-only, with a rowset size of 1. Also known as "cursorless queries."

 You must set this property before opening a connection; it has no effect on an existing connection.

VBA Code

```
Private Sub cmdDefaultCursorDriver_Click()

On Error GoTo cmdDefaultCursorDriver_ClickError

    Dim wks As Workspace
    Dim con As Connection

    'Create ODBCDirect workspace.
    Set wks = CreateWorkspace("ODBCWorkspace", _
        "admin", "", dbUseODBC)
    wks.DefaultCursorDriver = dbUseClientBatchCursor

    'Open connection.
    Set con = wks.OpenConnection("Headquarters Data", _
        dbDriverNoPrompt, , "ODBC;;;;DSN=HQ Data")

    'Display the name of the database connection, and
    'its default cursor type.
    Debug.Print "Database name: " & con.Database.Name
    Debug.Print "Updatable: " & con.Updatable
    con.Close

cmdDefaultCursorDriver_ClickExit:
    Exit Sub

cmdDefaultCursorDriver_ClickError:
    MsgBox "Error No: " & err.Number & "; Description: " & err.Description
    Resume cmdDefaultCursorDriver_ClickExit

End Sub
```

IsolateODBCTrans

Data Type

Integer (Object Browser); Boolean (Help)

Description

Sets or returns a value indicating whether multiple transactions involving the same Jet-connected ODBC data source are isolated. It applies to Jet workspaces only.

> SQL Server doesn't allow simultaneous transactions on one connection. If you need multiple transactions for SQL Server connections, set the IsolateODBCTrans property to **True** for each workspace when you open it, in order to force a separate connection for each workspace.

LoginTimeout

Data Type

Long (Object Browser); Integer (Help)

Description

Sets or returns the number of seconds before an error occurs while attempting to log on to an ODBC database. The default setting is 20 seconds, and if the property is set to zero, no timeout occurs. LoginTimeout can only be used with ODBC-Direct workspaces.

Name

Data Type

String

Description

The name of a workspace. The Name property is read/write for a workspace that has not been appended to the Workspaces collection and read-only for appended workspaces. A workspace's name is limited to 20 characters in length; it must start with a letter and may contain numbers and underscores, but not punctuation marks or spaces.

> The default workspace (`Workspaces(0)`) is always a member of the Workspaces collection, even if it is not specifically appended.

VBA Code

```
Private Sub cmdName_Click()

On Error GoTo cmdName_ClickError

    Dim wks As Workspace
    Dim wks1 As Workspace
    Dim wks2 As Workspace

    Set wks1 = Workspaces(0)
    Set wks2 = CreateWorkspace("Workspace1", "Admin", _
        "", dbUseJet)

    'List Workspace names for appended workspaces.
      For Each wks In Workspaces
          Debug.Print "Workspace name: " & wks.Name
      Next wks

    'List each workspace name separately.
    Debug.Print "Workspace 1 name" & wks1.Name
    Debug.Print "Workspace 2 name" & wks2.Name
    wks1.Close
    wks2.Close

cmdName_ClickExit:
    Exit Sub

cmdName_ClickError:
    MsgBox "Error No: " & err.Number & "; Description: " & err.Description
    Resume cmdName_ClickExit

End Sub
```

Type   `RO`

Data Type

Long

Description

Returns the workspace type, as listed in Table 4-7. Its value can also be set by supplying a value to the *UseType* argument of the DBEngine object's Create-Workspace method, but the property is read-only for an existing workspace.

Table 4-7. The Workspace Type Intrinsic Constants

Named Constant	Value	Description
dbUseJet	2	The Workspace is a Jet workspace.
dbUseODBC	1	The Workspace is an ODBC workspace.

UserName   `RO`

Data Type

String

Description

Represents the owner of a Workspace object. In the case of a Jet workspace, this is a User object in the Users collection, or a Group object in the Groups collection.

Workspace Object Methods

BeginTrans

object.BeginTrans

Description

Starts a new transaction during a workspace session. It is paired with the Commit-Trans method, which ends the transaction, or the Rollback method, which aborts the transaction.

VBA Code

This VBA code illustrates the use of the BeginTrans, CommitTrans, and Rollback methods to enclose a loop in which the user is asked to confirm increasing a price field by 10%. Apart from the individual choice offered for each record, the user has a chance to undo the entire transaction by selecting not to commit when all the records have been processed. If the user chooses to commit the transaction, the **wks.CommitTrans** method is used; otherwise, **wks.Rollback** is used to roll back (undo) the individual changes, leaving the prices unchanged:

```
Private Sub cmdBeginTrans_Click()

On Error GoTo cmdBeginTrans_ClickExit

    Dim strName As String
    Dim strMessage As String
    Dim wks As Workspace
    Dim dbs As Database
    Dim rstEmployees As Recordset
    Dim strAccessDir As String
    Dim strDBName As String
    Dim curUnitPrice As Currency

    'Get default Access directory from SysCmd function.
    strAccessDir = SysCmd(9)
    strDBName = strAccessDir & "Samples\Northwind.mdb"
    MsgBox "DBName: " & strDBName
```

```
'Get default Workspace.
Set wks = DBEngine.Workspaces(0)
Set dbs = OpenDatabase(strDBName)
Set rstEmployees = dbs.OpenRecordset("Products")

'Start transaction.
wks.BeginTrans

With rstEmployees

    'Loop through recordset and ask user if she wants to
    'raise the product price by 10%.
    Do Until .EOF
        strMessage = "Raise price of " & ![ProductName] & _
            & ", currently priced at $" & ![UnitPrice] & ", by 10%?"

        'Raise the price of the specified product if the user agrees.
        If MsgBox(strMessage, vbYesNo) = VbYes Then
            .Edit
            ![UnitPrice] = ![UnitPrice] + (![UnitPrice] * 0.03)
            .Update
        End If

        .MoveNext
    Loop

    'Ask if the user wants to commit to all the changes
    'made above.
    If MsgBox("Save all changes?", vbYesNo) = VbYes Then
        wks.CommitTrans
    Else
        wks.Rollback
    End If

    'Print updated prices.
    .MoveFirst
    Do While Not .EOF
        Debug.Print "New price: " & ![UnitPrice]
        .MoveNext
    Loop

    .Close
End With

dbs.Close

cmdBeginTrans_ClickExit:
    Exit Sub

cmdBeginTrans_ClickError:
    MsgBox "Error No: " & err.Number & "; Description: " & err.Description
    Resume cmdBeginTrans_ClickExit

End Sub
```

Close

`object.Close`

Closes a workspace. See the Append code sample for usage.

 Since the Delete method doesn't work with the Workspaces collection, the Close method of the Workspace object is the only way to remove a Workspace from the Workspaces collection.

CommitTrans

`object.CommitTrans`

Used at the end of a series of commands started with the BeginTrans method, to save all the changes. Instead of CommitTrans, you can use Rollback to undo the changes. See the BeginTrans method for a code sample illustrating the BeginTrans and CommitTrans methods.

CreateDatabase

`Set database = workspace.CreateDatabase(name, connect, option)`

Argument	Data Type	Description
database	Database object	A Database object.
workspace	Workspace object	A Workspace object.
name	String	The filename (including extension) of the database to be created. May include full path and can be in UNC convention (*server1**share1**dir1**db1.mdb*). If the file represented by *name* exists, runtime error 3207, "Database already exists," is generated.
connect	String	Sets the collating order for the database. See Table 4-8 for a list of constants that can be used for this argument and their integer values. You can create a password for the new database by concatenating the password string (starting with "`;pwd=`") with a constant in the *connect* argument, as in the VB Code example.
option	Integer	The format of the database. See Table 4-9 for a list of constants that can be used for this argument, and their integer values.

Creates a new empty Database object and saves it to the disk. After creating the database, you must fill it with objects (tables, queries, etc.) for it to be of use. Like the CompactDatabase method of the DBEngine object, the arguments of this method are listed inaccurately in Help as *name*, *locale*, and *options*.

To copy an existing database (rather than starting from scratch with a new database), use the CompactDatabase method of the DBEngine object.

Table 4-8. The Connect Intrinsic Constants

Named Constant	Value	Description
dbLangGeneral	";LANGID=0x0409;CP=1252;COUNTRY=0"	English, German, French, Portuguese, Italian, and Modern Spanish
dbLangArabic	";LANGID=0x0401;CP=1256;COUNTRY=0"	Arabic
dbLangChineseSimplified	";LANGID=0x0804;CP=936;COUNTRY=0"	Simplified Chinese
dbLangChineseTraditional	";LANGID=0x0404;CP=950;COUNTRY=0"	Traditional Chinese
dbLangCyrillic	";LANGID=0x0419;CP=1251;COUNTRY=0"	Russian
dbLangCzech	";LANGID=0x0405;CP=1250;COUNTRY=0"	Czech
dbLangDutch	";LANGID=0x0413;CP=1252;COUNTRY=0"	Dutch
dbLangGreek	";LANGID=0x0408;CP=1253;COUNTRY=0"	Greek
dbLangHebrew	";LANGID=0x040D;CP=1255;COUNTRY=0"	Hebrew
dbLangHungarian	";LANGID=0x040E;CP=1250;COUNTRY=0"	Hungarian
dbLangIcelandic	";LANGID=0x040F;CP=1252;COUNTRY=0"	Icelandic
dbLangJapanese	";LANGID=0x0411;CP=932;COUNTRY=0"	Japanese
dbLangKorean	";LANGID=0x0412;CP=949;COUNTRY=0"	Korean
dbLangNordic	";LANGID=0x041D;CP=1252;COUNTRY=0"	Nordic languages (Microsoft Jet database engine version 1.0 only)
dbLangNorwDan	";LANGID=0x0414;CP=1252;COUNTRY=0"	Norwegian and Danish
dbLangPolish	";LANGID=0x0415;CP=1250;COUNTRY=0"	Polish
dbLangSlovenian	";LANGID=0x0424;CP=1250;COUNTRY=0"	Slovenian

Table 4-8. The Connect Intrinsic Constants (continued)

Named Constant	Value	Description
dbLangSpanish	";LANGID=0x040A;CP=1252;COUNTRY=0"	Traditional Spanish
dbLangSwedFin	";LANGID=0x040B;CP=1252;COUNTRY=0"	Swedish and Finnish
dbLangThai	";LANGID=0x041E;CP=874;COUNTRY=0"	Thai
dbLangTurkish	";LANGID=0x041F;CP=1254;COUNTRY=0"	Turkish

Table 4-9. The Option Intrinsic Constants

Named Constant	Value	Description
dbEncrypt	2	Encrypts the database while compacting
dbVersion10	1	Creates a database that uses the Microsoft Jet database engine version 1.0 file format while compacting
dbVersion11	8	Creates a database that uses the Microsoft Jet database engine version 1.1 file format while compacting
dbVersion20	16	Creates a database that uses the Microsoft Jet database engine version 2.0 file format while compacting
dbVersion30	32	Creates a database that uses the Microsoft Jet database engine version 3.0 file format (compatible with version 3.5) while compacting

 When you create a database from Access VBA without specifying the path, it is created in the default database folder, as set in the Access Options dialog's General page. When you create a database from Outlook VBS without specifying a path, it is created in the *C:\ root* folder. In either case, you can specify a path if desired, either by hard-coding it, or picking it up from the Registry or from the Access SysCmd object, as in the VBScript code sample.

VBA Code

```
Private Sub cmdCreateDatabase_Click()

On Error GoTo cmdCreateDatabase_ClickError

    Dim wks As Workspace
    Dim dbs As Database
    Dim tdf As TableDef
    Dim fld As Field
    Dim prp As Property
    Dim strDBName As String
    Dim strLocale As Variant
```

```
      Set wks = DBEngine.Workspaces(0)
      strDBName = "TestDatabase.mdb"
      strLocale = dbLangGeneral & ";pwd=Edgar"

      'Delete database of this name, if it exists.
      On Error Resume Next
      Kill strDBName

      'Create new database with default properties in the
      'default Access folder, and close it.
      Set dbs = wks.CreateDatabase(strDBName, , strLocale)
      dbs.Close

cmdCreateDatabase_ClickExit:
   Exit Sub

cmdCreateDatabase_ClickError:
   MsgBox "Error No: " & err.Number & "; Description: " & err.Description
   Resume cmdCreateDatabase_ClickExit

End Sub
```

When using the DAO object model from Outlook VBScript, it is advisable to specify the DAO version after "DBEngine" or to write code that detects the Access or Office version and then sets a reference to the appropriate DAO version, as in the following code samples. Otherwise you may get an "Internal Application Error" message, caused by DAO version confusion.

Outlook VBS Code

```
Sub cmdCreateDatabase_Click()

   Dim dao
   Dim dbs
   Dim wks
   Dim strDBName

   strDBName = "FromOutlook.mdb"
   Set dao = Application.CreateObject("DAO.DBEngine.35")
   Set wks = DAO.Workspaces(0)
   Set dbs = wks.CreateDatabase(strDBName, _
            ";LANGID=0x0409;CP=1252;COUNTRY=0")
   dbs.Close

End Sub

   Dim dbe
   Dim dbs
   Dim wks
   Dim strDBName
```

```
Dim strOfficeDir
Dim StrOfficeVer
Dim objAccess
Dim strFolder

strDBName = "FromOutlook2.mdb"

'Pick up path to the Office folder and the Office version
'from the Access SysCmd method.
Set objAccess = Item.Application.CreateObject("Access.Application")
StrOfficeVer = objAccess.SysCmd(7)
strOfficeDir = objAccess.SysCmd(9)
MsgBox "Office version: " & strOfficeVer
MsgBox "Access folder: " & strOfficeDir
objAccess.Quit

strDBName = strOfficeDir & strDBName

'Set up reference to correct version of DAO depending
'on Office version.
If left(strOfficeVer, 1) = "8" Then
   'Office 97 DAO version
   MsgBox "Office 97; DAO 3.5"
   Set dbe = Application.CreateObject("DAO.DBEngine.35")
ElseIf left (strOfficeVer, 1) = "9" Then
   'Office 2000 DAO version
   MsgBox "Office 2000; DAO 3.6"
   Set dbe = Application.CreateObject("DAO.DBEngine.36")
Else
   MsgBox "Unknown Office version; canceling"
   Exit Sub
Enf If

Set wks = DAO.Workspaces(0)
Set dbs = wks.CreateDatabase(strDBName, _
         ";LANGID=0x0409;CP=1252;COUNTRY=0")
dbs.Close

End Sub
```

CreateGroup

```
Set group = object.CreateGroup(name, pid)
```

Argument	Data Type	Description
group	Group object	The Group object you are creating
object	User or Workspace object	A User or Workspace object for which you want to create the new Group object
name	String	The name of the new Group object
pid	String	The PID (Personal ID) of a group account; must contain from 4 to 20 alphanumeric characters

Creates a Group object containing a group of user accounts with common access permissions. Groups are used to implement database security within secure workgroups. This method allows you to implement or modify permissions from VBA code.

A Group object may be referenced by any of the following syntax variants:

```
Groups(0)
Groups("name")
Groups![name]
```

VBA Code

This example creates a new group, appends the Admin user to it, and lists its properties (other than the PID property, which is not readable for security reasons) and its users:

```
Private Sub cmdCreateGroup_Click()

On Error GoTo cmdCreateGroup_ClickError

    Dim wks As Workspace
    Dim grp As Group
    Dim grpTemp As Group
    Dim prp As Property
    Dim usr As User

    Set wks = DBEngine.Workspaces(0)

    With wks
        'Create and append new group.
        Set grp = .CreateGroup("NewGroup", "WIEUC72838XKSI8")
        .Groups.Append grp

'Make the Admin user a member of the new group.
        Set grpTemp = .Users("admin").CreateGroup("NewGroup")
        .Users("admin").Groups.Append grpTemp

        'List the Properties of NewGroup, other than the
        'write-only PID property.
        Debug.Print grp.Name & " Properties"
        For Each prp In grp.Properties
            On Error Resume Next
            If prp <> "" Then Debug.Print vbTab & prp.Name & " = " & prp
            On Error GoTo 0
        Next prp

        Debug.Print grp.Name & " Users collection"

        For Each usr In grp.Users
            Debug.Print vbTab & usr.Name
        Next usr
```

```
            'Delete the new Group object.
            .Groups.Delete "NewGroup"
        End With

    cmdCreateGroup_ClickExit:
        Exit Sub

    cmdCreateGroup_ClickError:
        MsgBox "Error No: " & err.Number & "; Description: " & err.Description
        Resume cmdCreateGroup_ClickExit

    End Sub
```

CreateUser

```
Set user = object.CreateUser(name, pid, password)
```

Argument	Data Type	Description
user	User object	The User object you are creating.
object	Group or Workspace object	A Group or Workspace object for which you want to create the new User object.
name	String	The name of the new User object.
pid	String	The PID (Personal ID) of a user account; it must contain from 4 to 20 alphanumeric characters.
password	String	The new User object's password; it can be up to 14 characters long and may contain any character except ASCII character 0 (null). If not set, the password is a zero-length string ("")."

Creates a User account for a Group in a secured workgroup. As with Create-Group, you can use this method to manipulate access permissions.

You can reference a User object by any of the following syntax variants:

```
[workspace | group].Users(0)
[workspace | group].Users("name")
[workspace | group].Users![name]
```

VBA Code

This example code creates a new user and a new group, appends the new user to the new group, and lists the user and group properties:

```
Private Sub cmdCreateUser_Click()

On Error GoTo cmdCreateUser_ClickError

    Dim wks As Workspace
    Dim grp As Group
    Dim grpTemp As Group
    Dim prp As Property
```

```
        Dim usr As User
        Dim usrTemp As User

        Set wks = DBEngine.Workspaces(0)

        With wks
            'Create and append new user.
            Set usr = .CreateUser("NewUser")
            usr.PID = "US82PECLWPWLO90"
            usr.Password = "OpenSesame"
            .Users.Append usr

            'Create and append new group.
            Set grp = .CreateGroup("NewGroup", "WIEUC72838XKSI8")
            .Groups.Append grp

            'Make the new user a member of the new group.
            Set usrTemp = .Groups("NewGroup").CreateUser("NewUser")
            .Groups("NewGroup").Users.Append usrTemp

            'List the properties of the new user.
            Debug.Print usr.Name & " Properties"
            For Each prp In usr.Properties
                On Error Resume Next
                If prp <> "" Then Debug.Print vbTab & prp.Name & " = " & prp
                On Error GoTo 0
            Next prp

            'List the properties of the new group, other than the
            'write-only PID property.
            Debug.Print grp.Name & " Properties"
            For Each prp In grp.Properties
                On Error Resume Next
                If prp <> "" Then Debug.Print vbTab & prp.Name & " = " & prp
                On Error GoTo 0
            Next prp

    'Delete the new User and Group object.
            .Users.Delete "NewUser"
            .Groups.Delete "NewGroup"
        End With

cmdCreateUser_ClickExit:
    Exit Sub

cmdCreateUser_ClickError:
    MsgBox "Error No: " & err.Number & "; Description: " & err.Description
    Resume cmdCreateUser_ClickExit

End Sub
```

OpenConnection

```
Set connection = object.OpenConnection(name, options, readonly, connect)
```

Argument	Data Type	Description
connection	Connection object	The Connection object to which the new connection will be assigned.
object	Workspace object	(Optional) A Workspace object that will contain the new connection.
name	String	If a registered DSN is specified for the *connect* argument, the *name* argument can be any valid string; if no DSN is specified, it must reference a valid ODBC DSN. If neither *name* nor *connect* references a valid DSN, the ODBC driver manager can be set to prompt the user for the connection information using the *options* argument.
options	Variant	(Optional) A Variant that sets various options for the connection, as specified in Table 4-10. Based on this value, the ODBC driver manager may prompt the user for connection information such as data source name (DSN), user name, and password.
readonly	Boolean	(Optional) True if the connection is to be opened for read-only access, and False if it is to be opened for read/write access (default).
connect	String	(Optional) An ODBC connect string composed of a database type specifier and zero or more parameters separated by semicolons. A prepended "ODBC;" is required. If *connect* is omitted, the UID and/or PWD will be taken from the UserName and Password properties of the Workspace object.

Opens a Connection object on an ODBC data source. It is only valid for ODBC-Direct workspaces.

Table 4-10. The Options Intrinsic Constants

Named Constant	Value	Description
dbDriverNoPrompt	1	The ODBC Driver Manager uses the connection string provided in *name* and *connect*. If you don't provide sufficient information, a run-time error occurs.
dbDriverPrompt	2	The ODBC Driver Manager displays the ODBC Data Sources dialog box, which displays any relevant information supplied in *name* or *connect*. The connection string is made up of the DSN that the user selects via the dialog boxes, or, if the user doesn't specify a DSN, the default DSN is used.

Table 4-10. The Options Intrinsic Constants (continued)

Named Constant	Value	Description
dbDriverComplete	0	(Default) If the *connect* argument includes all the necessary information to complete a connection, the ODBC Driver Manager uses the string in *connect*. Otherwise it behaves as it does when you specify dbDriverPrompt.
dbDriverCompleteRequired	3	This option behaves like dbDriverComplete, except the ODBC driver disables the prompts for any information not required to complete the connection.
dbRunAsync	1024	This executes the method asynchronously. This constant may be logically ORed with any of the other Options constants.

Before using a DSN (Data Source Name), you have to create it in the Control Panel's 32-bit ODBC Administrator applet, which was installed with Access. To create a DSN for an Access 97 database, open the applet, select the MS Access 97 Database data source from the list box on the User DSN tab (as Figure 4-2 shows), and click the Add button.

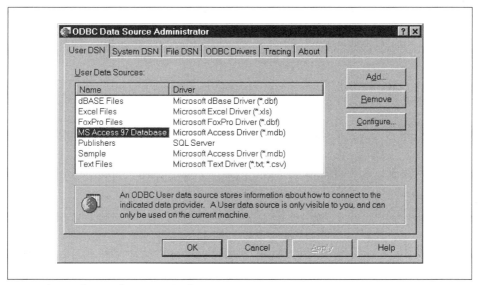

Figure 4-2. Selecting the Access 97 data source type to create a new DSN

On the next screen select the Microsoft Access driver, as shown in Figure 4-3, and click the Finish button.

On the next screen, which is shown in Figure 4-4, fill in the DSN name and description (the description is optional) as desired, and click the Select button to

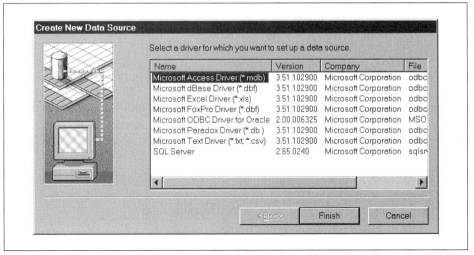

Figure 4-3. Selecting the Microsoft Access driver for the new DSN

select the *.mdb* file from a standard File Open dialog like the one shown in Figure 4-5.

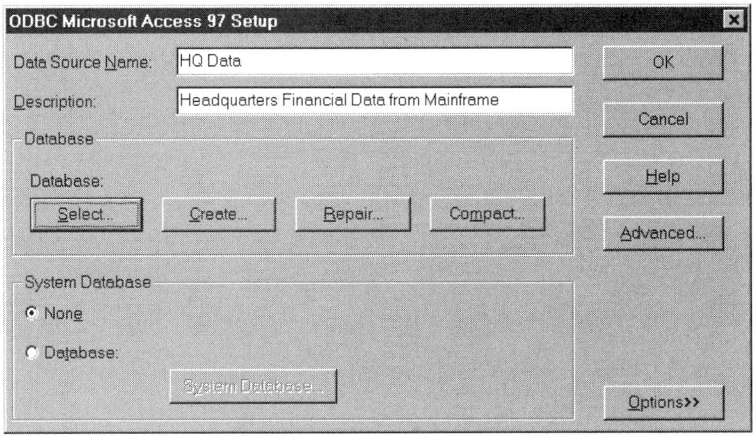

Figure 4-4. Naming the DSN

Click the OK button on the Select Database dialog and then on the two ODBC Setup screens to save the new DSN. Now you can reference the DSN by the name you assigned it, as in the code sample.

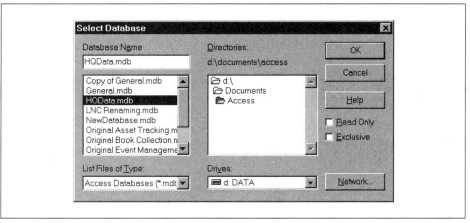

Figure 4-5. Selecting the database for the DSN

 For a standard Access database, it is easier to just open the database directly using the OpenDatabase method. However, for other (non-Access) databases, the OpenConnection method and a DSN may be the only available method for working with the data. If you don't see an appropriate driver for the database that you need to connect to in the 32-bit ODBC Setup list of available drivers, contact the manufacturer to obtain the appropriate driver (you may be able to download it from their web site).

VBA Code

```
Private Sub cmdOpenConnection_Click()

On Error GoTo cmdOpenConnection_ClickError

    Dim wks As Workspace
    Dim con As Connection

    'Create ODBCDirect workspace.
    Set wks = CreateWorkspace("NewODBCWorkspace", _
        "admin", "", dbUseODBC)

    'Open connection.
    Set con = wks.OpenConnection("Headquarters Data", _
        dbDriverNoPrompt, , "ODBC;;;;DSN=HQ Data")

    'Display the name of the database connection, and
    'its updatable value.
    Debug.Print "Database name: " & con.Database.Name
    Debug.Print "Updatable: " & con.Updatable
    con.Close
```

```
cmdOpenConnection_ClickExit:
    Exit Sub

cmdOpenConnection_ClickError:
    MsgBox "Error No: " & err.Number & "; Description: " & err.Description
    Resume cmdOpenConnection_ClickExit

End Sub
```

OpenDatabase

```
Set database = workspace.OpenDatabase(name, options, readonly, connect)
```

Argument	Data Type	Description
database	Database object	A Database object.
workspace	Workspace object	A Workspace object that will contain the database.
name	String	The name (optionally with path) of an existing Access database file, or the DSN of an ODBC data source. If *name* is a zero-length string and *connect* is "ODBC;", a dialog containing all the valid DSNs is displayed so the user can select one. If you are opening a database through an ODBCDirect workspace and providing the DSN in the *connect* argument, you can set *name* to a string that you can use to reference the database later in your code. An error occurs under the following conditions: • You try to open a database that has already been opened for exclusive access by another user. • You specify a name that doesn't correspond to an existing Access database or a valid DSN.
options	Variant	(Optional) A Variant that sets various options for the connection. For Jet workspaces (Access databases), **True** opens the database in exclusive mode, and **False** opens it in shared mode. For ODBC connections, use a named constant or Integer value (see Table 4-11).
readonly	Boolean	(Optional) **True** if the connection is to be opened for read-only access, and **False** if it is to be opened for read/write access (the default value).
connect	String	Consists of the database type, followed by a semicolon (;), such as "ODBC;" or "FoxPro 2.5;" and the optional arguments, in no particular order, separated by semicolons. One of the parameters may be the password.

This is probably the most widely used method of the Workspace object; it opens an existing database in the specified workspace and returns a reference to it, allowing you to work with the database and its contents.

Table 4-11. The Options Intrinsic Constants

Named Constant	Value	Description
dbDriverNoPrompt	1	The ODBC Driver Manager uses the connection string provided in *dbname* and *connect*. If you don't provide sufficient information, a run-time error occurs.
dbDriverPrompt	2	The ODBC Driver Manager displays the ODBC Data Sources dialog box, which displays any relevant information supplied in *dbname* or *connect*. The connection string is made up of the DSN that the user selects via the dialog boxes, or, if the user doesn't specify a DSN, the default DSN is used.
dbDriverComplete	0	(Default) If the *connect* argument includes all the necessary information to complete a connection, the ODBC Driver Manager uses the string in *connect*. Otherwise, it behaves as it does when you specify dbDriverPrompt.
dbDriverCompleteRequired	3	This option behaves like dbDriverComplete, except the ODBC driver disables the prompts for any information not required to complete the connection.

When a Jet database is opened with *options* set to False to open the database in shared mode, the Jet engine creates a temporary file (with an extension of *.ldb*) in the same directory as the database. This behavior can be problematic if the database resides on a read-only medium. In a case such as this, set *options* to True to open the database in exclusive mode.

VBA Code

```
Private Sub cmdOpenDatabase_Click()

    Dim wks As Workspace
    Dim dbs As Database

    Set wks = DBEngine.Workspaces(0)
    Set dbs = wks.OpenDatabase("D:\Documents\Access\Northwind.mdb", True)
    Debug.Print dbs.Name

End Sub
```

Outlook VBS Code

The VBScript code opens the Northwind database, opens a recordset based on the Customers table, and exports all the records in that table into Outlook contacts, using the default Contacts folder and Contact form with a Category of "Imported from Access." One of the imported contacts is shown in Figure 4-6.

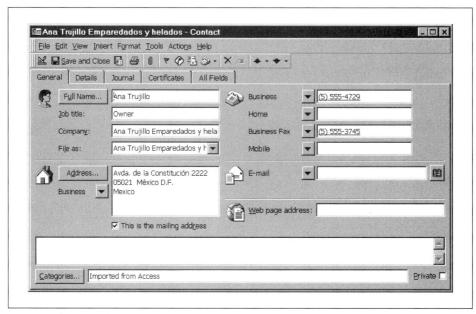

Figure 4-6. An Outlook contact imported from the Customers table in the Northwind database

```
Sub cmdOpenDatabase_Click()

    Dim dao
    Dim dbs
    Dim wks
    Dim strDBName
    Dim strOfficeDir
    Dim objAccess
    Dim strFolder

    strDBName = "Northwind.mdb"

    'Pick up path to the Office folder from Access SysCmd function.
    Set objAccess = Item.Application.CreateObject("Access.Application")
    strOfficeDir = objAccess.SysCmd(9) & "Samples\"
    objAccess.Quit

    strDBName = strOfficeDir & strDBName
    MsgBox "Opening " & strDBName

    'Set up reference to Access database.
    Set dao = Application.CreateObject("DAO.DBEngine.35")
    Set wks = dao.Workspaces(0)
    Set dbs = wks.OpenDatabase(strDBName)
```

```
'Open Access table containing data to import into Outlook.
Set rst = dbs.OpenRecordset("Customers")
intCount = rst.RecordCount
If intCount = 0 Then
   MsgBox "No customers to import"
   Exit Sub
Else
   MsgBox intCount & " customers to import"
End If


'Set up the Outlook folder and items and iterate
'through the Access table, adding one contact item using
'the custom form for each Access record.

Set nms = Application.GetNameSpace("MAPI")

'Set reference to default Contacts folder.
Set fld = nms.GetDefaultFolder(10)
Set itms = fld.Items

Do Until rst.EOF
   'If desired, a custom contact form can be specified instead
   'of the default form.
   Set itm = itms.Add("IPM.Contact")

   'Built-in Outlook properties.
   If IsNull(rst.CustomerID) = False Then _
           itm.CustomerID = rst.CustomerID
   If IsNull(rst.CompanyName) = False Then _
           itm.CompanyName = rst.CompanyName
   If IsNull(rst.ContactName) = False Then _
           itm.FullName = rst.ContactName
   If IsNull(rst.ContactTitle) = False Then _
           itm.JobTitle = rst.ContactTitle
   If IsNull(rst.Address) = False Then _
           itm.BusinessAddressStreet = rst.Address
   If IsNull(rst.City) = False Then _
           itm.BusinessAddressCity = rst.City
   If IsNull(rst.Region) = False Then _
           itm.BusinessAddressState = rst.Region
   If IsNull(rst.PostalCode) = False Then _
           itm.BusinessAddressPostalCode = rst.PostalCode
   If IsNull(rst.Country) = False Then _
           itm.BusinessAddressCountry = rst.Country
   If IsNull(rst.Phone) = False Then _
           itm.BusinessTelephoneNumber = rst.Phone
   If IsNull(rst.Fax) = False Then _
           itm.BusinessFaxNumber = rst.Fax
   itm.Categories = "Imported from Access"
   itm.Close(0)
   rst.MoveNext

Loop
rst.Close
```

```
    MsgBox "All contacts imported!"

End Sub
```

Rollback

workspace.Rollback

Rolls back (undoes) transactions made during a session. It is used in conjunction with the BeginTrans and CommitTrans methods; see the code sample in the BeginTrans section for an example of its usage.

5

Databases Collection and Database Object

The Databases collection includes all the open Database objects in a Workspace object; its position in the DAO object model is shown in Figure 5-1. Multiple databases can be opened in a workspace, as illustrated in the code sample for the Count method. When you open or create a Database object, it is automatically appended to the Databases collection; when you close a database (using the Close method), it is removed from the Databases collection. However, closing a database does not remove it from the disk, as databases are persistent objects, unlike workspaces. To remove a database, use the Kill method, as in Example 5-1.

Example 5-1. Removing a Database

```
Private Sub cmdKill_Click()

    Dim strAccessDir As String
    Dim strDBName As String
    Dim strTitle As String
    Dim strMessage As String
    Dim intReturn As Integer

    'Get default Access directory from SysCmd function.
    strAccessDir = SysCmd(9)
    strDBName = strAccessDir & "FromOutlook2.mdb"

    strTitle = "Question"
    strMessage = "Delete " & strDBName & " from hard drive?"
    intReturn = MsgBox(strMessage, vbYesNo + vbQuestion + _
        vbDefaultButton1, strTitle)

    If intReturn = vbNo Then
        Exit Sub
    ElseIf intReturn = VbYes Then
        Kill strDBName
```

Example 5-1. Removing a Database (continued)

```
   End If

End Sub
```

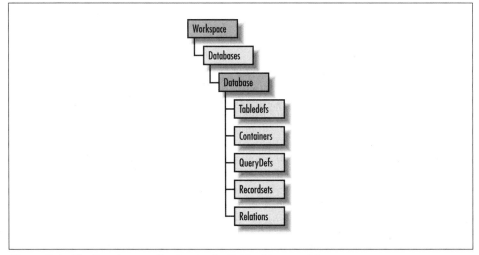

Figure 5-1. The Databases collection in the DAO object model

The Databases collection has only two properties—Count and Item The latter property is hidden by the Object Browser. In addition, according to both online Help and the Object Browser, it supports one method, Refresh. However, since Refresh can only be used with *persistent collections* (i.e., collections of objects that exist on the disk and not just in memory), it can't be used with the Databases collection.

You can reference a Database object in the Databases collection by any of the following syntax variants:

```
Databases(0)
Databases("name")
Databases![name]
```

The Database object has 6 collections (listed in Table 5-1 and covered in the following chapters), 13 properties (shown in Table 5-2), and 11 methods (which appear in Table 5-3).

Table 5-1. Database Object Collections

Collection	Description
Containers	Returns a collection of Container objects, each of which represents a group of related Document objects
QueryDefs	Returns a collection of QueryDef objects

Table 5-1. Database Object Collections (continued)

Collection	Description
Properties	Returns a collection of Property objects representing database properties
Recordsets	Returns a collection of Recordset objects associated with the database
Relations	Returns a collection of Relation objects for the database
TableDefs	Returns a collection of TableDef objects

Table 5-2. Database Object Properties

Property	Description
CollatingOrder	Defines the sequence used for comparing or sorting text
Connect	Provides information about the source of an open database, a database used in a pass-through query, or a linked table
Connection	Returns the Connection object used to open the database
Name	The name (including the path) of the open database
QueryTimeout	Determines the number of seconds to wait before timing out when executing a query on an ODBC data source
RecordsAffected	Indicates the number of records affected by the most recent Execute method
Replicable	Indicates whether a database can be replicated
ReplicableBool	(Jet 3.5 and higher) Indicates whether a database can be replicated
ReplicaID	Uniquely identifies each member of a replica set
ReplicationConflictFunction	Names a custom function that resolves conflicts that occur between replicas during synchronization
Transactions	Indicates whether a database or ODBC driver supports transactions
Updatable	Indicates whether a database can be changed or updated
V1xNullBehavior	Determines whether zero-length strings ("") used to fill text or memo fields are converted to Nulls
Version	Indicates the version of the Jet database (for Jet workspaces) or of DAO (for ODBCDirect workspaces)

Table 5-3. Database Object Methods

Method	Description
Close	Closes an open database
CreateProperty	Creates a custom property that can be added to the Database object's Properties collection
CreateQueryDef	Creates a new QueryDef object
CreateRelation	Defines a new database relation
CreateTableDef	Creates a new table definition

Table 5-3. Database Object Methods (continued)

Method	Description
Execute	Executes a query or SQL statement that does not return a recordset
MakeReplica	Makes a new replica from another database replica
NewPassword	Changes a database's password
OpenRecordset	Opens a recordset
PopulatePartial	Synchronizes a partial replica with a full database replica
Synchronize	Synchronizes two replicas that are members of the same replica set

Access to the Database Object

Creatable

No

Returned by

The Database property of the Connection object

The CreateDatabase method of the DBEngine object

The OpenDatabase method of the DBEngine object

The CreateDatabase method of the Workspace object

The Databases property of the Workspace object

The OpenDatabase method of the Workspace object

Databases Collection Properties

Count   `RO`

Data Type

Integer

Description

The number of objects in a collection. In previous versions of Access, Count was useful for setting up loops to process all objects in a collection, as in the following code; however, the `For Each...Next` loop is a more efficient way of iterating through the members of a collection. The following code lists the name of all the open databases in the Debug window. You should see four names listed—the three opened from code, plus the database from which the code is running.

The System database (*System.mdw*) is not a member of the Databases collection.

VBA Code

```
Private Sub cmdCount_Click()

    Dim wks As Workspace
    Dim dbs1 As Database
    Dim dbs2 As Database
    Dim dbs3 As Database
    Dim prp As Property
    Dim intCount As Integer
    Dim dbsCount As Integer

    Set wks = Workspaces(0)
    Set dbs1 = wks.OpenDatabase("D:\Documents\Northwind.mdb")
    Set dbs2 = wks.OpenDatabase("D:\Documents\Contacts.mdb")
    Set dbs3 = wks.OpenDatabase("D:\Documents\Test.mdb")

    'Iterate through Databases collection and list names.
    dbsCount = wks.Databases.Count
        For intCount = 1 To dbsCount - 1
            Debug.Print "Database " & intCount & vbTab & _
                        wks.Databases(intCount).Name
        Next intCount

    dbs1.Close
    dbs2.Close
    dbs3.Close

End Sub
```

Item   `R0`

```
Databases.Item(Index)
```

Argument	Data Type	Description
Index	Integer	The ordinal position of the Database object in the Databases collection, or a string containing the name of the Database object to be retrieved from the Databases collection

Data Type

Database object

Description

Retrieves a particular Database object from the Databases collection. A Database object can be retrieved based either on its ordinal position in the collection or on its name. Since Databases is a zero-based collection, the following code fragment returns the default workspace's first open database:

```
Dim dbs As Database
Set dbs = DBEngine.Workspaces(0).Databases.Items(0)
```

You can also retrieve a particular Database object by name. The following code fragment, for instance, retrieves the Northwind database by name:

```
Dim wks As Database
Set wks = DBEngine.Workspaces(0).Databases("C:\Documents\Northwind.mdb")
```

Note that the database's name as supplied to the Item property corresponds to its Name property, which includes its path as well as its filename. Since the Item property is the default member of the Databases collection, it does not need to be explicitly specified when retrieving a particular Database object. In other words, the following two statements are equivalent; both retrieve the same database:

```
Set dbs = DBEngine.Workspaces(0).Databases.Item(0)
Set dbs = DBEngine.Workspaces(0).Databases(0)
```

Similarly, the following two statements both retrieve the same database by name:

```
Set dbs = DBEngine.Workspaces(0).Databases.Item(strName)
Set dbs = DBEngine.Workspaces(0).Databases(strName)
```

Databases Collection Methods

Refresh

`collection.Refresh`

Although the Refresh method is listed as a method of the Databases collection in Help and the Object Browser, it actually can't be used with the Databases collection (although calling it does not generate an error) because Refresh only works with persistent collections, i.e., collections of objects that exist on the disk, not just in memory. This may seem paradoxical, as databases do exist on disk as *.mdb* files, but nevertheless the Databases collection is considered to be a nonpersistent collection.

Database Object Properties

CollatingOrder   RO

Data Type

Long

Description

For Jet workspaces only, one of the constants shown in Table 5-4 that defines the order of alphanumeric characters for string comparison or sorting. It corresponds to the *locale* argument of the CreateDatabase method when the database was created or of the CompactDatabase method when it was most recently compacted.

Table 5-4. The CollatingOrder Values

Constant	Value	Description
dbSortGeneral	1033	General (English, French, German, Portuguese, Italian, and Modern Spanish)
dbSortArabic	1025	Arabic
dbSortChineseSimplified	2052	Simplified Chinese
dbSortChineseTraditional	1028	Traditional Chinese
dbSortCyrillic	1049	Cyrillic
dbSortCzech	1029	Czech
dbSortDutch	1043	Dutch
dbSortGreek	1032	Greek
dbSortHebrew	1037	Hebrew
dbSortHungarian	1038	Hungarian
dbSortIcelandic	1039	Icelandic
dbSortJapanese	1041	Japanese
dbSortKorean	1042	Korean
dbSortNeutral	1024	Neutral
dbSortNorwDan	1030	Norwegian or Danish
dbSortPDXIntl	1033	Paradox International
dbSortPDXNor	1030	Paradox Norwegian or Danish
dbSortPDXSwe	1053	Paradox Swedish or Finnish
dbSortPolish	1045	Polish
dbSortSlovenian	1060	Slovenian
dbSortSpanish	1034	Spanish
dbSortSwedFin	1053	Swedish or Finnish
dbSortThai	1054	Thai
dbSortTurkish	1055	Turkish
dbSortUndefined	−1	Undefined or unknown

VBA Code

The following VBA and VBS codes list the collating order of the default Northwind database to the Debug window (curiously enough, it turns out to be 1033, or Paradox International):

```
Private Sub cmdCollatingOrder_Click()

    Dim dbs As Database
```

```
        Set dbs = OpenDatabase("D:\Documents\Northwind.mdb")
        Debug.Print "Northwind collating order: " & dbs.CollatingOrder

    End Sub
```

VBS Code

```
Sub cmdCollatingOrder_Click()

    Dim dao
    Dim dbs
    Dim wks
    Dim strDBName

    strDBName = "D:\Documents\Northwind.mdb"

    'Set up reference to Access database.
    Set dao = Application.CreateObject("DAO.DBEngine.35")
    Set wks = dao.Workspaces(0)
    Set dbs = wks.OpenDatabase(strDBName)

    'Display collating order.
    MsgBox "Northwind collating order: " & dbs.CollatingOrder

End Sub
```

Connect

Data Type

String

Description

A String containing information about the source of an open database or a database used in a pass-through query. The information in this property passes needed information to ODBC or ISAM drivers when making a connection.

The format of the Connect string is:

> *databasetype;parameters;*

This syntax is explained in Table 5-5.

Table 5-5. The Connect Property Arguments

Argument	Data Type	Description
databasetype	String	(Optional; see Table 5-6 for settings) Omit this argument for Jet databases, but include a semicolon (;) as a place-holder.
parameters	String	Additional parameters to pass to ODBC or installable ISAM drivers; use semicolons to separate parameters.

Table 5-6. The Databasetype Argument Settings

Database Type	Specifier	Example
Microsoft Jet Database	`[database];`	*drive:\path\filename.mdb*
dBASE III	`dBASE III;`	*drive:\path*
dBASE IV	`dBASE IV;`	*drive:\path*
dBASE 5	`dBASE 5.0;`	*drive:\path*
Paradox 3.x	`Paradox 3.x;`	*drive:\path*
Paradox 4.x	`Paradox 4.x;`	*drive:\path*
Paradox 5.x	`Paradox 5.x;`	*drive:\path*
FoxPro 2.0	`FoxPro 2.0;`	*drive:\path*
FoxPro 2.5	`FoxPro 2.5;`	*drive:\path*
FoxPro 2.6	`FoxPro 2.6;`	*drive:\path*
Excel 3.0	`Excel 3.0;`	*drive:\path\filename.xls*
Excel 4.0	`Excel 4.0;`	*drive:\path\filename.xls*
Excel 5.0 or Excel 95	`Excel 5.0;`	*drive:\path\filename.xls*
Excel 97	`Excel 97;`	*drive:\path\filename.xls*
HTML Import	`HTML Import;`	*drive:\path\filename*
HTML Export	`HTML Export;`	*drive:\path*
Text	`Text;`	*drive:\path*

ODBC	`ODBC; DATABASE=database;`
	`UID=user; PWD=password;`
	`DSN= datasourcename;`
	`[LOGINTIMEOUT=seconds;]`
		None

Exchange	`Exchange;` `MAPILEVEL=folderpath;` `[TABLETYPE={ 0	1 }];` `[PROFILE=profile;]` `[PWD=password;]` `[DATABASE=database;]`	*drive:\path\filename.mdb*

Many of the argument settings apply to Connection, TableDef, and QueryDef objects, not to Database objects; see Chapter 6, *Containers Collection and Container Object*, and Chapter 9, *Relations Collection and Relation Object*, for a discussion of the Connect property for TableDefs and QueryDefs.

Connection   `R0`

Data type

Connection Object

Description

For databases in ODBCDirect workspaces, returns the Connection object corresponding to the database. For Jet databases, attempting to retrieve this value raises runtime error 3251, "Operation is not supported for this type of object."

DesignMasterID

Data Type

GUID (16-byte value)

Description

For replicated databases in Jet workspaces, sets or returns a GUID property that uniquely identifies the Design Master in the replica set. Setting this property makes a specified replica of the Design Master in the replica set. The property is stored in the SchemaMaster field in the MSysRepInfo system table.

 Before using this property to make a different replica the Design Master for a replica set, synchronize it with all the replicas in the set and open it in exclusive mode.

 If you set this property so as to create a second Design Master in the replica set, you may end up with corrupted data or a partitioned replica set, preventing synchronization of data.

VBA Code

Figure 5-2 shows the database that just made the new Design Master of a replica set, using the following code. The MSysRepInfo table is open, showing the GUID.

```
Private Sub cmdDesignMasterID_Click()

    Dim dbsDMOld As Database
    Dim dbsDMNew As Database
    Dim strDMOld As String
    Dim strDMNew As String

    strDMOld = "D:\Documents\Companywide Contacts.mdb"
    strDMNew = "D:\Documents\Boston Contacts.mdb"

    'Open current Design Master in Exclusive mode.
    Set dbsDMOld = OpenDatabase(strDMOld, True)
```

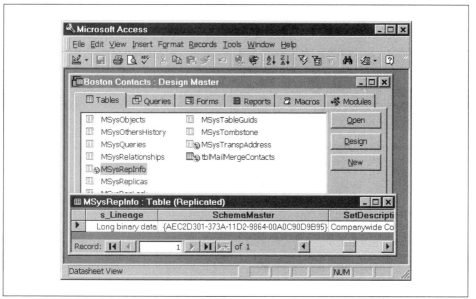

Figure 5-2. A new Design Master, showing the GUID

```
'Open new Design Master.
Set dbsDMNew = OpenDatabase(strDMNew)

'Make new database the Design Master.
dbsDMOld.DesignMasterID = dbsDMNew.ReplicaID
Debug.Print "Design Master ID: " & dbsDMNew.DesignMasterID

'Synchronize the two Design Masters two-way.
dbsDMOld.Synchronize strDMNew, dbRepImpExpChanges
dbsDMOld.Close
dbsDMNew.Close

End Sub
```

Name   `R0`

Data Type

String

Description

Displays the name of a database object. This is the actual filename (including the path), as distinguished from the variable name used to reference the database.

VBA Code

This code opens a database in the default database folder (as set in the Access Options dialog's General page) then lists its name (including path) to the Debug Window:

```
Private Sub cmdName_Click()

    Dim dbs As Database
    Dim strDBName As String

    strDBName = "Contacts.mdb"
    Set dbs = OpenDatabase(strDBName)
    Debug.Print "Database Name: " & dbs.Name
    dbs.Close

End Sub
```

QueryTimeout

Data Type

Integer

Description

Sets or returns the number of seconds to wait before timing out when executing a query on an ODBC data source. For databases, this value is applied to all queries associated with the database, although it can be overwritten for specific queries by setting their ODBCTimeout property. The default value is 60.

RecordsAffected   `RO`

Data Type

Long

Description

Tells you the number of records affected by the most recently invoked Execute method on the database. For an action query, this value contains the number of records deleted, updated, or inserted.

For ODBCDirect workspaces, RecordsAffected does not return a useful value from a SQL_DROP_TABLE action query.

VBA Code

```
Private Sub cmdRecordsAffected_Click()

    Dim dbs As Database
    Dim strDBName As String
    Dim qdf As QueryDef
    Dim strSQL As String

    strSQL = "INSERT INTO tblRecentOrders ( OrderDate, "
    strSQL = strSQL & "OrderID, CustomerID, EmployeeID, RequiredDate, "
    strSQL = strSQL & "ShippedDate, ShipVia, Freight, ShipName, "
    strSQL = strSQL & "ShipAddress, ShipCity, ShipRegion, "
    strSQL = strSQL & "ShipPostalCode, ShipCountry ) SELECT "
    strSQL = strSQL & "OrderDate, OrderID, CustomerID, EmployeeID, "
    strSQL = strSQL & "RequiredDate, ShippedDate, ShipVia, Freight, "
    strSQL = strSQL & "ShipName, ShipAddress, ShipCity, ShipRegion, "
    strSQL = strSQL & "ShipPostalCode, ShipCountry, * FROM Orders "
    strSQL = strSQL & "WHERE OrderDate>#1/6/96#;"
    strDBName = "D:\Documents\Northwind.mdb"
    Set dbs = OpenDatabase(strDBName)
    dbs.Execute strSQL
    Debug.Print "Northwind records affected: " & dbs.RecordsAffected

End Sub
```

Replicable

database.Properties("Replicable")

Data Type

Text

Description

Sets or returns a value indicating whether a database in a Jet workspace can be replicated. Making a database replicable means that you are making it a Design Master from which replicas can be created. In order for a database to be replicable, all the objects in it must also be replicable; otherwise, you will get an error when you append the property to the database's Properties collection.

This property does not exist by default; in order to use it, you must first create it using the CreateProperty method and then append it to the database's Properties collection.

The "`T`" setting is the only one that is usable; if you try to set the Replicable property to "`F`" after initially setting it to "`T`", you will get Run-time error 3459.

The standard *database*.`Replicable` syntax won't work with this property; if you use it, you will get a "Method or data member not found" error.

After adding the Replicable property to a database, appending it to the Properties collection, and setting it to "`T`", as in the following code, the database appears as a Design Master when you next open it, as shown in Figure 5-3.

VBA Code

```
Private Sub cmdReplicable_Click()

    Dim dbs As Database
    Dim strDBName As String
    Dim prp As Property

    strDBName = "D:\Documents\Eastwind.mdb"
    Set dbs = OpenDatabase(strDBName, True)

    With dbs
        On Error Resume Next
        Set prp = .CreateProperty("Replicable", dbText, "T")
        .Properties.Append prp
        .Properties("Replicable") = "T"
        Debug.Print "Name: " & dbs.Name
        Debug.Print "Replicable: " & dbs.Properties("Replicable")

    End With

End Sub
```

ReplicableBool

Data Type

Boolean

Description

If you are working with Jet 3.5 or higher you can use the ReplicableBool property instead of the awkward Replicable property. ReplicableBool takes a Boolean value rather than requiring creation of a custom property. Otherwise, its functionality is identical to the Replicable property.

Figure 5-3. A database converted into a Design Master by making its Replicable property equal to "T"

ReplicaID

Data Type

GUID (16-byte value)

Description

Uniquely identifies each member of a replica set (including the Design Master). It is automatically generated when a replica is created. The value is stored in the GlobalDbId field of the MSysRepInfo table, as shown in Figure 5-4.

VBA Code

```
Private Sub cmdReplicaID_Click()

    Dim dbsDMReplica As Database
    Dim strDMReplica As String

    strDMReplica = "D:\Documents\Companywide Contacts.mdb"

    'Open Replica database
    Set dbsDMReplica = OpenDatabase(strDMReplica)
```

Figure 5-4. The ReplicaID property as stored in the MSysRepInfo table in a replica database

```
Debug.Print "Replica GUID: " & dbsDMReplica.ReplicaID
dbsDMReplica.Close

End Sub
```

ReplicationConflictFunction

database.Properties("ReplicationConflictFunction")

Data Type

String

Description

Defines custom conflict resolution code that's used to resolve data conflicts between replicas being synchronized. To define such a custom procedure, simply assign the name of a function procedure (and not a sub procedure) to the ReplicationConflictFunction property.

ReplicationConflictFunction is not an intrinsic property; in order to use it, you must first create it using the CreateProperty method, and then append it to the database's Properties collection. In the call to CreateProperty method, the *DDL* argument should be set to `True` (-1).

Transaction `RO`

Data Type

Boolean

Description

Indicates whether the Database object supports transactions. For ODBCDirect workspaces it indicates whether the ODBC driver supports transactions. For Jet workspaces it always returns `False` for snapshots and forward-only recordsets. In the case of dynaset and table-type recordsets in Jet workspaces, it returns `True` if the Jet database engine is used and returns `False` otherwise.

Most commonly, this property is used to determine whether a Database object supports transactions prior to calling the BeginTrans method.

Updatable `RO`

Data Type

Boolean

Description

Indicates whether a database can be changed or updated. If it is `True`, the database can be updated; if it is `False`, it can't be updated.

VBA Code

```
Private Sub cmdUpdatable_Click()

    Dim dbs As Database

    Set dbs = OpenDatabase("Northwind.mdb")
    Debug.Print dbs.Name & " updatable? " & dbs.Updatable

End Sub
```

V1xNullBehavior

Data Type

Boolean

Description

Indicates whether zero-length strings used to fill Text or Memo fields are converted to Nulls. It applies only to Jet v. 1.x databases that have been converted to Jet 2.0 or 3.0 databases. The change takes effect after closing and reopening the database.

Version   `RO`

Data Type

String

Description

Tells you what version of Jet (for Jet workspaces) or DAO (for ODBCDirect workspaces) a database uses. Jet versions are shown in Table 5-7.

Table 5-7. Jet Versions and Microsoft Products

Microsoft Jet Version	Release Year	Access	Visual Basic	Excel	Visual C++
1.0	1992	1.0	N/A	N/A	N/A
1.1	1993	1.1	2.0	N/A	N/A
2.0	1994	2.0	N/A	N/A	N/A
2.5	1995	N/A	4.0 (16-bit)	N/A	N/A
3.0	1995	95 (7.0)	4.0 (32-bit)	95 (7.0)	4.x
3.5	1996	97 (8.0)	5.0	97 (8.0)	5.0
3.6	1999	2000 (9.0)	N/A	2000 (9.0)	N/A

VBA Code

```
Private Sub cmdVersion_Click()

    Dim dbsODBC As Database
    Dim wksODBC As Workspace
    Dim con As Connection
    Dim dbsJet As Database
    Dim wksJet As Workspace

    'Create ODBCDirect workspace.
    Set wksODBC = CreateWorkspace("ODBCWorkspace", _
        "admin", "", dbUseODBC)
    Set con = wksODBC.OpenConnection("HQ Data")

    'Set reference to default Jet workspace.
    Set wksJet = Workspaces(0)
    Set dbsJet = wksJet.OpenDatabase("D:\Documents\Eastwind.mdb")
    Debug.Print "ODBCDirect connection version: " & con.Database.Version
```

```
    Debug.Print "Jet engine version: " & dbsJet.Version

End Sub
```

The code prints the following information to the Debug Window:

```
ODBCDirect connection version: 03.51.1029.00
Jet engine version: 3.0
```

Database Object Methods

Close

database.Close

Closes a Database object and removes it from the Databases collection. If you try to close a database that has already been closed, runtime error 3420, "Object invalid or no longer set," occurs.

If you close a database without first closing any open recordsets in it, the recordsets will be closed without saving any pending edits and without a warning.

As an alternative to using the Close method to close a database, you can set its variable equal to Nothing.

VBA Code

This code opens a database based on *Northwind.mdb*, then opens a recordset based on its Customers table, lists all the company names to the Debug window, and finally closes the recordset and the database:

```
Private Sub cmdClose_Click()

    Dim wks As Workspace
    Dim dbs As Database
    Dim rst As Recordset

    Set wks = DBEngine.Workspaces(0)
    Set dbs = wks.OpenDatabase("D:\Documents\Access\Northwind.mdb", True)
    Set rst = dbs.OpenRecordset("Customers", dbOpenTable)
    Do While Not rst.EOF
        Debug.Print rst!CompanyName
        rst.MoveNext
```

```
    Loop
    rst.Close
    dbs.Close

End Sub
```

Outlook VBS Code

This code does much the same thing from Outlook 98 as the VBA code does, with the following syntactical differences, which are typical of the changes you need to make when converting code from VBA to VBS:

- In VBA the bang (!) operator is used to indicate a member of a collection, such as a field in a recordset. In Outlook VBS you must use the dot (.) operator for members of collections.

- In VBA you can use named constants (such as **dbOpenTable**) as function arguments. In Outlook VBS (with very few exceptions, such as **True** and **False**), you must use the argument's numeric value or explicitly define the constant using the **Const** statement.

- There are no data types in Outlook VBS (that is, VBScript supports only the variant data type), so you can't declare variables as any specific data type.

- Outlook VBS lacks the Debug window, so you need to replace Debug.Print calls with *MsgBox* functions.

 Unlike earlier versions of Outlook, Outlook 2000 has VBA, so in many cases you can write VBA code instead of VBS, thus avoiding the limitations listed.

```
Sub cmdCloseDatabase_Click()

    Dim dao
    Dim wks
    Dim dbs
    Dim rst

    Set dao = Application.CreateObject("DAO.DBEngine.35")
    Set wks = dao.Workspaces(0)
    Set dbs = wks.OpenDatabase("D:\Documents\Access\Northwind.mdb", True)
    Set rst = dbs.OpenRecordset("Customers", 1)
    Do While Not rst.EOF
        MsgBox rst.CompanyName
        rst.MoveNext
    Loop
    rst.Close
    dbs.Close

End Sub
```

CreateProperty

```
Set property = object.CreateProperty([name], [type], [value], [DDL])
```

Argument	Data Type	Description
property	Property object	An object variable representing the Property object you are creating.
object	Database, Field, Index, QueryDef, Document, or TableDef object	A Database, Field, Index, QueryDef, Document, or TableDef object variable used to create the new Property object.
name	String	(Optional) The name of the new Property object. Property names can be up to 64 characters in length.
type	Integer	(Optional) A named constant or Integer value (see Table 5-8) that specifies the property's data type.
value	Variant	(Optional) The initial property value.
DDL	Boolean	(Optional) If **True**, the Property is a DDL object, and users can't change or delete it unless they have **dbSecWriteDef** permission. If **False** (the default), it is not a DDL object and can be changed or deleted by users.

For Jet workspaces only, creates a new user-defined Property object in the Properties collection of a persistent object. See the Replicable section earler in this chapter for an important use for this method.

Table 5-8. The Type Intrinsic Constants

Named Constant	Value	Description
dbBigInt	16	Big Integer
dbBinary	9	Binary
dbBoolean	1	Boolean
dbByte	2	Byte
dbChar	18	Char
dbCurrency	5	Currency
dbDate	8	Date/Time
dbDecimal	20	Decimal
dbDouble	7	Double
dbFloat	21	Float
dbGUID	15	GUID
dbInteger	3	Integer
dbLong	4	Long
dbLongBinary	11	Long Binary (OLE Object)
dbMemo	12	Memo

Table 5-8. The Type Intrinsic Constants (continued)

Named Constant	Value	Description
dbNumeric	19	Numeric
dbSingle	6	Single
dbText	10	Text
dbTime	22	Time
dbTimeStamp	23	Time Stamp
dbVarBinary	17	VarBinary

You don't have to assign values to all the arguments when you create a property; you can set them later, before you append the Property to a Database object. After appending, some (but not all) of the property settings can be altered.

If you try to create a property with a name that already exists in the Properties collection (such as the name of a built-in property), an error occurs.

You may be familiar with Word custom document properties. If so, you are in for a surprise. Access custom database properties don't work exactly like Word custom document properties. In Word you can create custom document properties in the interface on the Custom tab of a template's properties sheet, and these properties are listed when you run code to display a document's custom properties. Likewise, when you create Word custom document properties from code and then open the document's properties sheet, you will see any properties you created from code in the interface.

Access lets you create custom database properties in the interface, as in Word. But when you run the following procedure to list a database's custom properties:

```
Public Function ListDatabaseProperties()

    Dim dbs As Database
    Dim prp As Object

    Set dbs = CurrentDb
    For Each prp In dbs.Properties
        On Error Resume Next
        Debug.Print prp.Name & "(" & prp.Value & ")"
    Next prp
    dbs.Close

End Function
```

you won't see any of the properties you created in the interface. Nor will you see the properties (such as Type, Location, Size, and Create Date) on the General page of the properties sheet. Instead, you will see a list like the following:

```
Name(D:\Documents\Access\General.mdb)
Connect()
Transactions(True)
Updatable(True)
CollatingOrder(1033)
QueryTimeout(60)
Version(3.0)
RecordsAffected(0)
ReplicaID()
DesignMasterID()
AccessVersion(07.53)
Build(4122)
Track Name AutoCorrect Info(0)
Perform Name AutoCorrect(0)
```

You can create custom database properties from code in Access, as in the following procedure:

```
Sub SetProperty(dbs As Database, strName As String, _
   strType As String, strValue As String)

On Error GoTo SetPropertyError

   Dim prp As Property
   Dim err As Error

   'Attempt to set the specified property.
   dbs.Properties(strName) = strValue
   On Error GoTo 0

SetPropertyExit:
   Exit Sub

SetPropertyError:
   If DBEngine.Errors(0).Number = 3270 Then
      'The property was not found.
      Set prp = dbs.CreateProperty(Name:=strName, _
         Type:=strType, Value:=strValue)
      dbs.Properties.Append prp
      Resume Next
   Else
      For Each err In DBEngine.Errors
         MsgBox "Error number: " & err.Number & vbCr & _
            err.Description
      Next err
   End If
   Resume SetPropertyExit
   dbs.Close

End Sub
```

After you create some properties from code, you will see them when you run the *ListDatabaseProperties* function listed in the CreateProperty entry along with some standard properties. But you won't see them in the interface. The properties you create in the interface are added to the Properties collection of a document called *UserDefined* in the Databases container; they can be listed using the following code:

```
Private Sub cmdListCustomProps_Click()

    Dim dbs As Database
    Dim strDBName As String
    Dim ctr As Container
    Dim doc As Document
    Dim prp As Property

    strDBName = "D:\Documents\Northwind.mdb"
    Set dbs = OpenDatabase(strDBName)
    Set ctr = dbs.Containers("Databases")
    Set doc = ctr.Documents("UserDefined")
    With doc
        Debug.Print "User-defined properties in database:"
            For Each prp In doc.Properties
                On Error Resume Next
                Debug.Print vbTab & prp.Name
            Next prp
    End With
    dbs.Close

End Sub
```

The following is a typical set of properties as listed by this procedure (note that some built-in properties are also included in this listing):

```
Name
Owner
UserName
Permissions
AllPermissions
Container
DateCreated
LastUpdated
NWVersion
HFCustomProp
```

Microsoft should rectify this confusing situation so that custom database properties created in code are appended to the same collection as ones created in the interface, and so that the behavior of custom properties is consistent among Office applications. However, there is one benefit to this situation: because custom database properties created in code are not visible in the interface, they are handy places to store odd bits of information you may need to use anywhere in an application, with the assurance that they can't be modified by users.

To set and retrieve the value of a custom database property, use code like the following procedures that call the SetProperty procedure listed earlier:

```
Private Sub cmdCreateProp_Click()

    Dim dbs As Database

    Set dbs = CurrentDb
    Call SetProperty(dbs, "PropFromCode", dbText, "Entered from code")

End Sub

Private Sub cmdReadProp_Click()

    Dim dbs As Database

    Set dbs = CurrentDb
    Debug.Print "Value of PropFromCode property: " _
        & dbs.Properties("PropFromCode")

End Sub
```

There is also a CreateProperty method for the Document, Field, Index, QueryDef, and TableDef objects.

VBA Code

The code creates a new property and appends it to the Northwind database's Properties collection then lists the names and values of any non-empty properties (including the newly created one) to the Debug window:

```
Private Sub cmdCreateProperty_Click()

    Dim wks As Workspace
    Dim dbs As Database
    Dim prp As Property
    Dim prpNew As Property

    Set wks = Workspaces(0)
    Set dbs = wks.OpenDatabase("D:\Documents\Northwind.mdb")
    Set prpNew = dbs.CreateProperty("Internal", dbBoolean, False)
    dbs.Properties.Append prpNew

    'Enumerate database properties.
    For Each prp In dbs.Properties
        On Error Resume Next
        Debug.Print prp.Name & " = " & prp
    Next prp

End Sub
```

CreateQueryDef

```
Set querydef = database.CreateQueryDef(name, sqltext)
```

Argument	Data Type	Description
querydef	QueryDef object	The QueryDef object being created.
object	Connection or Database object	The open Connection or Database object to contain the new QueryDef object.
name	String	The name of the new QueryDef. Querydef names can be up to 64 characters in length.
sqltext	String	(Optional) A SQL statement defining the QueryDef. If omitted, you can set this property before or after appending the QueryDef to a collection.

Creates a new QueryDef object (see Chapter 7, *QueryDefs Collection and Query-Def Object*, for more details on QueryDefs). QueryDefs may be either temporary (unnamed queries that are used in code, but not saved to the database) or saved as named queries. If you specify a name for the QueryDef, it is saved to the database as a permanent object; if you specify a zero-length string for the *name* argument, the QueryDef is temporary.

It is not necessary to append a new QueryDef to a collection.

If you try to create a QueryDef with a name that already exists in the QueryDefs collection, error 3012, "Object already exists," occurs.

VBA Code

The following VBA code creates a temporary QueryDef and lists its record count to the Debug Window. It then creates a permanent QueryDef and lists all the QueryDefs in the QueryDefs collection of the Northwind database. The permanent qryHighOrders query can later be used in the user interface just like a query created with the Query Designer:

```
Private Sub cmdCreateQueryDef_Click()

    Dim wks As Workspace
    Dim dbs As Database
    Dim qdf As QueryDef
    Dim qdfTemp As QueryDef
    Dim qdfPerm As QueryDef
    Dim strSQL As String
    Dim rst As Recordset

    Set wks = Workspaces(0)
    Set dbs = wks.OpenDatabase("D:\Documents\Northwind.mdb")
    strSQL = "SELECT * FROM Customers"
    Set qdfTemp = dbs.CreateQueryDef("", strSQL)
    Set rst = qdfTemp.OpenRecordset(dbOpenSnapshot)
    With rst
        .MoveLast
        Debug.Print "Number of records in temporary QueryDef: " & _
                    .RecordCount & vbCrLf
        .Close
    End With

    strSQL = "SELECT * FROM tblOrders WHERE OrderAmount >500;"
    Set qdfPerm = dbs.CreateQueryDef("qryHighOrders", strSQL)

    'Enumerate permanent QueryDefs in Northwind database
    For Each qdf In dbs.QueryDefs
        Debug.Print qdf.Name
    Next qdf
    dbs.Close

End Sub
```

CreateRelation

```
Set relation = database.CreateRelation(name, table, foreigntable, attributes)
```

Argument	Data Type	Description
relation	Relation object	The Relation object being created.
database	Database object	The Database object for which the new Relation object is being created.
name	String	(Optional) The name of the new Relation. Relation names can be up to 64 characters in length.
table	String	The primary table in the relation. If this table doesn't exist before the Relation object is appended, an error occurs.
foreigntable	String	The foreign table in the relation. If this table doesn't exist before the Relation object is appended, an error occurs.
attributes	Long	(Optional) One or more of the named constants or Long values shown in Table 5-9.

Creates a new Relation object (see Figure 5-5), representing a relationship between two fields in two TableDef or QueryDef objects. If you omit a value for one of the optional arguments, you can set it later, before you append the new Relation to a collection. However, you can't change any of the settings after appending. Before appending a new Relation to the Relations collection, you must set and append the Field objects needed to define the primary and foreign keys.

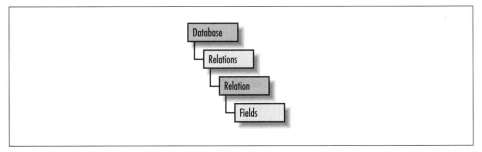

Figure 5-5. The Relations collection in the DAO object model

 A relation created by the CreateRelation method may not appear in the Relationships window.

 If you try to create a Relation with a name that represents an existing member of the Relations collection, an error occurs.

You can't set a relation between a replicated table and a local table.

You can reference a Relation object with any of the following syntax variations:

```
Relations(0)
Relations("name")
Relations![name]
```

Table 5-9. The Relation Attributes Intrinsic Constants

Named Constant	Value	Description
dbRelationUnique	1	The relationship is one-to-one.
dbRelationDontEnforce	2	The relationship isn't enforced (no referential integrity).
dbRelationInherited	4	The relationship exists in a non-current database that contains the two linked tables.
dbRelationUpdateCascade	256	Updates will cascade.

Table 5-9. The Relation Attributes Intrinsic Constants (continued)

Named Constant	Value	Description
dbRelationDeleteCascade	4096	Deletions will cascade.
dbRelationLeft	16777216	This constant is listed in the Object Browser but not in Help. No definition is provided, but presumably it indicates that the relationship is a left join.
dbRelationRight	33554432	This constant is listed in the Object Browser, but not in Help. No definition is provided, but presumably it indicates that the relationship is a right join.

VBA Code

```
Private Sub cmdCreateRelation_Click()

    Dim wks As Workspace
    Dim dbs As Database
    Dim tdfEmp As TableDef
    Dim tdfPhone As TableDef
    Dim fld As Field
    Dim rel As Relation
    Dim idx As Index

    Set wks = Workspaces(0)
    Set dbs = wks.OpenDatabase("D:\Documents\Northwind.mdb")

    With dbs
        'Create a Tabledef based on an existing table.
        Set tdfEmp = dbs.TableDefs("Employees")

        'Create new table.
        Set tdfPhone = dbs.CreateTableDef("Phones")

        'Append fields to new table.
        With tdfPhone
            .Fields.Append .CreateField("EmployeeID", dbLong)
            .Fields.Append .CreateField("PhoneNumber", dbText, 14)
            .Fields.Append .CreateField("PhoneDesc", dbText, 20)

            'Index the new table.
            Set idx = .CreateIndex("EmpIDIndex")

            'Add a field to the index and make it unique.
            idx.Fields.Append idx.CreateField("EmployeeID")
            idx.Unique = True
            .Indexes.Append idx
        End With
    .TableDefs.Append tdfPhone

        'Create a relation to join the new Phones table to the
        'existing Employees table.
```

```
            Set rel = .CreateRelation("EmployeePhones", _
                tdfEmp.Name, tdfPhone.Name, dbRelationUpdateCascade)

            'Create a Field object for the relation, and set
            'its Name and ForeignName properties.
            rel.Fields.Append rel.CreateField("EmployeeID")
            rel.Fields!EmployeeID.ForeignName = "EmployeeID"
            .Relations.Append rel
            .Close
        End With

    End Sub
```

CreateTableDef

```
Set tabledef = database.CreateTableDef(name, attributes, sourcetablename, connect)
```

Argument	Data Type	Description
tabledef	TableDef object	The TableDef object being created.
database	Database object	The Database object for which the new TableDef object is being created.
name	String	(Optional) The name of the new TableDef. This may be up to 64 characters in length.
attributes	Long	(Optional) One or more of the named constants or Long values shown in Table 5-10.
sourcetablename	String	The name of a table in an external database that is the source of the data. This becomes the SourceTableName property setting of the new TableDef object.
connect	String	(Optional) A String composed of a database type specifier and zero or more parameters separated by semicolons. This contains information about the source of an open database, a database used in a pass-through query, or a linked table.

Similar to the CreateQueryDef method, CreateTableDef creates a new TableDef object in a database (Jet workspaces only). Unlike CreateQueryDef, however, there is no way to create a TableDef that exists only in memory; any TableDefs you create are tables in the database that can be manipulated in the database the same as manually created tables. (However, to some extent Recordsets can be considered the "in memory" equivalent of TableDefs.) See Chapter 10, *TableDefs Collection and TableDef Object*, for more details on TableDefs.

Table 5-10. The TableDef Attributes Intrinsic Constants

Named Constant	Value	Description
dbAttachExclusive	65536	For databases that use the Jet database engine, the table is a linked table opened for exclusive use. You can set this constant on an appended TableDef object for a local table but not on a remote table.
dbAttachSavePWD	131072	For databases that use the Jet database engine, the user ID and password for the remotely linked table are saved with the connection information. You can set this constant on an appended Table-Def object for a remote table but not on a local table.
dbSystemObject	-2147483646	The table is a system table provided by the Jet database engine. You can set this constant on an appended TableDef object.
dbHiddenObject	1	The table is a hidden table provided by the Jet database engine. You can set this constant on an appended TableDef object.
dbAttachedTable	1073741824	The table is a linked table from a non-ODBC data source such as a Jet or Paradox database (read-only).
dbAttachedODBC	536870912	The table is a linked table from an ODBC data source, such as Microsoft SQL Server (read-only).

TableDefs created by the TableDef method don't appear immediately in the database window, but you can see them if you list Table-Defs to the Debug window, as in the following VBA code sample.

The following syntactical differences between the VBA and VBS code are typical of the changes you need to make when converting code from VBA to VBS. If you are using Office 2000, you may be able to write Outlook VBA code instead of VBScript, in which case you will not be bound by these limitations:

- There are no data types in Outlook VBS, so you can't declare variables as any specific data type.

- In VBA the bang (!) operator is used to indicate a member of a collection, such as a field in a recordset. In Outlook VBS you must use the dot (.) operator for members of collections.

- In VBA you can use named constants (such as **dbHiddenObject**) as function arguments. In Outlook VBS (with a very few exceptions, such as **True** and **False**) you must use the argument's numeric value, or you must explicitly define the constant in advance by using the VBScript **Const** statement.

- Outlook VBS lacks the Debug window, so you need to replace Debug.Print calls with *MsgBox* functions.

- The With...End With statement is not supported by VBS, so you have to use the full syntax when referencing variables.

- When using a looping code structure (such as For Each...Next), you can't specify the looping variable—just use Next instead of Next tdf.

VBA Code

The following VBA and VBS codes both create a new, hidden table in the Northwind database:

```
Private Sub cmdCreateTableDef_Click()

    Dim wks As Workspace
    Dim dbs As Database
    Dim tdf As TableDef
    Dim tdfNew As TableDef

    Set wks = Workspaces(0)
    Set dbs = wks.OpenDatabase("D:\Documents\Northwind.mdb")

    With dbs
        'Create new table.
        Set tdfNew = dbs.CreateTableDef("Stuff", dbHiddenObject)

        'Append fields to new table.
        With tdfNew
            .Fields.Append .CreateField("EmployeeID", dbLong)
            .Fields.Append .CreateField("Hobbies", dbText, 14)
            .Fields.Append .CreateField("VacationPreference", dbText, 20)
            .Fields.Append .CreateField("AnnualBonus", dbCurrency)
        End With

        .TableDefs.Append tdfNew
        For Each tdf In .TableDefs
            Debug.Print "Table Name: " & tdf.Name & vbTab & vbTab & _
                "Attributes: " & tdf.Attributes
        Next tdf
        .Close
    End With

End Sub
```

Outlook VBS Code

```
Sub cmdCreateTableDef_Click()

    Dim dao
    Dim wks
    Dim dbs
    Dim tdf
```

```
    Dim tdfNew

    Set dao = Application.CreateObject("DAO.DBEngine.35")
    Set wks = dao.Workspaces(0)
    Set dbs = wks.OpenDatabase("D:\Documents\Northwind.mdb")

    'Create new table.
    Set tdfNew = dbs.CreateTableDef("ExtraStuff", 1)

    'Append fields to new table.
    tdfNew.Fields.Append tdfNew.CreateField("EmployeeID", 4)
    tdfNew.Fields.Append tdfNew.CreateField("Hobbies", 10, 14)
    tdfNew.Fields.Append tdfNew.CreateField("VacationPreference", 10, 20)
    tdfNew.Fields.Append tdfNew.CreateField("AnnualBonus", 5)
    dbs.TableDefs.Append tdfNew

    For Each tdf In dbs.TableDefs
        MsgBox "Table Name: " & tdf.Name & "       " & "       " & _
               "Attributes: " & tdf.Attributes
    Next
    dbs.Close

End Sub
```

Execute

```
database.Execute query, [options]
querydef.Execute [options]
```

Argument	Data Type	Description
database	Database object	A Database object on which the query will run
querydef	QueryDef object	A QueryDef object whose SQL property specifies the SQL statement to execute
query	String	A SQL statement or the name of a QueryDef
options	Long	(Optional) One or more of the named constants or Long values shown in Table 5-11

Runs an action (make-table, append, update, or delete) query or executes a SQL statement for a Database object. Note that the Execute method does not return a recordset; hence, it cannot be used with a **SELECT** query or **SELECT** statement.

After the Execute method has completed, the RecordsAffected property of *database* or *querydef* indicates the number of records affected by the action query.

Table 5-11. The Options Intrinsic Constants

Named Constant	Value	Description
dbDenyWrite	1	Denies write permission to other users (Jet workspaces only).
dbInconsistent	16	(Default) Executes inconsistent updates (Jet workspaces only). This setting allows data to be updated in linked tables so as to cause a mismatch between the data in the joined tables, for example, a CustomerID in the Orders table that doesn't have a match in the Customers table.
dbConsistent	32	Executes consistent updates (Jet workspaces only). This only allows data to be updated so that it is consistent and data in linked tables matches.
dbSQLPassThrough	64	Executes a SQL pass-through query. Setting this option passes the SQL statement to an ODBC database for processing (Jet workspaces only).
dbFailOnError	128	Rolls back updates if an error occurs (Jet workspaces only).
dbSeeChanges	512	Generates a run-time error if another user is changing data that you are editing (Jet workspaces only).
dbRunAsync	1024	Executes the query asynchronously (ODBCDirect Connection and QueryDef objects only).
dbExecDirect	2048	Executes the statement without first calling the *SQLPrepare* ODBC API function (ODBCDirect Connection and QueryDef objects only).

VBA Code

The following two code samples run the same action query from a SQL statement. You could also run a stored action query using the Execute method. See the notes in the CreateTableDef section for an explanation of the syntactical differences between the VBA and VBS code:

```
Private Sub cmdExecute_Click()

    Dim wks As Workspace
    Dim dbs As Database
    Dim qdf As QueryDef
    Dim strSQL As String
    Dim tdf As TableDef

    Set wks = Workspaces(0)
    Set dbs = wks.OpenDatabase("D:\Documents\Northwind.mdb")
    strSQL = _
            "SELECT Orders.*, * INTO tmakRecentOrders " & _
            "FROM Orders WHERE OrderDate>#1/6/96#;"

    'Execute a SQL statement to produce the
    'tmakRecentOrders table
    dbs.Execute strSQL, dbFailOnError
```

```
    For Each tdf In dbs.TableDefs
        Debug.Print "Table Name: " & tdf.Name & vbTab & _
            vbTab & "Attributes: " & tdf.Attributes
    Next tdf
    dbs.Close

End Sub
```

Outlook VBS Code

```
Sub cmdExecute_Click()

    Dim dao
    Dim wks
    Dim dbs
    Dim strSQL

    Set dao = Application.CreateObject("DAO.DBEngine.35")
    Set wks = dao.Workspaces(0)
    Set dbs = wks.OpenDatabase("D:\Documents\Northwind.mdb")
    strSQL = _
            "SELECT Orders.*, * INTO tmakRecentOrders " & _
            "FROM Orders WHERE OrderDate>#1/6/96#;"

    'Execute a SQL statement to produce the tmakRecentOrders table.
    dbs.Execute strSQL, 128

    For Each tdf In dbs.TableDefs
        MsgBox "Table Name: " & tdf.Name
    Next
    dbs.Close

End Sub
```

MakeReplica

database.MakeReplica *pathname*, *description*, *options*

Argument	Data Type	Description
database	Database object	An existing replicated database (either the Design master or one of the replicas).
pathname	String	The path and filename of the new replica database. If an existing name is used, an error occurs.
description	String	The description of the replica database.
options	Integer	A named constant or Integer value (see Table 5-12).

When you are working with a replicated database, the MakeReplica method creates a new replica from any member of the replica set (the Design Master or any of the existing replicas).

Table 5-12. The Options Intrinsic Constants

Named Constant	Value	Description
dbRepMakePartial	1	Creates a partial replica.
dbRepMakeReadOnly	2	Prevents users from modifying the replicable objects of the new replica. However, when you synchronize the new replica with another member of the replica set, design and data changes will be propagated to the new replica.

VBA Code

This code creates a replica of a database in a remote folder:

```
Private Sub cmdMakeReplica_Click()

    Dim wks As Workspace
    Dim dbs As Database
    Dim strDBName As String
    Dim strReplicaName As String
    Dim strDescription As String

    Set wks = Workspaces(0)
    strDBName = "D:\Documents\Companywide Contacts.mdb"
    strReplicaName = "N:\Documents\Boston Contacts.mdb"
    strDescription = "Boston Replica of Companywide Contacts database"
    Set dbs = wks.OpenDatabase(strDBName)
    dbs.MakeReplica strReplicaName, strDescription

End Sub
```

NewPassword

`database.NewPassword bstrold, bstrnew`

Argument	Data Type	Description
database	Database object	The Database object whose password you want to change.
bstrold	String	The current password of the database. The password is a case-sensitive string up to 14 characters long and can include any characters except ASCII 0 (null).
bstrnew	String	The new password for the database. This can be up to 14 characters long and can include any characters except ASCII 0 (null).

Changes the password for an existing user account or database (for Jet workspaces only). You can change the database password even if the database is not secured. (See Chapter 12, *Users Collection and User Object*, for information on changing user account passwords.)

To clear a password, set the *newpassword* argument to a zero-length string.

VBA Code

The VBA code assigns a new password to an Access database that has a default zero-length string password:

```
Private Sub cmdNewPassword_Click()

    Dim wks As Workspace
    Dim dbs As Database
    Dim strPW As String

    Set wks = Workspaces(0)
    Set dbs = wks.OpenDatabase("D:\Documents\TestPW.mdb", True)

    dbs.NewPassword "", "N2828322K"

End Sub
```

OpenRecordset

Set *recordset* = *database*.OpenRecordset(*name*, [[[*type*], *options*], *lockedit*])

Argument	Data Type	Description
recordset	Recordset object	The Recordset object to be opened.
database	Database object	The Database object in which the recordset is to be opened.
name	String	The record source for the new Recordset object. May be a table name, a query name, or a SQL statement. For table-type Jet recordsets, only table names are allowable.
type	Integer	(Optional) A named constant or Integer value indicating the type of recordset to create (see Table 5-13).
options	Long	(Optional) A named constant or Long value (see Table 5-14).
lockedit	Integer	(Optional) A named constant or Integer value (see Table 5-15).

The OpenRecordset method of the Database object is probably the most useful method in the entire DAO object model. It is used to work with data in tables and queries (including temporary queries created by SQL statements). Using the *type* settings, you have a great deal of flexibility in opening recordsets of various types, on both native and attached tables.

A saved query or SQL statement used for the *name* argument must be a query that returns records, not an action query. If you specify an action query, an "Invalid Operation" error occurs.

Table 5-13. The Type Intrinsic Constants

Named Constant	Value	Description
dbOpenTable	1	Opens a table-type Recordset object (Jet workspaces only). This is the default value for Jet workspaces.
dbOpenDynamic	16	Opens a dynamic-type Recordset object, similar to an ODBC dynamic cursor (ODBCDirect workspaces only).
dbOpenDynaset	2	Opens a dynaset-type Recordset object, similar to an ODBC keyset cursor. This is the default value for linked tables or queries in Jet workspaces.
dbOpenSnapshot	4	Opens a snapshot-type Recordset object similar to an ODBC static cursor.
dbOpenForwardOnly	8	Opens a forward-only-type Recordset object. This is the default value for ODBCDirect workspaces.

Table 5-14. The Options Intrinsic Constants

Named Constant	Value	Description
dbAppendOnly	8	Allows users to append new records to the Recordset, but prevents them from editing or deleting existing records (Jet dynaset-type Recordset only).
dbSQLPassThrough	64	Passes a SQL statement to a Jet-connected ODBC data source for processing (Jet snapshot-type Recordset only).
dbSeeChanges	512	Generates a run-time error if one user is changing data that another user is editing (Jet dynaset-type Recordset only). This setting is useful in applications where multiple users have simultaneous read/write access to the same data.
dbDenyWrite	1	Prevents other users from modifying or adding records (Jet Recordset objects only).
dbDenyRead	2	Prevents other users from reading data in a table (Jet table-type Recordset only).
dbForwardOnly	256	Creates a forward-only Recordset (Jet snapshot-type Recordset only). It is provided only for backward compatibility; you should use the **dbOpenForwardOnly** constant in the *Type* argument instead of using this constant.
dbReadOnly	4	Prevents users from making changes to the Recordset (Jet only). The **dbReadOnly** constant in the *Lockedits* argument replaces this option, which is provided only for backward compatibility.

Table 5-14. The Options Intrinsic Constants (continued)

Named Constant	Value	Description
dbRunAsync	1024	Runs an asynchronous query (ODBCDirect workspaces only).
dbExecDirect	2048	Runs a query by skipping *SQLPrepare* and directly calling *SQLExecDirect* (ODBCDirect workspaces only). Use this option only when you're not opening a Recordset based on a parameter query.
dbInconsistent	16	Allows inconsistent updates (Jet dynaset-type and snapshot-type Recordset objects only). This setting allows data to be updated in linked tables so as to cause a mismatch between the data in the joined tables. (For example, a CustomerID in the Orders table that doesn't have a match in the Customers table.)
dbConsistent	32	Allows only consistent updates (Jet dynaset-type and snapshot-type Recordset objects only). This only allows data to be updated so that it is consistent and data in linked tables matches.

Table 5-15. The Lockedit Intrinsic Constants

Named Constant	Value	Description
dbReadOnly	4	Prevents users from making changes to the Recordset (default for ODBCDirect workspaces). You can use dbReadOnly in either the *Options* argument or the *Lockedit* argument, but not both. If you use it for both arguments, a run-time error occurs.
dbPessimistic	2	Uses pessimistic locking to determine how changes are made to the recordset in a multiuser environment. The page containing the record you're editing is locked as soon as you use the Edit method (default for Jet workspaces).
dbOptimistic	3	Uses optimistic locking to determine how changes are made to the recordset in a multi-user environment. The page containing the record is not locked until the Update method is executed.
dbOptimisticValue	1	Uses optimistic concurrency based on row values (ODBCDirect workspaces only).
dbOptimisticBatch	5	Enables batch optimistic updating (ODBCDirect workspaces only).

The recordset types and their uses are listed in Table 5-16.

Table 5-16. The Recordset Types and Their Uses

Recordset Type	Usage
Table	Represents a single base table. Supports the AddNew, Delete, and Seek methods, but not the Find* methods. (Jet only.)

Table 5-16. The Recordset Types and Their Uses (continued)

Recordset Type	Usage
Dynamic	Represents one or more base tables. Supports the AddNew and Delete methods, but not the Find* or Seek methods.
Dynaset	Represents a table or an updatable query. Supports the AddNew, Delete, and Find* methods, but not the Seek method.
Snapshot	A read-only recordset. Useful for finding data or printing. Does not allow updating, except in the case of an updatable Snapshot in an ODBCDirect workspace. Supports the Find* methods.
Forward-only	Similar to a snapshot, but only allows forward movement. Useful when you only need to make a single pass through a recordset. Does not support the Find* methods.

For a full listing of which methods and properties are supported by which recordset types, see the Recordset Object Help topic.

Access VBA Code

This code opens two types of recordsets, useful for different situations. The table-type recordset offers you the maximum utility to work with the recordset, allowing both reading and writing to it; the snapshot-type recordset is handy when you just want to examine a recordset, but don't need to write to it:

```
Private Sub cmdOpenRecordset_Click()

    Dim wks As Workspace
    Dim dbs As Database
    Dim rstTable As Recordset
    Dim rstSQL As Recordset
    Dim strTable As String
    Dim strSQL As String
    Dim fld As Field
    Dim flds As Fields

    Set wks = Workspaces(0)
    Set dbs = wks.OpenDatabase("D:\Documents\Northwind.mdb")
    strTable = "Orders"
    strSQL = "SELECT * FROM Customers"
    Set rstTable = dbs.OpenRecordset(strTable, dbOpenTable)
    Set rstSQL = dbs.OpenRecordset(strSQL, dbOpenSnapshot)

    'List fields from the two recordsets to the Debug window.
    Set flds = rstTable.Fields
    Debug.Print strTable & " fields:" & vbCrLf
    Debug.Print "Recordset type: " & rstTable.Type
    For Each fld In flds
```

```
        Debug.Print "Field name: " & fld.Name & vbTab & " = " & fld.Value
     Next fld

     Set flds = rstSQL.Fields
     Debug.Print "SQL recordset fields:" & vbCrLf
     Debug.Print "Recordset type: " & rstSQL.Type
     For Each fld In flds
        Debug.Print "Field name: " & fld.Name & vbTab & " = " & fld.Value
     Next fld

End Sub
```

Excel VBA Code

This code, which runs from the Worksheet_Open event of an Excel template, imports contacts from an Access table into a preformatted worksheet:

```
Private Sub Workbook_Open()

    Dim DAO As DBEngine
    Dim wks As Workspace
    Dim dbs As Database
    Dim rst As Recordset
    Dim strTemplateDir As String
    Dim strFullName As String
    Dim strAddress As String
    Dim strCityStateZip As String
    Dim strJobTitle As String
    Dim strCompany As String
    Dim strPhone As String
    Dim strFax As String
    Dim lngCount As Long
    Dim strEmpty As String
    Dim strRange As String
    Dim lngASC As Long
    Dim strASCII As String
    Dim i As Integer

    strEmpty = Chr$(34) & Chr$(34)

    'Get reference to data table.
    Set DAO = CreateObject("DAO.DBEngine.35")
    Set wks = DAO.Workspaces(0)
    Set dbs = wks.OpenDatabase("D:\Documents\Data for Import.mdb")
    Set rst = dbs.OpenRecordset("tblContacts", dbOpenTable, dbDenyRead)
    lngCount = rst.RecordCount
    If lngCount = 0 Then
       MsgBox "No records to import"
       Exit Sub
    Else
       MsgBox lngCount & " records to import into Excel"
    End If
```

```
'Adjust the counter to be 1 less than the row number of the
'first body row of the worksheet.
i = 3

'Initialize column letters with 64, so the first letter used will be A.
lngASCII = 64

'Loop through table, importing each record to a cell in the Word table.
Do Until rst.EOF
   With rst
      'Create variables from a record.
      strFullName = ![FullName]

      If ![BusinessAddressStreet] <> strEmpty Then
         strAddress = ![BusinessAddressStreet]
      End If

      If ![BusinessAddressCity] <> strEmpty Then
         strCityStateZip = (![BusinessAddressCity] & Chr$(44) & _
                           Chr$(32) & _
                           IIf(![BusinessAddressState] <> strEmpty, _
                           ![BusinessAddressState] & Chr$(32) _
                           & Chr$(32), ![BusinessAddressState]) & _
                           ![BusinessAddressPostalCode])
      End If

      If ![JobTitle] <> strEmpty Then
         strJobTitle = ![JobTitle]
         Debug.Print strJobTitle
      End If

      If ![CompanyName] <> strEmpty Then
         strCompany = ![CompanyName]
         Debug.Print strCompany
      End If

      If ![BusinessTelephoneNumber] <> strEmpty Then
         strPhone = ![BusinessTelephoneNumber]
         Debug.Print strPhone
      End If

      If ![BusinessFaxNumber] <> strEmpty Then
         strFax = ![BusinessFaxNumber]
         Debug.Print strFax
      End If

      i = i + 1
      lngASCII = lngASCII + 1
      strASCII = Chr(lngASCII)
      strRange = strASCII & CStr(i)
      Set objRange = Selection.Range(strRange)
      If strFullName <> strEmpty Then
         objRange.Value = strFullName
      End If
```

```
                  lngASCII = lngASCII + 1
                  strASCII = Chr(lngASCII)
                  strRange = strASCII & CStr(i)
                  Set objRange = Selection.Range(strRange)
                  objRange.Value = strJobTitle

                  lngASCII = lngASCII + 1
                  strASCII = Chr(lngASCII)
                  strRange = strASCII & CStr(i)
                  Set objRange = Selection.Range(strRange)
                  objRange.Value = strCompany

                  lngASCII = lngASCII + 1
                  strASCII = Chr(lngASCII)
                  strRange = strASCII & CStr(i)
                  Set objRange = Selection.Range(strRange)
                  objRange.Value = strAddress1

                  lngASCII = lngASCII + 1
                  strASCII = Chr(lngASCII)
                  strRange = strASCII & CStr(i)
                  Set objRange = Selection.Range(strRange)
                  objRange.Value = strAddress2

                  lngASCII = lngASCII + 1
                  strASCII = Chr(lngASCII)
                  strRange = strASCII & CStr(i)
                  Set objRange = Selection.Range(strRange)
                  objRange.Value = strCityStateZip

                  lngASCII = lngASCII + 1
                  strASCII = Chr(lngASCII)
                  strRange = strASCII & CStr(i)
                  Set objRange = Selection.Range(strRange)
                  objRange.Value = strPhone

                  lngASCII = lngASCII + 1
                  strASCII = Chr(lngASCII)
                  strRange = strASCII & CStr(i)
                  Set objRange = Selection.Range(strRange)
                  objRange.Value = strFax

                  lngASCII = 64

            End With
         rst.MoveNext
         Loop

      MsgBox "All Contacts imported!"

   End Sub
```

Set a reference to the DAO 3.5 type library in the Tools → References dialog in Word and Excel so that you can early bind the DAO object variables, declaring them as specific object types rather than generic Objects. See Figure 5-6.

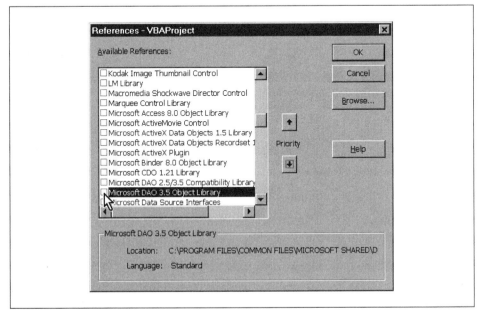

Figure 5-6. Setting a reference to the DAO 3.5 object library

Word VBA Code

This code (running from a Word template's AutoNew event) opens a table-type recordset and populates a Word table from the recordset. The Word table is sized for Avery #5160 labels, so the data will create sheets of labels:

```
Sub AutoNew()

    Dim DAO As DBEngine
    Dim wks As Workspace
    Dim dbs As Database
    Dim rst As Recordset
    Dim strTemplateDir As String
    Dim strLetter As String
    Dim strFullName As String
    Dim strAddress As String
    Dim lngCount As Long
    Dim intAddressType As Integer
    Dim strEmpty As String
```

```
strEmpty = Chr$(34) & Chr$(34)

'Get reference to data table.
Set DAO = CreateObject("DAO.DBEngine.35")
Set wks = DAO.Workspaces(0)
Set dbs = wks.OpenDatabase("D:\Documents\Data for Import.mdb")
Set rst = dbs.OpenRecordset("tblContacts", dbOpenTable, dbDenyRead)
lngCount = rst.RecordCount
If lngCount = 0 Then
    MsgBox "No records to import"
    Exit Sub
Else
    MsgBox lngCount & " records to import into Word"
End If

'Create 3-column Word table to fill with Access data.
ActiveDocument.Tables.Add Range:=Selection.Range, _
    NumRows:=2, NumColumns:=3

'Loop through table, importing each record to a cell in the Word table.
Do Until rst.EOF
    With rst
        'Create variables from a record.
        strFullName = ![FullName]
        Debug.Print strFullName
        strAddress = ![BusinessAddress]
        Debug.Print strAddress

        'Insert data into labels.
        Selection.TypeText Text:=strFullName
        Selection.TypeParagraph
        Selection.TypeText Text:=strAddress
        Selection.TypeParagraph
        Selection.MoveRight Unit:=wdCell
    End With
rst.MoveNext
Loop

Selection.HomeKey Unit:=wdStory
MsgBox "All Contacts imported!"

End Sub
```

Outlook VBS Code

This code fills a list box on an Outlook custom form with the contents of a record-set based on the Northwind Customers table. In a real application, you would probably want to run this code from the form's Open event, rather than from a command button.

See the notes in the CreateTableDef section for an explanation of the syntactical differences between the VBA and VBS code:

```
Sub cmdFillListBox_Click

    Dim rst
    Dim dao
    Dim wks
    Dim dbs
    Dim nms
    Dim strAccessDir
    Dim objAccess
    Dim CustomerArray(99, 2)

    'Pick up path to Access database directory from Access SysCmd function.
    Set objAccess = Item.Application.CreateObject("Access.Application")
    strAccessDir = objAccess.SysCmd(9)
    strDBName = strAccessDir & "Samples\Northwind.mdb"
    objAccess.Quit

    'Set up reference to Access database.
    Set dao = Application.CreateObject("DAO.DBEngine.35")
    Set wks = dao.Workspaces(0)
    Set dbs = wks.OpenDatabase(strDBName)

    'Retrieve Customer information from table.
    Set rst = dbs.OpenRecordset("Customers")
    Set ctl = Item.GetInspector.ModifiedFormPages("Message").
Controls("lstCustomers")

    ctl.ColumnCount = 3
    ctl.ColumnWidths = "50; 150 pt; 75 pt"

    'Assign Access data to an array of 3 columns and 100 rows.
    CustomerArray(99, 2) = rst.GetRows(100)

    ctl.Column() = CustomerArray(99, 2)

End Sub
```

PopulatePartial

database.PopulatePartial *dbpathname*

Argument	Data Type	Description
database	Object	A Database object representing the partial replica Database object to populate
dbpathname	String	The path and name of the full replica from which to populate the records in the partial replica

For replicated databases (Jet databases only), synchronizes a partial replica with the full replica, clears the data in the partial replica, and then repopulates the partial replica based on the current replica filters.

 You should run the PopulatePartial method when you change your replica filters for a partial filter, as this type of change may create orphan records. If you run Synchronize when there are orphan records, an error will occur.

VBA Code

```
Private Sub PopulatePartial()

    Dim tdf As TableDef
    Dim strFilter As String
    Dim dbs As Database
    Dim strPartial as String
    Dim strFull as String

    strPartial = "F:\DATA\Boston Replica.mdb"
    strFull = "C:\DATA\Full Replica.mdb"

    'Open the partial replica in exclusive mode.
    Set dbs = OpenDatabase(strPartial, True)

    With dbs
        Set tdf = .TableDefs("Contacts")

        'Synchronize with full replica
        'before setting replica filter.
        .Synchronize strFull

        strFilter = "AreaCode = '914'"
        tdf.ReplicaFilter = strFilter

'Repopulate records from the full replica.
        .PopulatePartial strFull

        .Close
    End With

End Sub
```

Synchronize

```
database.Synchronize dbpathname, exchangetype
```

Argument	Data Type	Description
database	Database object	A Database object that is a replica
dbpathname	String	The path to the target replica with which Database will be synchronized (the *.mdb* extension is optional)
exchangetype	Integer	A named constant or Integer value (see Table 5-17)

Synchronizes two replicas that are members of the same replica set. It applies only to Jet workspaces. You can do either one-way or two-way synchronization, by using the appropriate value for the Exchange argument.

You can't synchronize a partial replica with another partial replica. See the PopulatePartial method section for more details on partial replica synchronization.

Synchronization over the Internet requires the Replication Manager, which is available in the Office 97 Developer Edition or Microsoft Office 2000 Developer.

Table 5-17. The ExchangeType Intrinsic Constants

Named Constant	Value	Description
dbRepExportChanges	1	Sends changes from database to pathname
dbRepImportChanges	2	Sends changes from pathname to database
dbRepImpExpChanges	4	(Default) Sends changes from database to pathname, and vice-versa, also known as bidirectional exchange
dbRepSyncInternet	16	Exchanges data between files connected by an Internet pathway

VBA Code

The code does a two-way synchronization between a design master and one of its replicas:

```
Private Sub cmdSynchronize_Click()

    Dim wks As Workspace
    Dim dbs As Database
```

```
Dim strReplica As String
Dim strDesignMaster As String

Set wks = Workspaces(0)
strDesignMaster = "D:\Documents\Companywide Contacts.mdb"
strReplica = "D:\Documents\Boston Contacts.mdb"
Set dbs = wks.OpenDatabase(strDesignMaster)
dbs.Synchronize strReplica, dbRepImpExpChanges

End Sub
```

6

Containers Collection and Container Object

The Containers collection is a collection of all the Container objects in a Jet database. Its position in the DAO object model is shown in Figure 6-1. Containers are one of the more obscure components of the DAO object model, with a number of curious and unintuitive features. The Containers collection is subordinate to the Database object, yet within the Containers collection there is a Container object called—you got it—Databases! This paradoxical arrangement is explained in Help (none too clearly) by defining the Databases collection that is one of the Container objects as the collection of *saved* databases, while the Databases collection itself (the one directly under the Workspaces object) is defined as the collection of *open* databases within a workspace.

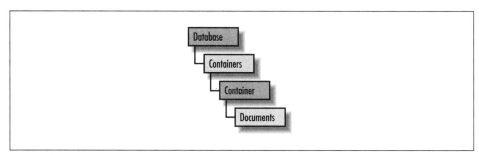

Figure 6-1. The Containers collection in the DAO object model

But that leaves out the most important difference between these objects—the members of the Documents collection contained in the Databases Container are not the familiar Access databases (with the *.mdb* extension) that we work with in the interface, but are some kind of internal storage databases with names like AccessLayout and MSysDb. This confusion could have been avoided if Microsoft had not used the same name for two different objects in the same object model.

The Databases Container object is not the only Container object with a confusing name; some of the other containers (listed in Table 6-1) also share names with other objects in the DAO object model. While the Container Object Help topic lists only three of these containers—Databases, Tables, and Relations (and one of them inaccurately; it is Relationships, not Relations)—all of the containers listed in Table 6-1 can be accessed by code, as in the VBA code example, which lists the Northwind database's Container objects and their properties to the Debug window.

VBA Code

```
Private Sub cmdListContainers_Click()

    Dim dbs As Database
    Dim strDBName As String
    Dim ctr As Container
    Dim prp As Property

    strDBName = "D:\Documents\Northwind.mdb"
    Set dbs = OpenDatabase(strDBName)
    With dbs
        For Each ctr In .Containers
            Debug.Print ctr.Name & " Container properties:"
            For Each prp In ctr.Properties
                On Error Resume Next
                Debug.Print vbTab & prp.Name & " = " & prp
            Next prp
        Next ctr
        .Close
    End With

End Sub
```

Table 6-1. The Container Objects in the Database Containers Collection

Container Name	Contains	Comments
Databases	Saved databases	These are internal database objects with names like AccessLayout and MSysDb.
Forms	Saved forms	Includes all forms, whether open or closed.
Modules	Saved modules	Includes only modules visible in the module tab of the database window; excludes CBF modules.
Relationships	Saved relationships	Includes relationships created in code, whether or not they are visible in the Relationships window.
Reports	Saved reports	Includes all reports, whether open or closed.
Scripts	Saved macros	Macros were known as scripts in the very earliest stages of Access, as is still evidenced in the Script icon used to represent them.

Table 6-1. The Container Objects in the Database Containers Collection (continued)

Container Name	Contains	Comments
SysRel	Undocumented	This mysterious Container object appears neither in Help nor in the Object Browser, but it is listed when you run code that lists all Containers (such as the code in the Owner section later in this chapter). Whatever this Container is, it has only one Document object in it, Admin.
Tables	Saved tables and queries	Includes both tables and queries in one container, while they are separated in other parts of the DAO object model.

There is another area of potential confusion: Each Container object has a Documents collection that includes the instances of objects stored in that Container, such as tables and queries for the Tables container. Don't confuse these Documents with Word documents! They are a very different type of object. Microsoft really should have used a different word here; this duplication of terminology can lead to confusion when selecting objects from the Object Browser or completing a line of code (or declaring a variable) using IntelliSense. (This points to the need for an internal Microsoft process that reviews all object-naming proposals in order to avoid these conflicts of meaning.)

Container objects are built-in, and thus you can't delete one or create a new one. You can reference a Container object by any of the following syntax variations:

```
Containers(0)
Containers("name")
Containers![name]
```

The primary use of the Containers branch of the DAO object model is to iterate through the documents in the Documents collection within a particular Container object. If you need to perform certain operations on all forms or all reports, the Forms and Reports Containers are useful. (The Forms and Reports collections in the Access object model include only the *open* forms or reports.) However, the Access 2000 object model includes new AllForms and AllReports collections, which are easier to use than the Containers collection. These new collections contain all saved forms (or reports), regardless of whether they are open or closed.

The following VBA code iterates through all the saved forms in a database, and the VBS code iterates through the saved reports, using a slightly different syntax. The following syntactical differences between the VBA and VBS code are typical of the changes you need to make when converting code from VBA to VBS:

- There are no data types in Outlook VBS, so you can't declare variables as any specific data type.

- In VBA the bang (!) operator is used to indicate a member of a collection, such as a field in a recordset. In Outlook VBS you must use the dot (.) operator for members of collections.

- In VBA you can use named constants (such as **dbHiddenObject**) as function arguments. In Outlook VBS (with very few exceptions, such as **True** and **False**) you must use the argument's numeric value.

- Outlook lacks the Debug window, so you need to replace Debug.Print calls with *MsgBox* functions.

- The **With...End With** statement is not supported by VBS, so you have to use the full syntax when referencing variables.

- When using a looping code structure (such as **For Each...Next**), you can't specify the looping variable—just use **Next** instead of **Next** *var*.

 If you have Office 2000, you can use the new Outlook VBA for many purposes instead of VBS, thus avoiding these limitations.

VBA Code

```
Private Sub cmdListForms_Click()

    Dim dbs As Database
    Dim strDBName As String
    Dim ctr As Container
    Dim doc As Document

    strDBName = "D:\Documents\Northwind.mdb"
    Set dbs = OpenDatabase(strDBName)
    Set ctr = dbs.Containers("Forms")
    With ctr
        Debug.Print "Forms in Forms Container:"
            For Each doc In ctr.Documents
                On Error Resume Next
                Debug.Print vbTab & doc.Name
            Next doc
    End With
    dbs.Close

End Sub
```

Outlook VBS Code

```
Sub cmdListReports_Click()

    Dim dao
    Dim dbs
    Dim wks
```

```
Dim strDBName
Dim ctr
Dim doc
Dim docs

strDBName = "D:\Documents\Northwind.mdb"

'Set up reference to Access database.
Set dao = Application.CreateObject("DAO.DBEngine.35")
Set wks = dao.Workspaces(0)
Set dbs = wks.OpenDatabase(strDBName)

'Set up reference to Access database.
Set dao = Application.CreateObject("DAO.DBEngine.35")
Set wks = dao.Workspaces(0)
Set dbs = wks.OpenDatabase(strDBName)
Set ctr = dbs.Containers("Reports")

For Each doc In ctr.Documents
    MsgBox doc.Name
Next

dbs.Close

End Sub
```

The Containers collection has two properties and one method (see Table 6-2). The Container object has two collections (the Documents collection and the Properties collection, which consists of one Property object for each property supported by the Container object), no methods, and six properties (see Table 6-3).

Table 6-2. Members of the Containers Collection

Type	Member	Description
Property	Count	Indicates the number of Container objects in the Containers collection
Property	Item	A property hidden in the Object Browser that returns a reference to a particular Container object
Method	Refresh	Updates the objects in the Containers collection

Table 6-3. Container Object Properties

Property	Description
AllPermissions	Returns all the permissions belonging to the current user of the Container object
Inherit	Determines whether new Document objects will inherit the permissions of their container
Name	The name of the Container object
Owner	Indicates the owner of a Container object

Table 6-3. Container Object Properties (continued)

Property	Description
Permissions	Indicates the permissions belonging to the user of a Container object
UserName	The name of the Container object's user

Access to the Container Object

Creatable

    No

Returned by

    The Containers property of the Database object

Containers Collection Properties

Count   `RO`

Data Type

Integer

Description

Indicates the number of objects in a collection. It can be used to iterate through the members of a collection, as in the following VBA code, though this method has generally been replaced by the more efficient **For Each...Next** looping structure.

VBA Code

```
Private Sub cmdCount_Click()

    Dim dbs As Database
    Dim strDBName As String
    Dim ctr As Container
    Dim doc As Document
    Dim docs As Documents
    Dim i As Integer
    Dim intCount As Integer

    strDBName = "D:\Documents\Northwind.mdb"
    Set dbs = OpenDatabase(strDBName)
    Set ctr = dbs.Containers("Reports")
    Set docs = ctr.Documents

    intCount = docs.Count
        Debug.Print intCount & " reports in Reports Container:"
            For i = 1 To intCount
                On Error Resume Next
                Debug.Print vbTab & docs(i).Name
```

```
        Next i
    dbs.Close

  End Sub
```

Item `RO`

```
Containers.Item(Index)
```

Argument	Data Type	Description
Index	Integer	The ordinal position of the Container object in the Containers collection, or a string representing the name of the Container object to be retrieved from the Containers collection

Data Type

Container object

Description

Retrieves a particular Container object from the Containers collection. A Container object can be retrieved either based on its ordinal position in the collection or based on its name. Since Containers is a zero-based collection, the following code fragment returns the first Container object:

```
Dim ctr As Container
Set ctr = Workspaces(0).Databases(0).Containers.Item(0)
```

You can also retrieve a particular Container object by name. The following code fragment, for instance, retrieves the Container object named Scripts:

```
Dim ctr As Container
Set ctr = Workspaces(0).Databases(0).Containers.Item("Scripts")
```

Note that, since the Item property is the default member of the Workspaces collection, it does not need to be explicitly specified when retrieving a particular Workspace object. In other words, the following two statements are equivalent; both retrieve the first container in the collection:

```
Set ctr = objDB.Containers.Item(0)
Set ctr = objDB.Containers(0)
```

Similarly, the following three statements are equivalent and retrieve the Scripts Container object by name:

```
Set ctr = objDB.Containers.Item("Scripts")
Set ctr = objDB.Containers("Scripts")
Set ctr = objDB.Containers![Scripts]
```

Containers Collection Methods

Refresh

```
Containers.Refresh
```

Updates the objects in a collection, taking into account any recently made changes, such as a newly created table.

VBA Code

This code should be run either from Access or from a VB or VBA project to which a reference to the Access object model has been added:

```
Private Sub cmdRefresh_Click()

    Dim dbs As Database

    Set dbs = CurrentDb
    dbs.Containers.Refresh

End Sub
```

Container Object Properties

AllPermissions `RO`

Data Type

Long

Description

Returns all the permissions belonging to the current user of the Container object, including both user-specific and group permissions. (By contrast, the Permissions property includes only the user's own permissions.) All Container objects can return the values listed in Table 6-4; in addition, the Databases container and all Document objects in a Documents collection may return the values in Table 6-5.

Table 6-4. The AllPermissions Return Values for Container Objects

Named Constant	Value	Description
dbSecReadDef	4	The user can read the table definition, including column and index information.
dbSecWriteDef	65548	The user can modify or delete the table definition, including column and index information.
dbSecRetrieveData	20	The user can retrieve data from the Document object.
dbSecInsertData	32	The user can add records.

Table 6-4. The AllPermissions Return Values for Container Objects (continued)

Named Constant	Value	Description
dbSecReplaceData	64	The user can modify records.
dbSecDeleteData	128	The user can delete records.

Table 6-5. Extra AllPermissions Return Values for Document Objects

Named Constant	Value	Description
dbSecDBAdmin	8	The user can replicate the database and change the database password.
dbSecDBCreate	1	The user can create new databases. This setting is valid only on the Databases container in the workgroup information file (*System.mdw*).
dbSecDBExclusive	4	The user has exclusive access to the database.
dbSecDBOpen	2	The user can open the database.

VBA Code

This code lists a number representing the sum of all the permissions for the user of each container in the Northwind database:

```
Private Sub cmdAllPermissions_Click()

    Dim dbs As Database
    Dim ctr As Container

    Set dbs = CurrentDb
    For Each ctr In dbs.Containers
        Debug.Print ctr.Name & " permissions:  " & ctr.AllPermissions
    Next ctr
    dbs.Close

End Sub
```

Inherit

Data Type

Boolean

Description

Used together with the Permissions property to set the permissions new documents will have when they are created. If it is set to **True**, then new documents will pick up their container's permissions; if set to **False**, they won't inherit properties from their container.

Setting the Inherit property to **True** only affects documents created from that point on—it won't affect the permissions of existing documents.

VBA Code

```
Private Sub cmdInherit_Click()

    Dim dbs As Database
    Dim strDBName As String
    Dim ctr As Container

    strDBName = "D:\Documents\Northwind.mdb"
    Set dbs = OpenDatabase(strDBName)
    Set ctr = dbs.Containers("Forms")
    ctr.Inherit = True
    ctr.Permissions = dbSecWriteSec
    dbs.Close

End Sub
```

Name   RO

Data Type

String

Description

Displays the name of a Container object.

VBA Code

This code lists the names of all the containers and all the documents in the Northwind database:

```
Private Sub cmdName_Click()

    Dim dbs As Database
    Dim strDBName As String
    Dim ctr As Container
    Dim doc As Document

    strDBName = "D:\Documents\Northwind.mdb"
    Set dbs = OpenDatabase(strDBName)
    With dbs
        For Each ctr In .Containers
            Debug.Print ctr.Name & " documents:"
            For Each doc In ctr.Documents
                On Error Resume Next
```

```
            Debug.Print vbTab & doc.Name
         Next doc
      Next ctr
      .Close
      End With

   End Sub
```

Owner

Data Type

String

Description

Sets or returns the owner of an object (for Jet workspaces only). It can be either the name of a User in the Users collection or a Group in the Groups collection.

VBA Code

```
Private Sub cmdOwner_Click()

   Dim dbs As Database
   Dim strDBName As String
   Dim ctr As Container
   Dim doc As Document

   strDBName = "D:\Documents\Northwind.mdb"
   Set dbs = OpenDatabase(strDBName)
   With dbs
      For Each ctr In .Containers
         Debug.Print ctr.Name & " documents and their users:"
         For Each doc In ctr.Documents
            On Error Resume Next
            Debug.Print vbTab & doc.Name & " user: " & doc.UserName
         Next doc
      Next ctr
      .Close
      End With

   End Sub
```

Permissions

Data Type

Long

Description

Sets or returns a value representing the permissions belonging to the user of a Container or Document object. Unlike the AllPermissions property, it includes only the specific permissions of the individual user, not the user's permissions that come from group membership.

The valid constants for this property differ by container type, as described in Tables 6-6 through 6-8.

Table 6-6. The Permissions Property Intrinsic Constants for Container Objects Other Than Tables and Databases

Named Constant	Value	Description
dbSecNoAccess	0	The user doesn't have access to the object. (This is not valid for Document objects.)
dbSecFullAccess	1048575	The user has full access to the object.
dbSecDelete	65536	The user can delete the object.
dbSecReadSec	131072	The user can read the object's security-related information.
dbSecWriteSec	262144	The user can alter access permissions.
dbSecWriteOwner	524288	The user can change the Owner property setting.

Table 6-7. The Permissions Property Intrinsic Constants for the Tables Container

Named Constant	Value	Description
dbSecCreate	1	The user can create new documents. (This is not valid for Document objects.)
dbSecReadDef	4	The user can read the table definition, including column and index information.
dbSecWriteDef	65548	The user can modify or delete the table definition, including column and index information.
dbSecRetrieveData	20	The user can retrieve data from the Document object.
dbSecInsertData	32	The user can add records.
dbSecReplaceData	64	The user can modify records.
dbSecDeleteData	128	The user can delete records.

Table 6-8. The Permissions Property Intrinsic Constants for the Databases Container

Named Constant	Value	Description
dbSecDBAdmin	8	The user can replicate a database and change the database password. (This is not valid for Document objects.)
dbSecDBCreate	1	The user can create new databases. This option is valid only on the Databases container in the workgroup information file (*System.mdw*). This constant isn't valid for Document objects.
dbSecDBExclusive	4	The user has exclusive access to the database.
dbSecDBOpen	2	The user can open the database.

VBA Code

This code lists the permissions of all Document objects in all containers in the Northwind database:

```
Private Sub cmdPermissions_Click()

    Dim dbs As Database
    Dim strDBName As String
    Dim ctr As Container
    Dim doc As Document

    strDBName = "D:\Documents\Northwind.mdb"
    Set dbs = OpenDatabase(strDBName)
    With dbs
       For Each ctr In .Containers
          Debug.Print ctr.Name & " documents and their permissions:"
          For Each doc In ctr.Documents
             On Error Resume Next
             Debug.Print vbTab & doc.Name & " permissions: " & _
                         doc.Permissions
          Next doc
       Next ctr
       .Close
       End With

    End Sub
```

UserName

Data Type

String

Description

Represents the name of a Container object's user. In Jet workspaces, this can be either a User object in the Users collection or a Group object in the Groups collection. It is a read-write property for containers.

VBA Code

This code lists the names and user names of all Containers in the Northwind database:

```
Private Sub cmdUserName_Click()

Dim dbs As Database
    Dim strDBName As String
    Dim ctr As Container
    Dim doc As Document

    strDBName = "D:\Documents\Northwind.mdb"
```

```
      Set dbs = OpenDatabase(strDBName)
      With dbs
         For Each ctr In .Containers
            Debug.Print "Container name: " & ctr.Name
               Debug.Print vbTab; " Owner: " & ctr.UserName
         Next ctr
         .Close
      End With

End Sub
```

7

QueryDefs Collection and QueryDef Object

The QueryDefs collection is the collection of all the QueryDef objects in a Database object (for Jet databases). Its position in the DAO object model is shown in Figure 7-1. QueryDefs are stored queries—the ones you see in the Query tab of the database window. When you create a query from the interface, it is a QueryDef; you can also create QueryDefs from code. QueryDefs are completely interchangeable, regardless of how they were created; you can view and work with QueryDefs created from code in the interface, and you can manipulate QueryDefs created in the interface from code.

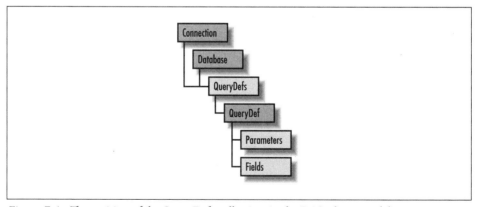

Figure 7-1. The position of the QueryDefs collection in the DAO object model

 A QueryDef represents the structure of a query, not its data. To work with query data, create a recordset based on the QueryDef using the OpenRecordset method.

To create a new QueryDef, use the CreateQueryDef method. Although there is an Append method, you don't need to append a new QueryDef to the QueryDefs collection; it is automatically appended, so long as you assign it a non-zero-length string name. QueryDefs created with zero-length string ("") names are temporary; they exist only in memory and can't be appended to the QueryDefs collection. The only way you can reference a temporary QueryDef is by the variable used to create it.

QueryDefs can be referenced by any of the following syntax variants:

```
QueryDefs(0)
QueryDefs("name")
QueryDefs![name]
```

The QueryDefs object has two properties (shown in Table 7-1) and three methods (see Table 7-2). The QueryDef object has 17 properties (see Table 7-3) and 5 methods (see Table 7-4), along with 2 collections (Parameters and Fields). For information on the Parameters collection, see Chapter 14, *Parameters Collection and Parameter Object*; for information on the Fields collection, see Chapter 13, *Fields Collection and Field Object*.

Table 7-1. QueryDefs Collection Properties

Property	Description
Count	Indicates the number of QueryDef objects in the collection
Item	(Hidden) Returns an individual QueryDef object based either on its ordinal position in the QueryDefs collection or on its name

Table 7-2. QueryDefs Collection Methods

Method	Description
Append	Adds a new QueryDef object to the collection
Delete	Removes a QueryDef object from the collection
Refresh	Updates the QueryDefs collection

Table 7-3. QueryDef Object Properties

Property	Description
CacheSize	Number of records retrieved from an ODBC data source that will be cached locally
Connect	Stores information about the source of a QueryDef's data
DateCreated	Indicates the date and time the QueryDef was created
KeepLocal	Determines whether the QueryDef remains local when the database is replicated
LastUpdated	Indicates the date and time the QueryDef was last updated
LogMessages	Determines whether messages returned from a Jet-connected ODBC data source are recorded in a log file

Table 7-3. QueryDef Object Properties (continued)

Property	Description
MaxRecords	Defines the maximum number of records to return from a query
Name	Provides the name of the QueryDef object
ODBCTimeout	Defines the number of seconds to wait before timing out when executing a query on an ODBC data source
Prepare	In ODBCDirect workspaces, determines whether the query should be prepared on the server as a temporary stored procedure prior to execution, or just executed
RecordsAffected	Indicates the number of records affected by the most recent Execute method
Replicable	A custom string property that indicates whether a QueryDef object in a Jet workspace can be replicated
ReplicableBool	(Jet 3.5 and higher) A custom Boolean property that indicates whether a QueryDef object in a Jet workspace can be replicated
ReturnsRecords	Determines whether a QueryDef object in a Jet workspace can be replicated
SQL	Indicates whether a SQL pass-through query to an external database returns records
StillExecuting	Indicates whether an asynchronous operation has finished executing
Type	Indicates the type of a QueryDef object
Updatable	Determines whether a QueryDef can be changed or updated

Table 7-4. QueryDef Object Methods

Method	Description
Cancel	Cancels execution of a pending asynchronous method call
Close	A nonfunctional method
CreateProperty	Adds a new user-defined Property object to the QueryDef object's Properties collection
Execute	Runs an action query
OpenRecordset	Creates a new Recordset object

VBA Code

This VBA code lists all the Northwind database's permanent QueryDefs to the Debug window:

```
Private Sub cmdListQueryDefs_Click()

    Dim dbs As Database
    Dim strDBName As String
    Dim qdf As QueryDef
    Dim strSQL As String
```

```
    strDBName = "D:\Documents\Northwind.mdb"
    Set dbs = OpenDatabase(strDBName)

    Debug.Print "QueryDefs in " & dbs.Name
    For Each qdf In dbs.QueryDefs
       Debug.Print qdf.Name
    Next qdf
    dbs.Close

End Sub
```

Access to the QueryDef Object

Creatable

Yes

Returned by

The CreateQueryDef method of the Connection object
The QueryDefs property of the Connection object
The CreateQueryDef method of the Database object
The OpenQueryDef method of the Database object
The QueryDefs property of the Database object
The CopyQueryDef method of the Recordset object

QueryDefs Collection Properties

Count   RO

Data Type

Integer

Description

Returns the number of permanent QueryDefs in a database. It can be used to iterate through the members of the collection, as in the VBA example, though this method has generally been replaced by the more efficient **For Each...Next** looping structure.

VBA Code

```
Private Sub cmdCount_Click()

    Dim dbs As Database
    Dim strDBName As String
    Dim qdfs As QueryDefs
    Dim i As Integer
    Dim intCount As Integer

    strDBName = "D:\Documents\Northwind.mdb"
```

```
Set dbs = OpenDatabase(strDBName)
Set qdfs = dbs.QueryDefs
intCount = qdfs.Count
Debug.Print "Number of QueryDefs in the " & _
   strDBName & " database: " & intCount
dbs.Close

End Sub
```

Item   RO

QueryDefs.Item(*Index*)

Argument	Data Type	Description
Index	Integer	The ordinal position of the QueryDef object in the QueryDefs collection or a string containing the name of the QueryDef object to be retrieved from the collection

Data Type

QueryDef object

Description

Retrieves a particular QueryDef object from the QueryDefs collection. A QueryDef object can be retrieved either based on its ordinal position in the collection or based on its name. Since QueryDefs is a zero-based collection, the following code fragment returns the first QueryDef:

```
Dim qdf As QueryDef
Set qdf = DBEngine.Workspaces(0).Databases(0).QueryDefs.Item(0)
```

You can also retrieve a particular QueryDef object by name. The following code fragment, for instance, retrieves the QueryDef named "Sales by Year":

```
Dim qdf As QueryDef
Set qdf = _
    DBEngine.Workspaces(0).Databases(0).QueryDefs.Item("Sales by Year")
```

Since the Item property is the default member of the QueryDefs collection, it does not need to be explicitly specified to retrieve a particular QueryDef object. In other words, the following two statements are equivalent; both retrieve the same QueryDef:

```
Set qdf = DBEngine.Workspaces(0).Databases(0).QueryDefs.Item(0)
Set qdf = DBEngine.Workspaces(0).Databases(0).QueryDefs(0)
```

Similarly, the following three statements all retrieve the same QueryDef by name:

```
Set qdf = _
    DBEngine.Workspaces(0).Databases(0).QueryDefs.Item("Sales by Year")
Set qdf = DBEngine.Workspaces(0).Databases(0).QueryDefs("Sales by Year")
Set qdf = DBEngine.Workspaces(0).Databases(0).QueryDefs![Sales by Year]
```

Finally, if a **dbs** variable has been set already, the folowing syntax can be used:

```
set qdf = dbs.QueryDefs("Sales by Year")
```

QueryDefs Collection Methods

Append

QueryDefs.Append *object*

Normally, the Append method adds a new object to a collection—in this case the QueryDefs collection. However, the Append method has only limited utility for QueryDefs, since when a QueryDef is created as a named object, it is automatically appended to the QueryDefs collection.

 You can assign a name to a temporary QueryDef, created with a zero-length string name, then set its Name property to a non-zero-length string, and append it to the QueryDefs collection. However, if you do this using a name that has already been used for a permanent query in the database, you will get runtime error 3214, "Invalid Operation." You can avoid this error by deleting any query that uses this name, for example, by using DeleteObject, as in the following VBA sample code. However, in a real-life application it would be wiser to have more sophisticated error-trapping and to stop code execution with an informative message, rather than just deleting the existing query. See the Delete method section for an example of such error-trapping.

When you assign a name to a query originally created as a temporary query, it is not counted as one of the database's permanent queries; that happens only if the variable is originally assigned as a permanent query, as in the last assignment in the following code sample. (Actually, a temporary QueryDef with a zero-length string name does have a name, **#Temporary QueryDef#**, which you can see if you print *qdf.Name* to the Debug window. In fact, all temporary QueryDefs share this internal name, even though they are different queries. See the following VBA code for a demonstration of this phenomenon.)

VBA Code

```
Private Sub cmdAppend_Click()

    Dim dbs As Database
    Dim strDBName As String
    Dim qdfs As QueryDefs
    Dim i As Integer
    Dim intCount As Integer
    Dim qdfTemp As QueryDef
```

```
Dim qdfTemp2 As QueryDef
Dim qdfPerm As QueryDef
Dim strSQL As String

strDBName = "D:\Documents\Northwind.mdb"
Set dbs = OpenDatabase(strDBName)
Set qdfs = dbs.QueryDefs
intCount = qdfs.Count
Debug.Print "Number of QueryDefs before creating temporary " & _
            "QueryDef: " & intCount

'Create temporary QueryDef.
strSQL = "SELECT * FROM Orders WHERE OrderAmount >500;"
Set qdfTemp = dbs.CreateQueryDef("", strSQL)

intCount = qdfs.Count
Debug.Print "Number of QueryDefs after creating temporary " & _
            "QueryDef: " & intCount

'Create another temporary QueryDef.
strSQL = "SELECT * FROM Customers"
Set qdfTemp2 = dbs.CreateQueryDef("", strSQL)

intCount = qdfs.Count
Debug.Print "Number of QueryDefs after creating another " & _
            "temporary QueryDef: " & intCount

Debug.Print "First temporary query name: " & _
   qdfTemp.Name & vbCrLf & vbTab & qdfTemp.SQL & vbCrLf
Debug.Print "Second temporary query name: " & _
   qdfTemp2.Name & vbCrLf & vbTab & qdfTemp2.SQL & vbCrLf

'Delete qryTemp in case it already exists.
On Error Resume Next
DoCmd.DeleteObject acQuery, "qryTemp"

'Assign a name to a temporary QueryDef.
qdfTemp.Name = "qryTemp"

Debug.Print "Number of QueryDefs after naming one of the " & _
            "temporary QueryDefs: " & intCount

'Create a new permanent QueryDef.
strSQL = "SELECT * FROM Orders WHERE OrderAmount > 500;"
Set qdfPerm = dbs.CreateQueryDef("qryPermanent", strSQL)
qdfs.Append qdfPerm
intCount = qdfs.Count
Debug.Print "Number of QueryDefs after appending a permanent " & _
            "QueryDef: " & intCount
dbs.Close

End Sub
```

Delete

`QueryDefs.Delete` *name*

Deletes a QueryDef from the QueryDefs collection. Attempting to delete a nonexistent QueryDef object generates runtime error 3265, "Item not found in this collection." This error can be avoided by use of an error-handling structure, as in the following example.

VBA Code

```
    Private Sub cmdDelete_Click()

    On Error GoTo cmdDelete_ClickError

        Dim dbs As Database
        Dim strDBName As String

        strDBName = "D:\Documents\Northwind.mdb"
        Set dbs = OpenDatabase(strDBName)
        dbs.QueryDefs.Delete "qryTemp"

    cmdDelete_ClickExit:
        Exit Sub

    cmdDelete_ClickError:
        If err.Number = 3265 Then
            MsgBox "No such query exists in the database; exiting"
        Else
            MsgBox "Error No: " & err.Number & "; Description: " & _
                    err.Description
        End If
        Resume cmdDelete_ClickExit

    End Sub
```

Refresh

`QueryDefs.Refresh`

Updates the objects in a collection, taking into account any recently made changes, such as creating or deleting a QueryDef.

As far as I can tell, using the Refresh method on the QueryDefs collection is redundant, since QueryDefs are automatically appended, and the collection count decreases automatically when a QueryDef is deleted. However, in a multiuser environment where other users may add or delete queries, the Refresh method may be useful.

VBA Code

This code shows that the count of a QueryDefs collection is automatically adjusted after deleting a QueryDef created in the previous code sample; using the Refresh method does nothing extra:

```
Private Sub cmdRefresh_Click()

    Dim dbs As Database
    Dim strDBName As String
    Dim qdfs As QueryDefs
    Dim i As Integer
    Dim intCount As Integer
    Dim qdfTemp As QueryDef
    Dim strSQL As String

    strDBName = "D:\Documents\Northwind.mdb"
    Set dbs = OpenDatabase(strDBName)
    Set qdfs = dbs.QueryDefs
    intCount = qdfs.Count
    Debug.Print "Initial number of QueryDefs: " & intCount

    'Delete a QueryDef.
    qdfs.Delete "qryPermanent"

    'Count again after deleting a QueryDef.
    intCount = qdfs.Count
    Debug.Print "Number of QueryDefs after deleting a QueryDef: " & _
            intCount

    'Count again after refreshing the QueryDefs collection.
    qdfs.Refresh
    intCount = qdfs.Count
    Debug.Print "Number of QueryDefs after refreshing the QueryDefs " & _
            "collection: " & intCount
    dbs.Close

End Sub
```

QueryDef Object Properties

CacheSize

Data Type

Long

Description

Sets or returns the number of records retrieved from an ODBC data source that will be cached locally. The value must be between 5 and 1200, but it can't be greater than available memory permits. Setting CacheSize to 0 turns off caching. Using a cache can improve performance, since retrieving data from a local cache is faster than retrieving it from the server. Attempting to set or return the value of the CacheSize property for a Jet database generates runtime error 3251, "Operation is not supported for this type of object." See the CacheSize property section in Chapter 8, *Recordsets Collection and Recordset Object,* for more details on using a cache.

Connect   RO

```
querydef.Connect = databasetype;parameters;
```

Argument	Data Type	Description
querydef	QueryDef object	The QueryDef object whose Connect property is being returned
databasetype	String	(Optional; see Table 7-5 for settings) Omit this argument for Jet databases, but include a semicolon (;) as a place-holder
parameters	String	Additional parameters to pass to ODBC or installable ISAM drivers; use semicolons to separate parameters

Data Type

String

Description

Returns a String value containing information about the source of a QueryDef's data.

Table 7-5. The Databasetype Argument Settings

Database type	Specifier	Example
Microsoft Jet Database	`[database];`	*drive:\path\filename.mdb*
dBASE III	`dBASE III;`	*drive:\path*
dBASE IV	`dBASE IV;`	*drive:\path*
dBASE 5	`dBASE 5.0;`	*drive:\path*
Paradox 3.x	`Paradox 3.x;`	*drive:\path*
Paradox 4.x	`Paradox 4.x;`	*drive:\path*
Paradox 5.x	`Paradox 5.x;`	*drive:\path*
FoxPro 2.0	`FoxPro 2.0;`	*drive:\path*
FoxPro 2.5	`FoxPro 2.5;`	*drive:\path*
FoxPro 2.6	`FoxPro 2.6;`	*drive:\path*
Excel 3.0	`Excel 3.0;`	*drive:\path\filename.xls*
Excel 4.0	`Excel 4.0;`	*drive:\path\filename.xls*
Excel 5.0 or Excel 95	`Excel 5.0;`	*drive:\path\filename.xls*

Table 7-5. The Databasetype Argument Settings (continued)

Database type	Specifier	Example
Excel 97	Excel 97;	*drive:\path\filename.xls*
HTML Import	HTML Import;	*drive:\path\filename*
HTML Export	HTML Export;	*drive:\path*
Text	Text;	*drive:\path*
ODBC	ODBC; DATABASE=database; UID=user; PWD=password; DSN= datasourcename; [LOGINTIMEOUT=seconds;]	None
Exchange	Exchange; MAPILEVEL=folderpath; [TABLETYPE={ 0 | 1 }]; [PROFILE=profile;] [PWD=password;] [DATABASE=database;]	*drive:\path\filename.mdb*

VBA Code

```
Private Sub cmdConnect_Click()

    Dim dbs As Database
    Dim strDBName As String
    Dim qdf As QueryDef

    strDBName = "D:\Documents\Examples\Northwind.mdb"
    Set dbs = OpenDatabase(strDBName)
    Set qdf = dbs.QueryDefs("qryDenverEmployees")
    Debug.Print "QueryDef Connect string: " & qdf.Connect

End Sub
```

DateCreated   `R0`

Data Type

Date/Time

Description

Returns the date and time the QueryDef was created.

VBA Code

```
Private Sub cmdDateCreated_Click()

    Dim dbs As Database
    Dim strDBName As String
    Dim qdf As QueryDef

    strDBName = "D:\Documents\Examples\Northwind.mdb"
```

```
Set dbs = OpenDatabase(strDBName)
Set qdf = dbs.QueryDefs("qryDenverEmployees")
Debug.Print "Date Created: " & qdf.DateCreated

End Sub
```

KeepLocal

querydef.Properties("KeepLocal")

Data Type

String

Description

The KeepLocal property, when set to "T", keeps the QueryDef local when the database is replicated. The property must be set before replication; it can't be changed after the QueryDef has been replicated.

 The KeepLocal property is not a built-in property; it must be created using the CreateProperty method and appended to the QueryDef's Properties collection before it can be set.

VBA Code

```
Private Sub cmdKeepLocal_Click()

    Dim dbs As Database
    Dim strDBName As String
    Dim qdf As QueryDef
    Dim prp As Property

    strDBName = "D:\Documents\Examples\Northwind.mdb"
    Set dbs = OpenDatabase(strDBName)
    Set qdf = dbs.QueryDefs("qryUSOrders")

    'Create KeepLocal property and append it.
    Set prp = qdf.CreateProperty("KeepLocal", dbText, "T")
    qdf.Properties.Append prp
    qdf.Properties("KeepLocal") = "T"
    Debug.Print "KeepLocal property: " & qdf.Properties("KeepLocal")

End Sub
```

LastUpdated   `RO`

Data Type

Variant (Date/Time subtype)

Description

Returns the date and time the QueryDef was last updated—in other words, when the data in the base table(s) was last changed.

VBA Code

```
Private Sub cmdLastUpdated_Click()

    Dim dbs As Database
    Dim strDBName As String
    Dim qdf As QueryDef

    strDBName = "D:\Documents\Examples\Northwind.mdb"
    Set dbs = OpenDatabase(strDBName)
    Set qdf = dbs.QueryDefs("Quarterly Orders")
    Debug.Print "Date Created: " & qdf.DateCreated
    Debug.Print "Last Updated: " & qdf.LastUpdated

End Sub
```

LogMessages

querydef.Properties("LogMessages")

Data Type

Boolean

Description

For Jet workspaces the LogMessages property sets or returns a value specifying whether the messages returned from a Jet-connected ODBC data source are recorded in a log file. As with the KeepLocal property you must first create and append this property to the QueryDef's Properties collection.

VBA Code

```
Private Sub cmdLogMessages_Click()

    Dim dbs As Database
    Dim strDBName As String
    Dim qdf As QueryDef
    Dim prp As Property

    strDBName = "D:\Documents\Examples\Northwind.mdb"
    Set dbs = OpenDatabase(strDBName)
    Set qdf = dbs.QueryDefs("qryUSOrders")

    'Create LogMessages property and append it.
    Set prp = qdf.CreateProperty("LogMessages", dbText, "T")
    qdf.Properties.Append prp
    qdf.Properties("LogMessages") = "T"
    Debug.Print "LogMessages property: " & qdf.Properties("LogMessages")

End Sub
```

MaxRecords

Data Type

Long

Description

Sets or returns the number of records to return from a query, which can be handy in case a query could return huge numbers of records, causing problems for the application. The default value is 0, which sets no limits on the number of records returned.

Name

Data Type

String

Description

The name of a QueryDef; this property is generally set when the QueryDef is created either by using the CreateQueryDef method in code or by using the interface. Although typically the Name property of objects is read-only, it is read-write in the case of most QueryDef objects. For example, you can rename a temporary QueryDef object created with a zero-length string name that originally has the name (assigned by Jet) `"#Temporary QueryDef#"`, as in the example for the Append method section earlier in this chapter.

The string assigned to the Name property can be up to 64 characters in length.

VBA Code

This code lists the Name (and several other properties) of all the QueryDefs in the Northwind database to the Debug window:

```
Private Sub cmdName_Click()

    Dim dbs As Database
    Dim strDBName As String
    Dim qdf As QueryDef

    strDBName = "D:\Documents\Northwind.mdb"
    Set dbs = OpenDatabase(strDBName)

    Debug.Print "QueryDefs in " & dbs.Name
    For Each qdf In dbs.QueryDefs
        Debug.Print "Name: " & qdf.Name
        Debug.Print "SQL: " & qdf.SQL
        Debug.Print "Type: " & qdf.Type
```

```
        Debug.Print "Updatable: " & qdf.Updatable & vbCrLf
    Next qdf
    dbs.Close

End Sub
```

ODBCTimeout

Data Type

Integer

Description

The number of seconds to wait before timing out when executing a query on an ODBC data source. Setting the value to 0 prevents timeout errors from occurring; setting it to –1 lets the value default to the ODBCTimeout value of the Database or Connection object that contains the QueryDef object.

Prepare

Data Type

Long

Description

For ODBCDirect workspaces, this value (see Table 7-6) indicates whether the query should be prepared on the server as a temporary stored procedure (using the ODBC *SQLPrepare* API function) prior to execution or just executed using the ODBC *SQLExecDirect* API function.

Table 7-6. The Prepare Setting Intrinsic Constants

Named Constant	Value	Description
dbQPrepare	1	(Default) The statement is prepared (that is, the ODBC *SQLPrepare* API is called).
dbQUnprepare	2	The statement is not prepared (that is, the ODBC *SQLExecDirect* API is called).

RecordsAffected   RO

Data Type

Long

Description

Tells you the number of records affected by the most recently invoked Execute method on the database. For an action query this value contains the number of records deleted, updated, or inserted.

 For ODBCDirect workspaces RecordsAffected does not return a useful value from a SQL DROP TABLE action query. For any workspaces it does not return a useful value from a temporary query.

VBA Code

```
Private Sub cmdRecordsAffected_Click()

    Dim dbs As Database
    Dim strDBName As String
    Dim qdf As QueryDef
    Dim strSQL As String

    strDBName = "D:\Documents\Northwind.mdb"
    Set dbs = OpenDatabase(strDBName)
    Set qdf = dbs.QueryDefs("qappRecentOrders")
    qdf.Execute

    Debug.Print "Query records affected: " & qdf.RecordsAffected

End Sub
```

Replicable

querydef.Properties("Replicable")

Data Type

String

Description

Sets or returns a value indicating whether a QueryDef object in a Jet workspace can be replicated. Making a QueryDef replicable means that it can be replicated when you synchronize a Design Master or replica.

This property does not exist by default; in order to use it, you must first create it using the CreateProperty method and then append it to the QueryDef's Properties collection.

The "T" setting is the only one that is usable; if you try to set the Replicable property to "F" after initially setting it to "T", you will get Run-time error 3459.

The standard *querydef*.Replicable syntax won't work with this property; if you use it, you will get a "Method or data member not found" error.

When you create a query in a replicated database, it is initially set as Local (its Replicable property is set to "F"). After making a QueryDef replicable, as in the following code, when you next open the database, it has the Replicable icon beside it in the database window, as shown in Figure 7-2. (Note also that qryAllHires—another query created in the interface after making the database replicable—lacks this icon.)

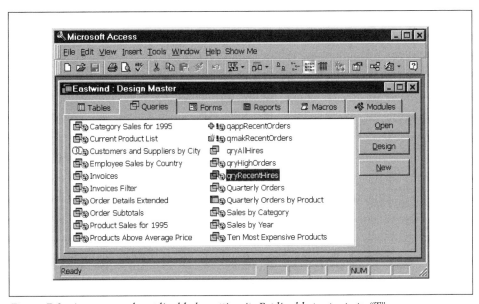

Figure 7-2. A query made replicable by setting its Replicable property to "T"

VBA Code

```
Private Sub cmdReplicable_Click()

    Dim dbs As Database
    Dim strDBName As String
    Dim qdf As QueryDef
    Dim prp As Property

    strDBName = "D:\Documents\Eastwind.mdb"
    Set dbs = OpenDatabase(strDBName, True)
```

```
    Set qdf = dbs.QueryDefs("qryRecentHires")
    With qdf
        On Error Resume Next
        Set prp = .CreateProperty("Replicable", dbText, "T")
        .Properties.Append prp
        .Properties("Replicable") = "T"
        Debug.Print "Query name: " & qdf.Name
        Debug.Print "Replicable: " & qdf.Properties("Replicable")
    End With

End Sub
```

ReplicableBool

Data Type

Boolean

Description

If you are using Jet 3.5 or higher, you can use the ReplicableBool property (which is not listed in either Help or the Object Browser) instead of the Replicable property. ReplicableBool takes a Boolean value, rather than requiring creation of a custom property. Otherwise, its functionality is identical to that of the Replicable property.

ReturnsRecords

Data Type

Boolean

Description

Sets or returns a value indicating whether a SQL pass-through query to an external database will return records.

You must first set the Connect property before you can set the ReturnsRecords property.

SQL

Data Type

String

Description

Sets or returns the SQL statement that defines the query executed by a QueryDef object. See the Name section code sample for an example of usage.

StillExecuting   `RO`

Data Type

Boolean

Description

For ODBCDirect workspaces only, indicates whether an asynchronous operation (one called with the **dbRunAsync** option) has finished executing. The return value is **True** if the query is still executing and **False** if it has finished executing. The Cancel property can be used to cancel execution if the StillExecuting property is **True**.

Type   `RO`

Data Type

Integer

Description

Indicates the query type of a QueryDef object. Possible values are listed in Table 7-7. See the Name section for an example using the Type property.

Table 7-7. The Type Setting Return Values Intrinsic Constants

Named Constant	Value	Description
dbQAction	240	Action
dbQAppend	64	Append
dbQCompound	160	Compound
dbQCrosstab	16	Crosstab
dbQDDL	96	Data-definition
dbQDelete	32	Delete
dbQMakeTable	80	Make-table
dbQProcedure	224	Procedure (ODBCDirect workspaces only)
dbQSelect	0	Select
dbQSetOperation	128	Union
dbQSPTBulk	144	Used with **dbQSQLPassThrough** to specify a query that doesn't return records (Microsoft Jet workspaces only)

Table 7-7. The Type Setting Return Values Intrinsic Constants (continued)

Named Constant	Value	Description
dbQSQLPassThrough	112	Pass-through (Microsoft Jet workspaces only)
dbQUpdate	48	Update

Updatable `RO`

Data Type

Boolean

Description

Indicates whether a QueryDef can be changed or updated. If it is **True**, the QueryDef can be updated; if it is **False**, it can't be updated. See the Name section later in this chapter for an example of using this property.

QueryDef Object Methods

Cancel

querydef.Cancel

Cancels execution of a pending asynchronous method call. It only applies to QueryDefs in ODBCDirect workspaces, since it requires use of the **dbRunAsync** value for the Execute method's Options argument. See the StillExecuting section later in this chapter for an example of usage of this method.

Close

querydef.Close

Although the Close method is listed as a method of the QueryDef object in Help, and it won't cause an error if you use it in code (at least if you use a real query name), it doesn't actually do anything. To remove a QueryDef from the Query-Defs collection, use the Delete method.

CreateProperty

Set *property* = *querydef*.CreateProperty(*name*, *type*, *value*, *DDL*)

Argument	Data Type	Description
property	Property object	An object variable representing the Property object you are creating.
querydef	QueryDef object	The QueryDef object variable used to create the new Property object.

Argument	Data Type	Description
name	Variant (String subtype)	The name of the new Property object. Property names can be up to 64 characters in length.
type	Integer	A named constant or Integer value indicating the data type of the property (see Table 7-8).
value	Variant	(Optional) The initial property value.
DDL	Variant (Boolean subtype)	If `True`, the Property is a DDL object, and users can't change or delete it unless they have `dbSecWriteDef` permission. If `False`, it is not a DDL object and can be changed or deleted by users.

(For Jet workspaces only.) Creates a new user-defined Property object in the Properties collection of a QueryDef object. See the KeepLocal section earlier in this chapter for one important use for this method. You can also use this method to create custom properties that store values in a database where they will be available for your code to use, but not visible to (or modifiable by) users.

Table 7-8. The Type Intrinsic Constants

Named Constant	Value	Description
`dbBigInt`	16	Big Integer
`dbBinary`	9	Binary
`dbBoolean`	1	Boolean
`dbByte`	2	Byte
`dbChar`	18	Char
`dbCurrency`	5	Currency
`dbDate`	8	Date/Time
`dbDecimal`	20	Decimal
`dbDouble`	7	Double
`dbFloat`	21	Float
`dbGUID`	15	GUID
`dbInteger`	3	Integer
`dbLong`	4	Long
`dbLongBinary`	11	Long Binary (OLE Object)
`dbMemo`	12	Memo
`dbNumeric`	19	Numeric
`dbSingle`	6	Single
`dbText`	10	Text
`dbTime`	22	Time
`dbTimeStamp`	23	Time Stamp
`dbVarBinary`	17	VarBinary

You don't have to assign values to all the arguments when you create a property; you can set them later, before you append the Property to an object. After appending, some (but not all) of the property
settings can be altered.

If you try to create a property with a name that already exists in the
Properties collection (such as the name of a built-in property), an
error occurs.

VBA Code

This VBA code creates a new property, appends it to the Northwind database's
properties collection, then lists the names and values of any nonempty properties
(including the newly created one) to the Debug window:

```
Private Sub cmdCreateProperty_Click()

    Dim dbs As Database
    Dim prp As Property
    Dim prpNew As Property
    Dim qdf As QueryDef
    Dim strDbname As String

    strDbname = "D:\Documents\Northwind.mdb"
    Set dbs = OpenDatabase(strDbname)
    Set qdf = dbs.QueryDefs("qryHighOrders")
    Set prpNew = qdf.CreateProperty("Temporary", dbBoolean, False)

    qdf.Properties.Append prpNew

    'Enumerate database properties.
    For Each prp In qdf.Properties
       If prp <> "" Then
          On Error Resume Next
          Debug.Print prp.Name & " = " & prp
       End If
    Next prp

End Sub
```

Execute

```
object.Execute query, options
querydef.Execute options
```

Argument	Data Type	Description
object	Connection or Database object	A Connection or Database object on which the query will run
querydef	QueryDef object	A QueryDef object whose SQL property specifies the SQL statement to execute
query	String	A SQL statement or the name of a QueryDef
options	Long	A named constant or Long value (see Table 7-9)

Runs an action query (make-table, append, update, or delete query) either from a saved QueryDef or from one created from a SQL statement.

Table 7-9. The Options Intrinsic Constants

Named Constant	Value	Description
dbDenyWrite	1	Denies write permission to other users (Jet workspaces only).
dbInconsistent	16	(Default) Executes inconsistent updates (Jet workspaces only).
dbConsistent	32	Executes consistent updates (Jet workspaces only).
dbSQLPassThrough	64	Executes a SQL pass-through query. Setting this option passes the SQL statement to an ODBC database for processing (Jet workspaces only).
dbFailOnError	128	Rolls back updates if an error occurs (Jet workspaces only).
dbSeeChanges	512	Generates a run-time error if another user is changing data you are editing (Jet workspaces only).
dbRunAsync	1024	Executes the query asynchronously (ODBCDirect Connection and QueryDef objects only).
dbExecDirect	2048	Executes the statement without first calling the *SQLPrepare* ODBC API function (ODBCDirect Connection and QueryDef objects only).

VBA Code

These VBA and VBS code samples run the same action query, the VBA version from a SQL statement, and the VBS version from a previously created stored query in the Northwind database. The action query itself writes all records from the Order table that are dated after January 6, 1996 to a table named tmakNewOrders, which is created on the fly. The following syntactical differences between the VBA and VBS code are typical of the changes you need to make when converting code from VBA to VBS; if you have Office 2000, you may be able to use Outlook VBA instead of VBS, thus avoiding these limitations:

- There are no data types in Outlook VBS, so you can't declare variables as any specific data type.

- In VBA the bang (!) operator is used to indicate a member of a collection, such as a field in a recordset. In Outlook VBS you must use the dot (.) operator for members of collections.

- In VBA you can use named constants (such as **dbHiddenObject**) as function arguments. In Outlook VBS (with very few exceptions, such as **True** and **False**) you must use the argument's numeric value.

- Outlook lacks the Debug window, so you need to replace Debug.Print calls with *MsgBox* functions.

- The **With...End With** statement is not supported by VBS, so you have to use the full syntax when referencing variables.

- When using a looping code structure (such as **For Each...Next**), you can't specify the looping variable—just use **Next** instead of **Next tdf**:

```
Private Sub cmdExecute_Click()

    Dim wks As Workspace
    Dim dbs As Database
    Dim qdf As QueryDef
    Dim strSQL As String
    Dim tdf As TableDef

    Set wks = Workspaces(0)
    Set dbs = wks.OpenDatabase("D:\Documents\Northwind.mdb")
    strSQL = _
      "SELECT Orders.*, * INTO tmakNewOrders FROM Orders WHERE OrderDate>#1/6/96#;"
    Set qdf = dbs.CreateQueryDef("qmakTestQuery", strSQL)

    'Execute a make-table query to produce the tmakRecentOrders table.
    qdf.Execute

    For Each tdf In dbs.TableDefs
       Debug.Print "Table Name: " & tdf.Name & vbTab & vbTab & _
          "Attributes: " & tdf.Attributes
    Next tdf
    dbs.Close

End Sub
```

Outlook VBS Code

```
Sub cmdExecuteQDF_Click()

    Dim dao
    Dim wks
    Dim dbs
    Dim strSQL
    Dim qdf
```

```
Set dao = Application.CreateObject("DAO.DBEngine.35")
Set wks = dao.Workspaces(0)
Set dbs = wks.OpenDatabase("D:\Documents\Northwind.mdb")
Set qdf = dbs.QueryDefs("qmakRecentOrders")

'Execute a SQL statement to produce the tmakRecentOrders table.
qdf.Execute

For Each tdf In dbs.TableDefs
    MsgBox "Table Name: " & tdf.Name
Next
dbs.Close

End Sub
```

OpenRecordset

Set *recordset* = *querydef*.OpenRecordset(*type*, *options*, *lockedit*)

Argument	Data Type	Description
recordset	Recordset object	The Recordset object to be opened
querydef	QueryDef object	The Querydef object from which the recordset is to be opened
type	Integer	A named constant or Integer value indicating the type of recordset to be created (see Table 7-10)
options	Long	A named constant or Long value (see Table 7-11)
lockedit	Integer	A named constant or Integer value defining the recordset's locking scheme (see Table 7-12)

Creates a new Recordset object in memory (recordsets are temporary objects only) and appends it to the Recordsets collection. See Chapter 8 for more information on recordsets.

Table 7-10. The Type Intrinsic Constants

Named Constant	Value	Description
dbOpenTable	1	Opens a table-type Recordset object (Jet workspaces only)
dbOpenDynamic	16	Opens a dynamic-type Recordset object, similar to an ODBC dynamic cursor (ODBCDirect workspaces only)
dbOpenDynaset	2	Opens a dynaset-type Recordset object, similar to an ODBC keyset cursor
dbOpenSnapshot	4	Opens a snapshot-type Recordset object similar to an ODBC static cursor
dbOpenForwardOnly	8	Opens a forward-only-type Recordset object

Table 7-11. The Options Intrinsic Constants

Named Constant	Value	Description
dbAppendOnly	8	Allows users to append new records to the Recordset but prevents them from editing or deleting existing records (Jet dynaset-type recordset only).
dbSQLPassThrough	64	Passes a SQL statement to a Jet-connected ODBC data source for processing (Jet snapshot-type Recordset only).
dbSeeChanges	512	Generates a run-time error if one user is changing data that another user is editing (Jet dynaset-type recordset only). This setting is useful in applications where multiple users have simultaneous read/write access to the same data.
dbDenyWrite	1	Prevents other users from modifying or adding records (Jet Recordset objects only).
dbDenyRead	2	Prevents other users from reading data in a table (Jet table-type recordset only).
dbForwardOnly	256	Creates a forward-only recordset (Jet snapshot-type Recordset only). It is provided only for backward compatibility; you should use the **dbOpenForwardOnly** constant in the *type* argument instead of using this option.
dbReadOnly	4	Prevents users from making changes to the Recordset (Jet only). The **dbReadOnly** constant in the *lockedit* argument replaces this option, which is provided only for backward compatibility.
dbRunAsync	1024	Runs an asynchronous query (ODBCDirect workspaces only).
dbExecDirect	2048	Runs a query by skipping the ODBC *SQLPrepare* function and directly calling *SQLExecDirect* (ODBCDirect workspaces only). Use this option only when you're not opening a recordset based on a parameter query.
dbInconsistent	16	Allows inconsistent updates (Jet dynaset-type and snapshot-type Recordset objects only).
dbConsistent	32	Allows only consistent updates (Jet dynaset-type and snapshot-type Recordset objects only).

Table 7-12. The LockEdit Intrinsic Constants

Named Constant	Value	Description
dbReadOnly	4	Prevents users from making changes to the recordset (default for ODBCDirect workspaces). You can use dbReadOnly in either the *options* argument or the *lockedit* argument, but not in both. If you use it for both arguments, a run-time error occurs.
dbPessimistic	2	Uses pessimistic locking to determine how changes are made to the recordset in a multiuser environment. The page containing the record you're editing is locked as soon as you use the Edit method (default for Jet workspaces).

Table 7-12. The LockEdit Intrinsic Constants (continued)

Named Constant	Value	Description
dbOptimistic	3	Uses optimistic locking to determine how changes are made to the recordset in a multiuser environment. The page containing the record is not locked until the Update method is executed.
dbOptimisticValue	1	Uses optimistic concurrency based on row values (ODBCDirect workspaces only).
dbOptimisticBatch	5	Enables batch optimistic updating (ODBCDirect workspaces only).

Access VBA Code

This code opens a recordset based on a stored query and lists a selection of the recordset's data to the Debug window:

```
Private Sub cmdOpenRecordset_Click()

    Dim dbs As Database
    Dim rstTable As Recordset
    Dim rstSQL As Recordset
    Dim strTable As String
    Dim strSQL As String
    Dim qdf As QueryDef
    Dim rst As Recordset
    Dim fld As Field
    Dim flds As Fields

    Set dbs = OpenDatabase("D:\Documents\Northwind.mdb")
    Set qdf = dbs.QueryDefs("Products by Category")
    Set rst = qdf.OpenRecordset

    'List fields from the two recordsets to the Debug window.
    With rst
        Do While Not .EOF
            Debug.Print !ProductName & " units in stock: " _
                & !UnitsInStock
            .MoveNext
        Loop
    End With

End Sub
```

Word VBA Code

The Word VBA code (running from the New Document event of a Word template) opens a recordset that filters contacts by the BusinessState field, and populates a Word table from the recordset. The Word table is sized for Avery #5160 labels, so the data will create sheets of labels. The code uses early binding of DAO objects, so you need to set a reference to the DAO object library in the References dialog in the Word VBE window, as shown in Figure 7-3.

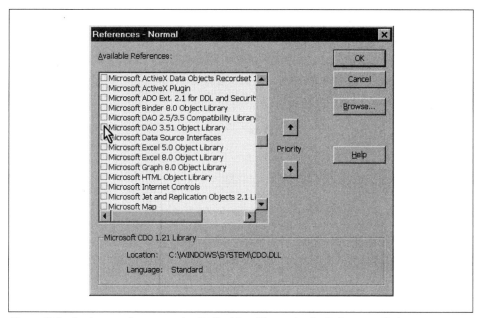

Figure 7-3. Setting a reference to the DAO object library in the References dialog

```
Private Sub Document_New

    Dim DAO As DBEngine
    Dim wks As Workspace
    Dim dbs As Database
    Dim qdf As QueryDef
    Dim rst As Recordset
    Dim strTemplateDir As String
    Dim strLetter As String
    Dim strFullName As String
    Dim strAddress As String
    Dim lngCount As Long
    Dim intAddressType As Integer
    Dim strEmpty As String

    strEmpty = Chr$(34) & Chr$(34)

    'Get reference to data table.
    Set DAO = CreateObject("DAO.DBEngine.35")
    Set wks = DAO.Workspaces(0)
    Set dbs = wks.OpenDatabase("D:\Documents\Data for Import.mdb")
    Set qdf = dbs.QueryDefs("qryMTContacts")
    Set rst = qdf.OpenRecordset

    'Need next step to ensure accurate record count.
    rst.MoveLast
    lngCount = rst.RecordCount
    If lngCount = 0 Then
        MsgBox "No records to import"
```

```
        Exit Sub
    Else
        MsgBox lngCount & " records to import into Word"
    End If

    'Create 3-column Word table to fill with Access data.
    ActiveDocument.Tables.Add Range:=Selection.Range, _
        NumRows:=2, NumColumns:=3

'Loop through table, importing each record to a cell in the Word table.
    Do Until rst.EOF
        With rst
            'Insert data into labels
            Selection.TypeText Text:=![FullName]
            Selection.TypeParagraph
            Selection.TypeText Text:=![BusinessAddress]
            Selection.TypeParagraph
            Selection.MoveRight Unit:=wdCell
        End With
    rst.MoveNext
    Loop

    Selection.HomeKey Unit:=wdStory
    MsgBox "All Contacts imported!"

End Sub
```

Outlook VBS Code

This code fills a list box on an Outlook custom form with the contents of a record-set based on the Northwind Customers table, using a previously created query. In a real application you would probably want to run this code from the form's Open event, rather than from a command button.

See the notes in the Execute section for an explanation of the syntactical differences between VBA and VBS code. In this case, you probably would need to use VBS code, even in Outlook 2000, since you are working with a listbox on an Outlook form, and Outlook form programming still uses the VBS dialect in Outlook 2000.

```
Sub cmdFillListBoxQDF_Click

    Dim rst
    Dim dao
    Dim wks
    Dim dbs
    Dim qdf
    Dim nms
    Dim objAccess
    Dim CustomerArray(99, 2)

    'Set up reference to Access database.
    Set dao = Application.CreateObject("DAO.DBEngine.35")
```

```
Set wks = dao.Workspaces(0)
strDBName = "D:\Documents\Northwind.mdb"
Set dbs = wks.OpenDatabase(strDBName)
Set qdf = dbs.QueryDefs("qryCustomers")

'Retrieve Customer information from table.
Set rst = qdf.OpenRecordset
Set ctl = _
    Item.GetInspector.ModifiedFormPages("Message").Controls("lstCustomers")

ctl.ColumnCount = 3
ctl.ColumnWidths = "50; 150 pt; 75 pt"

'Assign Access data to an array of 3 columns and 100 rows.
CustomerArray(99, 2) = rst.GetRows(100)

ctl.Column() = CustomerArray(99, 2)

End Sub
```

Recordsets Collection and Recordset Object

The Recordset object is the primary object used to manipulate data in Access databases (and other databases as well, via ODBC connections). Although there is a Recordsets collection (the collection of all open Recordset objects in a database), it is not much use, except to list the open recordsets and their SQL statements, as in the following code sample:

```
Private Sub cmdListRecordsets_Click()

    Dim dbs As Database
    Dim rst As Recordset
    Dim strDBName As String
    Dim intCount As Integer
    Dim strTable As String

    strTable = "Orders"
    strDBName = "D:\Documents\Northwind.mdb"
    Set dbs = OpenDatabase(strDBName)
    intCount = dbs.Recordsets.Count
    Debug.Print intCount & _
        " recordsets in current database (before opening a recordset)"
    Set rst = dbs.OpenRecordset(strTable, dbOpenTable)
    intCount = dbs.Recordsets.Count
    Debug.Print intCount & _
        " recordsets in current database (after opening a recordset)"

    For Each rst In dbs.Recordsets
        Debug.Print "Open recordset: " & rst.Name
    Next rst

End Sub
```

A new Recordset object is automatically added to the Recordsets collection when you open the recordset, and it is automatically removed when you close it. Note that when you first count the recordsets in the preceding code, the count is 0; after setting a recordset variable, it is 1. The position of the Recordsets collection in the DAO object model is shown in Figure 8-1.

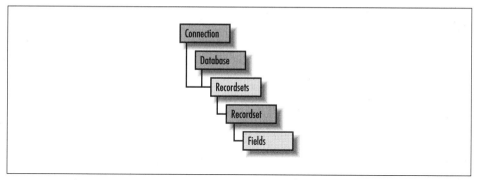

Figure 8-1. The Recordsets collection in the DAO object model

You can create as many recordset variables as you want, and different recordsets can access the same tables, queries, or fields without causing a problem. You can even open two recordsets from the same data source, and this is not a problem, so long as you refer to the recordsets by the variables used to assign them, not by their names.

> See the Name property section later in this chapter for a discussion of why it is unwise to use the Name property to reference a recordset.

There are five types of recordsets: Table-type, Dynaset, Snapshot, Forward-only, and Dynamic. (See the Type property section for a discussion of recordset types.) Each Recordset object contains a collection of Fields that represents the fields in the underlying table(s). You can list the field names and values, but you will just get the values in the current record, unless you first go to a particular record. For example, the following code moves to the last record in a recordset and lists the field names and values for that record:

```
Private Sub cmdListFields_Click()

    Dim dbs As Database
    Dim rst As Recordset
    Dim strDBName As String
    Dim strTable As String
    Dim fld As Field

    strTable = "Categories"
    strDBName = "D:\Documents\Northwind.mdb"
    Set dbs = OpenDatabase(strDBName)
```

```
Set rst = dbs.OpenRecordset(strTable, dbOpenTable)
With rst
    .MoveLast
    For Each fld In .Fields
        Debug.Print fld.Name & " value: " & fld.Value
    Next fld
    .Close
End With

End Sub
```

Although you can reference a Recordset object in the Recordsets collection by any of the following syntax variants, it is advisable to use its variable instead to avoid possible ambiguity.

```
Recordsets(0)
Recordsets("name")
Recordsets![name]
```

The Recordsets collection has two properties and one method, which are shown in Table 8-1.

Table 8-1. Members of the Recordsets Collection

Type	Name	Description
Property	Count	Indicates the number of Recordset objects in the Recordsets collection
Property	Item	Retrieves a Recordset object either by its index in the collection or by its name
Method	Refresh	A nonfunctional method

The Recordset object has 32 properties (shown in Table 8-2) and 24 methods (listed in Table 8-3). It also has two collections: the Fields collection, a collection of the individual fields in the recordset; and the Properties collection, a collection of the individual properties supported by the Recordset object.

Table 8-2. Recordset Object Properties

Property	Description
AbsolutePosition	The relative position of the current record
BatchCollision-Count	Number of records that did not complete the last batch update
BatchCollisions	Array of bookmarks representing rows that had a collision during the last batch update
BatchSize	For batch updates, the number of statements to send back to the server in each batch
BOF	Flag indicating whether the record pointer is at the beginning of the file
Bookmark	Value that uniquely identifies a particular record in the recordset

Table 8-2. Recordset Object Properties (continued)

Property	Description
Bookmarkable	Indicates whether a recordset supports bookmarks
CacheSize	Determines the number of records from an ODBC data source that will be cached locally
CacheStart	The bookmark of the first record to be cached locally
Connection	The Connection object that owns the recordset
DateCreated	Date and time the recordset was created
EditMode	Indicates the recordset's editing state
EOF	Flag indicating whether the record pointer is at the end of the file
Filter	Expression that filters records from the recordset
Index	Name of the current index
LastModified	Bookmark indicating the most recently modified record
LastUpdated	Date and time the recordset was last updated
LockEdits	The type of locking in effect when editing
Name	The name of the Recordset object
NoMatch	Flag indicating whether a search was successful
PercentPosition	Relative position of the current record in the recordset
RecordCount	Number of records in the recordset
RecordStatus	The update status of the current record in the next batch update
Restartable	Indicates whether a recordset supports the Requery method
Sort	Expression defining the sort order of records
StillExecuting	Indicates whether an asynchronous operation has finished executing
Transactions	Indicates whether the recordset supports transactions
Type	The recordset (or cursor) type
Updatable	Indicates whether the recordset can be updated
UpdateOptions	Indicates how the SQL WHERE clause is constructed for each record during a batch update and whether the update should use an UPDATE statement or a DELETE followed by an INSERT
ValidationRule	Defines a validation rule used to validate data as it is changed
ValidationText	Text displayed when a record fails to meet the validation criteria

Table 8-3. Recordset Object Methods

Method	Description
AddNew	Adds a new record to an updatable recordset
Cancel	Cancels execution of a pending asynchronous method call
CancelUpdate	Cancels any pending updates
Clone	Creates a duplicate Recordset object
Close	Closes the recordset

Table 8-3. Recordset Object Methods (continued)

Method	Description
CopyQueryDef	Returns a copy of the QueryDef object originally used to create the recordset
Delete	Deletes the current record
Edit	Prepares a record for editing
FillCache	Fills all or part of a recordset's local cache
FindFirst	Finds the first record that meets designated criteria
FindLast	Finds the last record that meets designated criteria
FindNext	Finds the next record that meets designated criteria
FindPrevious	Finds the previous record that meets designated criteria
GetRows	Retrieves rows into a two-dimensional array
Move	Moves the record pointer either forward or backward
MoveFirst	Moves to the first record of the recordset
MoveLast	Moves to the last record of the recordset
MoveNext	Moves to the next record of the recordset
MovePrevious	Moves to the previous record of the recordset
NextRecordset	Retrieves the next set of records returned by a multipart SELECT query
OpenRecordset	Creates a new recordset
Requery	Reissues the query that created the recordset
Seek	Locates a record that meets the criteria based on the current index
Update	Saves changes to a record

Access to the Recordset Object

Creatable

No

Returned by

The OpenRecordset method of the Connection object
The Recordsets property of the Connection object
The OpenRecordset method of the Database object
The Recordsets property of the Database object
The Clone method of the Recordset object
The OpenRecordset method of the Recordset object
The OpenRecordset method of the TableDef object

Recordsets Collection Properties

Count `RO`

Data Type

Integer

Description

Indicates the number of recordsets in the Recordsets collection. See the code sample in the introduction to this chapter for an example of its usage. As far as I can see, there is little (if any) practical use for this property.

Item `RO`

Recordsets.Item(*Index*)

Argument	Data Type	Description
Index	Integer	The ordinal position of the Recordset object in the Recordsets collection, or a string containing the name of the Recordset object to be retrieved from the collection

Data Type

Recordset object

Description

Retrieves a particular Recordset object from the Recordsets collection. A Recordset object can be retrieved either based on its ordinal position in the collection or based on its name. (But see the Name section later in this chapter for the reasons why it is unwise to reference a recordset based on its name.) Mostly, recordsets are manipulated by means of the variable used to set them, since this is the best way to assure that you are working with the correct recordset.

Recordsets Collection Methods

Refresh

Recordsets.Refresh

Although the documentation lists Refresh as a method of the Recordsets object in Help and the Object Browser, actually this method is inapplicable to the Recordset object, since Refresh applies only to persistent objects. (Since recordsets exist only in memory, the Recordsets collection is not a collection of persistent objects.) Calling the method, however, does not generate an error; it simply has no effect.

Recordset Object Properties

Table 8-4 summarizes which properties apply to each type of Recordset object and whether the property setting is read/write (RW) or read-only (RO) for Jet (J) and ODBCDirect (O) databases, or for both Jet and ODBCDirect workspaces (JO). A blank cell indicates that the property does not apply to either type of workspace. In cases where the property is always read-only with a value of **False**, that is indicated by an F in the cell.

Table 8-4. Recordset Property Summary

Property	Table	Dynaset	Snapshot	Forward-Only	Dynamic
AbsolutePosition		RW	RW		RW
		JO	JO		O
BatchCollisionCount		RO	RO	RO	RO
		O	O	O	O
BatchCollisions		RO	RO	RO	RO
		O	O	O	O
BatchSize		RW	RW	RW	RW
		O	O	O	O
BOF	RO	RO	RO	RO	RO
	J	JO	JO	JO	O
Bookmark	RW	RW	RW		RW
	J	JO	JO		O
Bookmarkable	RO	RO	RO		RO
	J	JO	JO		O
CacheSize		RW/RO	RO		RO
		J/O	O		O
CacheStart		RW			
		J			
Connection		RW	RW	RW	RW
		O	O	O	O
DateCreated	RO				
	J				
EditMode	RO	RO	RO	RO	RO
	J	JO	JO	JO	O

Table 8-4. Recordset Property Summary (continued)

Property	Table	Dynaset	Snapshot	Forward-Only	Dynamic
EOF	RO	RO	RO	RO	RO
	J	JO	JO	JO	O
Filter		RW	RW	RW	
		J	J	J	
Index	RW				
	J				
LastModified	RO	RO	RO		RO
	J	JO	O[a]		O
LastUpdated	RO				
	J				
LockEdits	RW	RW/RO	RW/RO	RW	RO
	J	J/O	J/O	J	O
Name	RO	RO	RO	RO	RO
	J	JO	JO	JO	O
NoMatch	RO	RO	RO		
	J	J	J		
PercentPosition	RW	RW	RW		RW
	J	JO	JO		O
RecordCount	RO	RO	RO	RO	RO
	J	JO	JO	JO	O
RecordStatus		RO	RO	RO	RO
		O	O	O	O
Restartable	F	RO	RO	RO	RO
	J	JO	JO	JO	O
Sort		RW	RW		
		J	J		
StillExecuting		RO	RO	RO	RO
		O	O	O	O
Transactions	RO	RO	RO (F)	RO (F)	
	J	J	J	J	
Type	RO	RO	RO	RO	RO
	J	JO	JO	JO	O
Updatable	RO	RO	F/RO	F/RO	RO
	J	JO	J/O[a]	J/O[a]	O
UpdateOptions		RW	RW	RW	RW
		O	O	O	O

Table 8-4. Recordset Property Summary (continued)

Property	Table	Dynaset	Snapshot	Forward-Only	Dynamic
ValidationRule	RO	RO	RO	RO	
	J	J	J	J	
ValidationText	RO	RO	RO	RO	
	J	J	J	J	

a In an ODBCDirect workspace a snapshot-type Recordset may be updatable, depending on the ODBC driver. The LastModified property is available and the Updatable property is True only on ODBCDirect snapshot-type Recordset objects if the ODBC driver supports updatable snapshots.

AbsolutePosition

Data Type

Long

Description

This misleadingly named property sets or returns the relative record number of a recordset's current record. It is a zero-based number corresponding to the ordinal position of the current record in the recordset, ranging from zero to one less than the record count. If there is no current record (for example, for an empty recordset), AbsolutePosition returns –1.

 Despite the "Absolute" in the property name, this property is not stable and certainly is not a record number. It changes every time records are added to or deleted from a recordset. Use the Bookmark property to set a variable you can use to return to a particular record after moving the record pointer by a search or requerying.

VBA Code

This code displays the ordinal number of the record in a recordset while iterating through it:

```
Private Sub cmdAbsolutePosition_Click()

    Dim dbs As Database
    Dim strDBName As String
    Dim rst As Recordset

    strDBName = "D:\Documents\Northwind.mdb"
    Set dbs = OpenDatabase(strDBName)
    Set rst = dbs.OpenRecordset("Employees", dbOpenSnapshot)
    With rst
```

```
        .MoveFirst
        Do While Not .EOF
            Debug.Print !LastName & " record--No. " & .AbsolutePosition + 1
            .MoveNext
        Loop
        .Close
    End With
    dbs.Close

End Sub
```

BatchCollisionCount ▫RO▫

Data Type

Long

Description

For ODBCDirect workspaces only, this property returns the number of records that did not complete in the last batch update. It corresponds to the number of Bookmarks in the BatchCollisions property.

BatchCollisions ▫RO▫

Data Type

Variant Array

Description

For ODBCDirect workspaces only, this property returns a variant containing an array of bookmarks, representing rows that had a collision during the last batch Update call. The number of elements in the array can be determined by retrieving the value of the BatchCollisionCount property.

BatchSize

Data Type

Long

Description

For ODBCDirect workspaces only, this property sets or returns the number of statements sent back to the server in each batch. The default value is 15. Setting BatchSize to 1 causes each statement to be sent separately; you might do this when working with those database servers that don't support batch updates.

BOF

Data Type

Boolean

Description

The BOF property (the name is derived from "Beginning of File") indicates that the current record position is before the first record in a recordset. It is useful for determining whether you have gone beyond the beginning of the records in a recordset when moving backward. In a recordset with no objects, this property is True. However, if you delete the last remaining record in a recordset, BOF may remain False until you attempt to reposition the record pointer. See Table 8-5 for a summary of what happens when you use the Move methods with different combinations of the BOF and EOF properties.

Table 8-5. The Move Methods with BOF and EOF

BOF/EOF	MoveFirst, MoveLast	MovePrevious, Move < 0	Move 0	MoveNext, Move > 0
BOF=True, EOF=False	Allowed	Error	Error	Allowed
BOF=False, EOF=True	Allowed	Allowed	Error	Error
Both True	Error	Error	Error	Error
Both False	Allowed	Allowed	Allowed	Allowed

Table 8-6 shows what happens to the BOF and EOF properties after using Move methods that don't find a record.

Table 8-6. When Move Methods Don't Find a Record

	BOF	EOF
MoveFirst, MoveLast	True	True
Move 0	No change	No change
MovePrevious, Move < 0	True	No change
MoveNext, Move > 0	No change	True

VBA Code

This code uses the BOF marker to prevent going beyond the first record when iterating backward through a recordset:

```
Private Sub cmdBOF_Click()

    Dim dbs As Database
    Dim rst As Recordset
```

```
    Dim strDBName As String
    Dim strTable As String
    Dim fld As Field

    strTable = "Categories"
    strDBName = "D:\Documents\Northwind.mdb"
    Set dbs = OpenDatabase(strDBName)
    Set rst = dbs.OpenRecordset(strTable, dbOpenTable)
    With rst
       .MoveLast
       Do While Not .BOF
          Debug.Print !CategoryName
          .MovePrevious
       Loop
       .Close
    End With

End Sub
```

Bookmark

Data Type

Variant array of Byte data

Description

Uniquely identifies the current record in a recordset. By retrieving the value of a record's Bookmark property, you can later return the record pointer to that record. It is the closest thing Access has to a record number. You can use bookmarks on recordsets whose Bookmarkable property is **True**, which is always the case for recordsets based entirely on Jet tables. For recordsets based on other databases, Bookmarkable may not be **True**, in which case you can't use bookmarks.

VBA Code

See the code sample in the Requery section for an example of using the Bookmark property to return to the same record after requerying; the following code sample shows another way the Bookmark property can be useful in returning to the previous record after a failed search:

```
Private Sub cmdBookmark_Click()

    Dim dbs As Database
    Dim rst As Recordset
    Dim strDBName As String
    Dim strTable As String
    Dim varBookmark As Variant

    strTable = "Categories"
```

```
strDBName = "D:\Documents\Northwind.mdb"
Set dbs = OpenDatabase(strDBName)
Set rst = dbs.OpenRecordset(strTable, dbOpenTable)
With rst
   If .Bookmarkable = False Then
      MsgBox "This recordset is not bookmarkable -- exiting!"
      Exit Sub
   Else
      MsgBox "This recordset is bookmarkable -- continuing!"
   End If
   varBookmark = .Bookmark
   .Index = "PrimaryKey"
   .Seek "=", 5
   If .NoMatch Then .Bookmark = varBookmark
   Debug.Print !CategoryName
   .Close
End With

End Sub
```

Bookmarkable

[RO]

Data Type

Boolean

Description

The Bookmarkable property indicates whether you can use bookmarks in a recordset. If you are not sure that the tables underlying a recordset are all Jet tables, you can check this property before attempting to use bookmarks. See the Bookmark section for an example of its usage.

CacheSize

Data Type

Long

Description

Sets or returns the number of records retrieved from an ODBC data source that will be cached locally. The value must be between 5 and 1200, but it can't be greater than available memory permits. Setting CacheSize to 0 turns off caching. Using a cache can improve performance, since retrieving data from a local cache is faster than retrieving it from the server.

CacheStart

Data Type

String

Description

The CacheStart property (used in conjunction with CacheSize and FillCache) sets or returns a value that specifies the bookmark of the first record in a dynaset-type recordset containing the data to be locally cached from an ODBC data source in a Jet workspace.

Connection

Data Type

Connection Object

Description

Sets or returns the Connection object that owns the recordset, for ODBCDirect workspaces only.

DateCreated

`RO`

Data Type

Date/Time

Description

Returns the date and time the recordset was created. Note that this is usually different than the date the underlying table was created.

VBA Code

```
Private Sub cmdDateCreated_Click()

    Dim dbs As Database
    Dim rst As Recordset
    Dim strDBName As String
    Dim strTable As String

    strTable = "Categories"
    strDBName = "D:\Documents\Northwind.mdb"
    Set dbs = OpenDatabase(strDBName)
    Set rst = dbs.OpenRecordset(strTable, dbOpenTable)
    Debug.Print rst.Name & " recordset created on " & rst.DateCreated

End Sub
```

EditMode   `RO`

Data Type

Long

Description

Indicates the state of editing, as listed in Table 8-7.

Table 8-7. The EditMode Property Settings

Named Constant	Value	Description
dbEditNone	0	No editing operation is in progress.
dbEditInProgress	1	The Edit method has been invoked, and the current record is in the copy buffer.
dbEditAdd	2	The AddNew method has been invoked, and the current record in the copy buffer is a new record that hasn't been saved in the database.

The value of the EditMode property can be useful in determining whether you should use the Update or CancelUpdate method when editing is interrupted. The following code sample shows the EditMode value for various stages of editing records.

VBA Code

```
Private Sub cmdEditMode_Click()

    Dim dbs As Database
    Dim rst As Recordset
    Dim strDBName As String
    Dim strTable As String

    strTable = "Categories"
    strDBName = "D:\Documents\Northwind.mdb"
    Set dbs = OpenDatabase(strDBName)
    Set rst = dbs.OpenRecordset(strTable, dbOpenTable)

    With rst
        .Move 3
        Debug.Print "EditMode before editing: " & .EditMode
        .Edit
        Debug.Print "EditMode after Edit : " & .EditMode
        !Description = "New description of this category"
        .Update
        Debug.Print "EditMode after updating: " & .EditMode
        .AddNew
        Debug.Print "EditMode after AddNew: " & .EditMode
        .CancelUpdate
        Debug.Print "EditMode after canceling editing: " & .EditMode
        .Close
```

```
      End With

   End Sub
```

EOF   RO

Data Type

Boolean

Description

The EOF property (derived from "End of File") indicates that the current record position is after the last record in a recordset. It is useful for determining whether you have gone beyond the end of the records in a recordset when moving forward. In a recordset with no objects, this property is **True**. However, if you delete the last remaining record in a recordset, EOF may remain **False** until you attempt to reposition the record. See Table 8-5 in the BOF section for a summary of what happens when you use the Move methods with different combinations of the BOF and EOF properties, and Table 8-6 for a listing of what happens to the BOF and EOF properties after using Move methods that don't find a record.

VBA Code

This code uses the EOF marker to prevent going beyond the last record when iterating through a recordset:

```
   Private Sub cmdEOF_Click()

      Dim dbs As Database
      Dim rst As Recordset
      Dim strDBName As String
      Dim strTable As String
      Dim fld As Field

      strTable = "Categories"
      strDBName = "D:\Documents\Northwind.mdb"
      Set dbs = OpenDatabase(strDBName)
      Set rst = dbs.OpenRecordset(strTable, dbOpenTable)
      With rst
         Do While Not .EOF
            Debug.Print !CategoryName
            .MoveNext
         Loop
         .Close
      End With

   End Sub
```

Filter

Data Type

String

Description

Sets or returns a value that filters the records in a recordset (for Jet workspaces only). Basically, it is the **WHERE** clause of a SQL statement without the word **WHERE**. You can use Filter with dynaset-, snapshot-, or forward-only-type recordsets.

 After using the Filter property with a recordset, you don't see the results of filtering immediately—you must open another recordset from the filtered recordset to see the results.

VBA Code

This code sample illustrates using the Filter property to filter records by country, opening a second recordset of UK employees based on the original, unfiltered recordset:

```
Private Sub cmdFilter_Click()

    Dim dbs As Database
    Dim strDBName As String
    Dim rstEmployees As Recordset
    Dim rstUKEmployees As Recordset
    Dim strSearch As String

    strDBName = "D:\Documents\Northwind.mdb"
    Set dbs = OpenDatabase(strDBName)
    Set rstEmployees = dbs.OpenRecordset("Employees", dbOpenDynaset)

    'Create a filtered recordset based on the first recordset
    rstEmployees.Filter = "Country = 'UK'"
    Set rstUKEmployees = rstEmployees.OpenRecordset()

    With rstUKEmployees
        Debug.Print vbCrLf & "Filtered recordset:"
        Do While Not .EOF
            Debug.Print "Name: " & !LastName & ", country: " & !Country
            .MoveNext
        Loop
    End With

End Sub
```

Using the Filter property on a recordset is generally less efficient than just applying a filter to a recordset and opening it in one step, using a SQL statement with a WHERE clause.

Index

Data Type

String

Description

Sets or returns the name of the index to use for a table-type recordset in a Jet workspace. It must be the name of an existing index in the Indexes collection of the TableDef object that is the data source of the Recordset object. The Index property is used with the Seek method for locating records in an indexed recordset. See the Seek section later in this chapter for an example of usage.

LastModified   RO

Data Type

Variant array of Byte data

Description

Returns a bookmark indicating which record in a recordset was most recently added or modified. It applies to table-type or dynaset-type recordsets only. The primary use of this property is to return to the record that was most recently modified in code by setting the Bookmark property equal to LastModified.

 The value of LastModified only reflects changes made to the recordset itself; if a record was changed in the interface or directly in the table, this change is not reflected in the LastModified property.

VBA Code

This code loops through tblCustomers (a copy of the Northwind Customers table), modifying records that meet a criterion, and then returns to the last modified record. I'm using the RecordCount property (–1) to avoid being at the EOF marker after looping; otherwise, there would be an error on the first Debug.Print line:

```
Private Sub cmdLastModified_Click()

    Dim dbs As Database
    Dim rst As Recordset
    Dim strTable As String
    Dim intCount As Integer
    Dim i As Integer

    strTable = "tblCustomers"
    Set dbs = CurrentDb
    Set rst = dbs.OpenRecordset(strTable, dbOpenTable)
    intCount = rst.RecordCount - 1

    With rst
        For i = 1 To intCount
            If !Country = "UK" Then
                .Edit
                !Country = "United Kingdom"
                .Update
                Debug.Print "Changed " & !CompanyName & " record"
            End If
            .MoveNext
        Next i

        Debug.Print "After looping, at " & !CompanyName & " record"
        'Go to most recently modified record
        .Bookmark = .LastModified
        Debug.Print "Last record modified: " & !CompanyName & " record"
        .Close
    End With

End Sub
```

LastUpdated   RO

Data Type

Date/Time

Description

Returns the date and time the recordset was last updated—in other words, when the data in the base table(s) was last changed. The changes can be made either in the interface or in code (unlike the LastModified property).

VBA Code

```
Private Sub cmdLastUpdated_Click()

    Dim dbs As Database
```

```
    Dim rst As Recordset
    Dim strDBName As String
    Dim strTable As String

    strTable = "Categories"
    strDBName = "D:\Documents\Northwind.mdb"
    Set dbs = OpenDatabase(strDBName)
    Set rst = dbs.OpenRecordset(strTable, dbOpenTable)
    Debug.Print "Date Created: " & rst.DateCreated
    Debug.Print "Last Updated: " & rst.LastUpdated

End Sub
```

LockEdits

Data Type

Boolean

Description

For updatable recordsets the LockEdits property sets or returns a value indicating the type of locking in effect while editing, as shown in Table 8-8. Pessimistic locking (**True**) means that the page containing the record being edited is unavailable to other users until you are through editing and use the Update method to save the record. Optimistic locking (**False**) means that other users can access the same record you are working on, except just briefly while you are actually updating the record. Optimistic locking is more risky (two users can simultaneously change a record), but pessimistic locking may cause delays while records are unnecessarily locked.

Table 8-8. The LockEdits Values/Settings

Named Constant	Value	Description
True	−1	(Default) Pessimistic locking is in effect. The 2K page containing the record you're editing is locked as soon as you call the Edit method.
False	0	Optimistic locking is in effect for editing. The 2K page containing the record is not locked until the Update method is executed.

 The LockEdits value can be preset by setting the *lockedit* argument of the OpenRecordset method; setting the *lockedit* argument to dbPessimistic sets the LockEdits property to **True**, and setting it to any other value sets LockEdits to **False**. When working with ODBC data sources, LockEdits is always set to **False**, allowing only optimistic locking.

Name   `RO`

Data Type

String

Description

For recordsets, the Name property is either the name of the underlying table or query, or, if the recordset is based on a SQL statement, the first 256 characters of the SQL statement. This makes the Name property unreliable as a means of referencing a particular recordset. To reference a recordset, just use the variable it was set with.

VBA Code

The code lists the names of several recordsets created based on a table, a query, and a SQL statement:

```
Private Sub cmdName_Click()

    Dim dbs As Database
    Dim rstTable As Recordset
    Dim rstQuery As Recordset
    Dim rstSQL As Recordset
    Dim rst As Recordset
    Dim strDBName As String
    Dim intCount As Integer
    Dim strTable As String
    Dim strQuery As String
    Dim strSQL As String

    strDBName = "D:\Documents\Northwind.mdb"
    Set dbs = OpenDatabase(strDBName)
    strTable = "Orders"
    strQuery = "Ten Most Expensive Products"
    strSQL = "SELECT * FROM Customers"
    Set rstTable = dbs.OpenRecordset(strTable, dbOpenTable)
    Set rstSQL = dbs.OpenRecordset(strSQL, dbOpenSnapshot)
    Set rstQuery = dbs.OpenRecordset(strQuery, dbOpenSnapshot)

    For Each rst In dbs.Recordsets
        Debug.Print rst.Name
    Next rst

End Sub
```

NoMatch   `RO`

Data Type

Boolean

Description

Indicates whether a search was successful. It applies to searches done with the Seek method or one of the Find methods.

If a search is unsuccessful (NoMatch = **True**), the current record will no longer be valid. To avoid problems, save the record's bookmark to a variable so you can return to it after an unsuccessful search, as in the code sample in the Seek section.

PercentPosition

Data Type

Single

Description

Sets or returns a value between 0 and 100, representing the position of the current record in a recordset. For dynaset- or snapshot-type recordsets, move to the last record before using this method to ensure an accurate record count. The following code prints the percent position to the Debug window after each successful find of a record meeting a search criterion.

You can use Percent Position with a scroll bar control on a form or text box to indicate the position of the current record in a recordset.

VBA Code

```
Private Sub cmdPercentPosition_Click()

    Dim dbs As Database
    Dim strDBName As String
    Dim rst As Recordset
    Dim strSearch As String

    strDBName = "D:\Documents\Northwind.mdb"
    Set dbs = OpenDatabase(strDBName)
    Set rst = dbs.OpenRecordset("Employees", dbOpenSnapshot)
    strSearch = "[Title] = 'Sales Rep'"

    'MoveLast to ensure an accurate count of records.
    With rst
        .MoveLast
        .MoveFirst
        .FindFirst strSearch
        Debug.Print !LastName & " record -- " & .PercentPosition & "%"
        .FindNext strSearch
```

```
        Debug.Print !LastName & " record -- " & .PercentPosition & "%"
        .Close
    End With
    dbs.Close

End Sub
```

RecordCount   `RO`

Data Type

Long

Description

Returns the number of records in a recordset. In case of dynaset-, snapshot-, or forward-only-type recordsets, you need to access all the records in the recordset before getting an accurate count of the records. See the following code sample for an example of usage of RecordCount for this purpose. This is not necessary for table-type recordsets.

VBA Code

```
Private Sub cmdRecordCount_Click()

    Dim dbs As Database
    Dim strDBName As String
    Dim rst As Recordset
    Dim intCount As Integer

    strDBName = "D:\Documents\Northwind.mdb"
    Set dbs = OpenDatabase(strDBName)
    Set rst = dbs.OpenRecordset("Employees", dbOpenSnapshot)

    Debug.Print "Record count before traversing recordset: " & _
            rst.RecordCount

    'MoveLast to ensure an accurate count of records.
    rst.MoveLast

    Debug.Print "Record count after traversing recordset: " & _
            rst.RecordCount
    rst.Close
    dbs.Close

End Sub
```

RecordStatus   `RO`

Data Type

Long

Description

Indicates the update status of the current record, if it is part of a batch update (for ODBCDirect workspaces only). The value returned indicates whether (and how) the current record will be involved in the next optimistic batch update. See Table 8-9 for a listing of the constants that may be returned.

Table 8-9. The RecordStatus Return Value Intrinsic Constants

Named Constant	Value	Description
dbRecordUnmodified	0	(Default) The record has not been modified or has been updated successfully.
dbRecordModified	1	The record has been modified and not updated in the database.
dbRecordNew	2	The record has been inserted locally with the AddNew method, but not yet inserted into the database.
dbRecordDeleted	3	The record has been deleted locally, but not yet deleted in the database.
dbRecordDBDeleted	4	The record has been deleted locally and in the database.

Restartable   `RO`

Data Type

Boolean

Description

Indicates whether a recordset supports the Requery method. If the value is **True**, Requery can be used to re-execute the query on which the recordset is based; if it is **False**, the query can't be re-executed.

VBA Code

The following code opens three different types of recordsets, examines the Restartable property of each, and requeries those that are restartable:

```
Private Sub cmdRestartable_Click()

    Dim dbs As Database
    Dim rstTable As Recordset
    Dim rstQuery As Recordset
    Dim rstSQL As Recordset
    Dim rst As Recordset
    Dim strDBName As String
    Dim intCount As Integer
    Dim strTable As String
    Dim strQuery As String
    Dim strSQL As String
```

```
strDBName = "D:\Documents\Northwind.mdb"
Set dbs = OpenDatabase(strDBName)
strTable = "Orders"
strQuery = "Ten Most Expensive Products"
strSQL = "SELECT * FROM Customers"
Set rstTable = dbs.OpenRecordset(strTable, dbOpenTable)
Set rstSQL = dbs.OpenRecordset(strSQL, dbOpenSnapshot)
Set rstQuery = dbs.OpenRecordset(strQuery, dbOpenSnapshot)

'Determine whether each recordset is restartable,
'and requery it if so.
For Each rst In dbs.Recordsets
    Debug.Print rst.Name & " restartable? " & rst.Restartable
    If rst.Restartable = True Then rst.Requery
Next rst

End Sub
```

Sort

Data Type

String

Description

Sets or returns the sort order for records in a recordset (for Jet workspaces only). Basically, it is the ORDER BY clause of a SQL statement without the phrase ORDER BY. You can use Sort with dynaset- and snapshot-type recordsets only. As with the Filter property, the Sort property only takes effect when a new recordset is created from the sorted recordset. The Sort property overrides any sort order that might be specified for a QueryDef on which a recordset is based.

 Using the Sort property on a recordset is generally less efficient than just applying a sort order to a recordset and opening it in one step, using a SQL statement with an ORDER BY clause.

VBA Code

The following code applies a Sort order to a recordset and then opens a second recordset based on the sorted original recordset:

```
Private Sub cmdSort_Click()

    Dim dbs As Database
    Dim strDBName As String
    Dim rst As Recordset
    Dim rstSort As Recordset
```

```
strDBName = "D:\Documents\Northwind.mdb"
Set dbs = OpenDatabase(strDBName)
Set rst = dbs.OpenRecordset("Employees", dbOpenDynaset)
rst.Sort = "Region"
Set rstSort = rst.OpenRecordset

With rstSort
    Do Until .EOF
        Debug.Print "State: " & !Region & " for "; !LastName
        .MoveNext
    Loop
End With

End Sub
```

StillExecuting   `RO`

Data Type

Boolean

Description

For ODBCDirect workspaces only, indicates whether an asynchronous operation (one called with the **dbRunAsync** option) has finished executing. The return value is **True** if the query is still executing and **False** if it has finished executing. The Cancel method can be called to cancel execution if the value is **True**.

Transactions   `RO`

Data Type

Boolean

Description

This property is **True** if the recordset supports transactions, and **False** if it does not. For ODBC workspaces the Transactions property indicates whether the ODBC driver supports transactions. The property can be used for dynaset- or table-type recordsets in Jet workspaces; for snapshot- and forward-only-type recordsets in Jet workspaces, it is always **False**. For dynaset- or table-type recordsets in Jet workspaces, the Transactions property is always **True**, indicating that you can use transactions.

 You should always check the Transactions property and make sure it returns **True** before working with transactions using the Begin-Trans, CommitTrans, and Rollback methods.

VBA Code

This code creates a recordset from the QueryDefs in Northwind and lists the Transactions value for each one:

```
Private Sub cmdTransactions_Click()

    Dim dbs As Database
    Dim strDBName As String
    Dim qdf As QueryDef
    Dim rst As Recordset

    strDBName = "D:\Documents\Northwind.mdb"
    Set dbs = OpenDatabase(strDBName)

    Debug.Print "QueryDefs in " & dbs.Name
    For Each qdf In dbs.QueryDefs
        On Error Resume Next
        Set rst = dbs.OpenRecordset(qdf.Name)
        Debug.Print "Recordset name and type: " & rst.Name & vbTab & _
                    rst.Type
        Debug.Print "Transactions possible?: " & rst.Transactions
    Next qdf
    dbs.Close

End Sub
```

Type   `RO`

Data Type

Integer

Description

Indicates the recordset type of a Recordset object. The possible values are listed in Table 8-10.

Table 8-10. The Type Setting Return Values Intrinsic Constants

Named Constant	Value	Description
dbOpenTable	1	Table (Jet workspaces only)
dbOpenDynamic	16	Dynamic (ODBC workspaces only)
dbOpenDynaset	2	Dynaset
dbOpenSnapshot	4	Snapshot
dbOpenForwardOnly	96	Forward-only

Using the Type property on recordsets can be useful when you don't know what type the recordset is. Note that the recordset type is not the same as the QueryDef type. There are many more QueryDef type constants than Recordset constants, and the available constants are different for the two types of objects.

VBA Code

The following code sample lists the recordset type of recordsets based on all the queries in Northwind:

```
Private Sub cmdType_Click()

    Dim dbs As Database
    Dim strDBName As String
    Dim qdf As QueryDef
    Dim rst As Recordset

    strDBName = "D:\Documents\Northwind.mdb"
    Set dbs = OpenDatabase(strDBName)

    Debug.Print "QueryDefs in " & dbs.Name
    For Each qdf In dbs.QueryDefs
        Debug.Print "Query name and type: " & qdf.Name & vbTab & qdf.Type
        Set rst = dbs.OpenRecordset(qdf.Name)
        Debug.Print "Recordset name and type: " & rst.Name & vbTab & _
                    rst.Type
    Next qdf
    dbs.Close

End Sub
```

Updatable ![RO]

Data Type

Boolean

Description

Indicates whether a recordset can be changed or updated. If it is **True**, the recordset can be updated; if it is **False**, it can't be updated.

VBA Code

This code creates recordsets from all the Northwind queries and reports on whether they are updatable:

```
Private Sub cmdUpdatable_Click()

    Dim dbs As Database
    Dim strDBName As String
    Dim qdf As QueryDef
    Dim rst As Recordset

    strDBName = "D:\Documents\Northwind.mdb"
```

```
Set dbs = OpenDatabase(strDBName)

Debug.Print "QueryDefs in " & dbs.Name
For Each qdf In dbs.QueryDefs
   On Error Resume Next
   Set rst = dbs.OpenRecordset(qdf.Name)
   Debug.Print "Recordset name and type: " & rst.Name & vbTab & _
               rst.Type
   Debug.Print "Recordset updatable?: " & rst.Updatable
Next qdf
dbs.Close

End Sub
```

UpdateOptions

Data Type

Long

Description

Indicates how the WHERE clause is constructed for each record during a batch
update and whether the update should use an UPDATE statement or a DELETE followed by an INSERT (for ODBCDirect workspaces only). The UpdateOptions
value can be any of the constants in Table 8-11.

Table 8-11. The UpdateOptions Return Value/Settings Intrinsic Constants

Named Constant	Value	Description
dbCriteriaKey	1	(Default) Uses just the key column(s) in the where clause.
dbCriteriaModValues	2	Uses the key column(s) and all updated columns in the where clause.
dbCriteriaAllCols	4	Uses the key column(s) and all the columns in the where clause.
dbCriteriaTimeStamp	8	Uses just the timestamp column if available (will generate a run-time error if no timestamp column is in the result set).
dbCriteriaDeleteInsert	16	Uses a set of DELETE and INSERT statements for each modified row.
dbCriteriaUpdate	32	(Default) Uses an UPDATE statement for each modified row.

ValidationRule   `RO`

Data Type

String

Description

Returns a value used to validate data as it is being changed or added to a field in a recordset's underlying data source table. It only applies to Jet workspaces. The ValidationRule phrase describes a comparison in the form of a SQL WHERE clause without the WHERE keyword. If the data does not meet the validation criteria, a trappable run-time error is generated, and the error message contains the text of the ValidationText property, if specified, or else the text of the expression specified by the ValidationRule property. See the ValidationRule section in Chapter 10, *TableDefs Collection and TableDef Object*, for more information on this property.

ValidationRule comparison strings are limited to referencing the field; they can't contain references to user-defined functions or queries.

VBA Code

This code lists the fields in the Northwind Customers table and their validation rules and validation text, if any:

```
Private Sub cmdValidationRule_Click()

    Dim dbs As Database
    Dim rst As Recordset
    Dim strDBName As String
    Dim strTable As String
    Dim fld As Field

    strTable = "Employees"
    strDBName = "D:\Documents\Northwind.mdb"
    Set dbs = OpenDatabase(strDBName)
    Set rst = dbs.OpenRecordset(strTable, dbOpenTable)
    With rst
        .MoveLast
        For Each fld In .Fields
            Debug.Print fld.Name
            If fld.ValidationRule <> "" Then
                Debug.Print "Validation Rule: " & fld.ValidationRule
                Debug.Print "Validation Text: " & fld.ValidationText
            End If
        Next fld
        .Close
    End With

End Sub
```

ValidationText   RO

Data Type

String

Description

The ValidationText property returns a value specifying the text of the message that
appears when data for a field fails the validation rule specified by the Validation-
Rule property. It applies only to Jet workspaces. See the ValidationText section in
Chapter 10 for more information on this property. See the code sample in the ValidationRule section for an example of usage of this property.

Recordset Object Methods

Table 8-12 summarizes the Recordset type supported by each method and whether
it applies to Jet (J) or ODBCDirect (O) workspaces, or both (JO). A blank cell
indicates that the property does not apply to either type of workspace.

Table 8-12. Recordset Method Summary

Method	Table	Dynaset	Snapshot	Forward-Only	Dynamic
AddNew	J	JO	O[a]	O	O
Cancel		O	O	O	O
CancelUpdate	J	JO	O[a]	O	O
Clone	J	J	J		
Close	J	JO	JO	JO	O
CopyQueryDef		J	J	J	
Delete	J	JO	O[a]	O	O
Edit	J	JO	O[a]	O	O
FillCache		J			
FindFirst		J	J		
FindLast		J	J		
FindNext		J	J		
FindPrevious		J	J		
GetRows	J	JO	JO	JO	O
Move	J	JO	JO	[b]	O
MoveFirst	J	JO	JO		O
MoveLast	J	JO	JO		O
MoveNext	J	JO	JO	JO	O
MovePrevious	J	JO	JO		O

Table 8-12. Recordset Method Summary (continued)

Method	Table	Dynaset	Snapshot	Forward-Only	Dynamic
NextRecordset		O	O	O	O
OpenRecordset	J	J	J		
Requery		JO	JO	JO	O
Seek	J				
Update	J	JO	O^a	O	O

^a In an ODBCDirect workspace, a snapshot-type recordset may be updatable, depending on the ODBC driver. The AddNew, Edit, Delete, Update, and CancelUpdate methods are only available on ODBC-Direct snapshot-type Recordset objects if the ODBC driver supports updatable snapshots.

^b Only with forward moves that don't use a bookmark offset.

The recordset types and their uses are listed in Table 8-13.

Table 8-13. Recordset Types and Their Uses

Recordset Type	Usage
Table	Represents a single base table. Supports the AddNew, Delete, and Seek methods, but not the Find* methods. (Jet only.)
Dynamic	Represents one or more base tables. Supports the AddNew and Delete methods, but not the Find* or Seek methods.
Dynaset	Represents a table or an updatable query. Supports the AddNew, Delete, and Find* methods, but not the Seek method.
Snapshot	A read-only recordset; useful for finding data or printing. Does not allow updating, except in the case of an updatable Snapshot in an ODBCDirect workspace. Supports the Find* methods.
Forward-only	Similar to a snapshot, but only allows forward movement. Useful when you only need to make a single pass through a recordset. Does not support the Find* methods.

AddNew

`recordset.AddNew`

Adds a new record to an updatable recordset (table-type or dynaset recordsets only). For dynasets the new records are added at the end of the recordset. For indexed dynasets, the new record is placed in indexed order; if the dynaset is not indexed, the new record is added to the end of the recordset.

Don't confuse AddNew and Append. The DAO AddNew method is the equivalent of Append in other database languages, such as dBASE, while the Append method in DAO is used to add new members to collections.

After adding a new record with the AddNew method, you need to use the Update method to save the new record, as in the following code sample. If you omit the Update, you won't get a warning, and the new record will be lost when you move to another record or close the recordset.

Note that in VBA code, you should use the dot (.) operator for recordset methods and properties, and the bang (!) operator for fields. In VBS code use the dot operator for methods, properties, and fields.

 If you get an "Item not found in this collection" error message when updating a recordset, it is probably the result of a misspelled field name (fields are members of the Fields collection within the recordset).

VBA Code

This code first lists the categories in the Northwind Categories table, then adds a new record, then lists the categories again, showing the newly added one:

```
Private Sub cmdAddNew_Click()

    Dim dbs As Database
    Dim rst As Recordset
    Dim strDBName As String
    Dim strTable As String

    strTable = "Categories"
    strDBName = "D:\Documents\Northwind.mdb"
    Set dbs = OpenDatabase(strDBName)
    Set rst = dbs.OpenRecordset(strTable, dbOpenTable)

    'List categories before adding new record
    Debug.Print "Categories before adding new record:" & vbCrLf
    rst.MoveFirst
    Do Until rst.EOF
        Debug.Print rst!CategoryName
        rst.MoveNext
    Loop

    'Add new category
    With rst
        .AddNew
        !CategoryName = "Dried Foods"
        !Description = _
            "Freeze-dried and sun-dried fruits, vegetables, and meats"
        .Update
    End With
```

```
      'List categories after adding new record
      Debug.Print vbCrLf & "Categories after adding new record:" & vbCrLf
      rst.MoveFirst
      Do Until rst.EOF
          Debug.Print rst!CategoryName
          rst.MoveNext
      Loop
      rst.Close

   End Sub
```

Cancel

recordset.Cancel

Cancels execution of a pending asynchronous method call. It only applies to recordsets in ODBCDirect workspaces since it requires use of the **dbRunAsync** value for the MoveLast method's *Options* argument. See the StillExecuting section for an example that uses this method.

CancelUpdate

recordset.CancelUpdate *updatetype*

Argument	Data Type	Description
recordset	Recordset object	The Recordset object for which you are canceling pending updates
updatetype	Integer	A named constant or Integer value (see Table 8-14)

Cancels any pending updates for a Recordset object, such as would result from use of the Edit or AddNew methods. Before using the CancelUpdate method, you should check the EditMode property of the recordset to find out if there is a pending operation that can be canceled.

Table 8-14. The UpdateType Intrinsic Constants

Named Constant	Value	Description
dbUpdateRegular	1	(Default) Cancels pending changes that aren't cached
dbUpdateBatch	4	Cancels pending changes in the update cache

The *type* argument settings in Table 8-14 can only be used if batch updating is enabled. In an ODBCDirect workspace (only), this is done by setting the DefaultCursorDriver property to **dbUseClient-BatchCursor** when the connection is opened, and the recordset must be opened using OpenRecordset with the *locktype* argument set to dbOptimisticBatch.

VBA Code

This code illustrates the use of CancelUpdate to allow a user to confirm adding a new record to the Categories table in the Northwind database:

```
Private Sub cmdCancelUpdate_Click()

    Dim dbs As Database
    Dim strDBName As String
    Dim rst As Recordset
    Dim intReturn As Integer
    Dim strCategory As String
    Dim strDescription As String

    strDBName = "D:\Documents\Northwind.mdb"
    Set dbs = OpenDatabase(strDBName)
    Set rst = dbs.OpenRecordset("Categories")
    With rst
        .AddNew
        strCategory = "Test"
        strDescription = "Test new food category"
        !CategoryName = strCategory
        !Description = strDescription
        intReturn = MsgBox("Add " & strCategory & " -- " & _
            strDescription & " as a food category?", vbYesNo)
        If intReturn = VbYes Then
            .Update
            MsgBox strCategory & " -- " & strDescription & _
                " added as a food category"
        Else
            .CancelUpdate
            MsgBox strCategory & " -- " & strDescription & _
                " not added as a food category"
        End If
    End With

End Sub
```

Clone

```
Set duplicate = original.Clone
```

Argument	Data Type	Description
duplicate	Recordset object	The duplicate Recordset object being created
original	Recordset object	The original Recordset object being duplicated

Creates a duplicate Recordset object that references the original Recordset object. The original and duplicate recordsets can have different current records. (Note, though, that after the cloning operation, the *duplicate* recordset initially has no current record.) Using the Clone method allows you to share bookmarks between Recordset objects, since their bookmarks are interchangeable.

VBA Code

This code sets up a recordset based on the Northwind Categories table, then clones it, and moves to different records in the original and duplicate recordsets:

```
Private Sub cmdClone_Click()

    Dim dbs As Database
    Dim strDBName As String
    Dim rstO As Recordset
    Dim rstD As Recordset
    Dim strSearch As String
    Dim strText As String

    strDBName = "D:\Documents\Northwind.mdb"
    Set dbs = OpenDatabase(strDBName)
    Set rstO = dbs.OpenRecordset("Categories", dbOpenDynaset)
    Set rstD = rstO.Clone
    strText = "Dried Food"
    strSearch = "[CategoryID] = 2"
    rstO.FindFirst strSearch
    strSearch = "[CategoryID] = 8"
    rstD.FindFirst strSearch

    'Report on where pointer is in the two recordsets.
    Debug.Print "At "; rstO!CategoryName & " record in original recordset"
    Debug.Print "At "; rstD!CategoryName & _
                " record in duplicate recordset"
    rstO.Close
    rstD.Close
    dbs.Close

End Sub
```

Close

`recordset.Close`

Closes a recordset. You should always use this method to close a recordset before closing a database, because otherwise your pending edits and updates will be canceled.

If you try to close a recordset that has already been closed, run-time error 3420, "Object invalid or no longer set," occurs.

See the code sample in the Clone section for an example of usage.

CopyQueryDef

```
Set querydef = recordset.CopyQueryDef
```

Argument	Data Type	Description
querydef	QueryDef object	The QueryDef object you want to create
recordset	Recordset object	The Recordset object you are creating

Returns a QueryDef object that is a copy of the QueryDef object originally used to create the Recordset object. A recordset must be created using the OpenRecordset method before using the CopyQueryDef method. This method can only be used in Jet workspaces. CopyQueryDef can be useful when you need to recreate a QueryDef from a recordset passed to a procedure.

An error occurs if you use this method on a recordset that was not based on a QueryDef.

VBA Code

The *cmdCopyQueryDef_Click* event procedure calls the CreateRecordset function, which sets a recordset variable, *rst*. (Note that the *rst* recordset variable is declared in the Declarations section of the module to make it public in scope.) When control returns to the event procedure, the CopyQueryDef method is used to recreate the QueryDef. The contents of one of the QueryDef's fields are then listed to the Debug window:

```
Private Function CreateRecordset()

    Dim dbs As Database
    Dim strDBName As String
    Dim qdf As QueryDef

    strDBName = "D:\Documents\Northwind.mdb"
    Set dbs = OpenDatabase(strDBName)
    Set qdf = dbs.QueryDefs("Sales by Category")
    Set rst = qdf.OpenRecordset

End Function

Private Sub cmdCopyQueryDef_Click()

    Dim qdf As QueryDef
    Call CreateRecordset
    Set qdf = rst.CopyQueryDef

    With rst
```

```
        Do While Not .EOF
            Debug.Print !CategoryName
            .MoveNext
        Loop
        .Close
    End With

End Sub
```

Delete

recordset.Delete

Deletes the current record from an updatable recordset. If the deleted record is in the primary table in a relationship set to permit cascading deletes, one or more records in the related table may also be deleted. The deleted record remains current (although it can't be edited or used) until you move to another record. It is not necessary to use Update after calling the Delete method.

If you want to be able to undo deletions, you can use transactions and the Rollback method. Transactions are covered in Chapter 4, *Workspaces Collection and Workspace Object*.

VBA Code

This code goes to the last record in a recordset and deletes it:

```
Private Sub cmdDelete_Click()

    Dim dbs As Database
    Dim rst As Recordset
    Dim strDBName As String
    Dim strTable As String
    Dim intCount As Integer

    strTable = "Categories"
    strDBName = "D:\Documents\Northwind.mdb"
    Set dbs = OpenDatabase(strDBName)
    Set rst = dbs.OpenRecordset(strTable, dbOpenTable)
    intCount = rst.RecordCount
    Debug.Print intCount & " records in recordset"

    With rst
        .MoveLast
        .Delete
        intCount = .RecordCount
        .Close
    End With
```

```
Debug.Print intCount & " records in recordset (after delete)"

End Sub
```

Edit

`recordset.Edit`

The Edit method prepares a record in an updatable recordset for editing by placing it in a temporary copy buffer. Generally, you must use the Edit method before making any changes to a record; however, the AddNew and Delete methods are exceptions (no need to use Edit before using either of them). After making changes to a record, you need to use the Update method to save the record.

 You must have a current record in order to use the Edit method.

 If you edit a record and don't use the Update method to save the changes, they will be lost without warning or an error message when you close the recordset or move to another record.

VBA Code

```
Private Sub cmdEdit_Click()

    Dim dbs As Database
    Dim rst As Recordset
    Dim strDBName As String
    Dim strTable As String

    strTable = "Categories"
    strDBName = "D:\Documents\Northwind.mdb"
    Set dbs = OpenDatabase(strDBName)
    Set rst = dbs.OpenRecordset(strTable, dbOpenTable)

    With rst
      .MoveLast
      Debug.Print "Description value before editing: " & !Description
      .Edit
      !Description = "New description of this category"
      .Update
      Debug.Print "Description value after editing: " & !Description
      .Close
    End With

End Sub
```

FillCache

recordset.FillCache *rows, startbookmark*

Argument	Data Type	Description
recordset	Recordset object	A Recordset object created from an ODBC data source, such as a TableDef representing a linked table.
rows	Integer	The number of rows to store in the cache (if omitted, the CacheSize property value is used).
startbookmark	String	The Bookmark specifying the record from which the cache is filled (if omitted, the CacheStart property setting is used).

For Jet-connected ODBC data sources only, this method fills all or part of a record-set's local cache. Caching can improve performance, as data can be retrieved faster from the local cache than from the remote data source.

VBA Code

The following VBA code compares the performance when iterating through a recordset based on a linked table, with or without caching. According to Help, performance should be better with caching, but when I ran this code with a table linked to Northwind, the time was actually slightly longer with caching.

```
Private Sub cmdFillCache_Click()

    Dim dbs As Database
    Dim rst As Recordset
    Dim strTable As String
    Dim sngStart As Single
    Dim sngEnd As Single
    Dim sngNoCache As Single
    Dim sngCache As Single
    Dim intCount As Integer
    Dim strTemp As String

    'Set up a recordset based on a linked table.
    strTable = "tblContacts"
    Set dbs = CurrentDb
    Set rst = dbs.OpenRecordset(strTable, dbOpenDynaset)

    'Iterate through recordset and time the operation.
    With rst
        .MoveFirst
        Do While Not .EOF
            sngStart = Timer
            strTemp = !LastName
            .MoveNext
        Loop

        sngEnd = Timer
        sngNoCache = sngEnd
```

```
'Display performance results.
Debug.Print "Without cache: " & Format(sngNoCache, "##0,000.000") _
           & " seconds"

'Cache the first 100 records and time the operation again.
intCount = 0
.MoveFirst
.CacheSize = 100
.FillCache
sngStart = Timer
.MoveFirst
Do While Not .EOF
    strTemp = !LastName
    intCount = intCount + 1
    .MoveNext
    If intCount Mod 100 = 0 Then
        On Error Resume Next
        .CacheStart = .Bookmark
        .FillCache
    End If
Loop

sngEnd = Timer
sngCache = sngEnd

'Display performance results.
Debug.Print "With cache: " & Format(sngCache, "##0,000.000") _
           & " seconds"
.Close
End With

End Sub
```

FindFirst

```
recordset.FindFirst criteria
```

Argument	Data Type	Description
recordset	Recordset object	An existing dynaset-type or snapshot-type Recordset object
criteria	String	A search string used to locate a record, similar to the WHERE clause in a SQL statement, but without the word WHERE

For Jet workspaces only, the FindFirst method locates the first record in a dynaset or snapshot-type recordset that meets the specified criteria and makes that record the current record. If no matching record is found, the NoMatch property is set to True, making this property useful in determining the success or failure of the FindFirst method, as shown in the following code sample.

To locate a record in a table-type recordset, use the Seek method instead of the FindFirst method.

VBA Code

```
Private Sub cmdFindFirst_Click()

    Dim dbs As Database
    Dim rst As Recordset
    Dim strDBName As String
    Dim strTable As String
    Dim strSearch As String
    Dim strName As String

    strTable = "Employees"
    strDBName = "D:\Documents\Northwind.mdb"
    Set dbs = OpenDatabase(strDBName)
    Set rst = dbs.OpenRecordset(strTable, dbOpenDynaset)
    strName = Chr(39) & "Smith" & Chr(39)
    strSearch = "[LastName] = " & strName
    With rst
        .FindFirst strSearch
        Debug.Print strName & " found? " & Not .NoMatch
        .Close
    End With

End Sub
```

FindLast

recordset.FindLast *criteria*

Argument	Data Type	Description
recordset	Recordset object	An existing dynaset-type or snapshot-type Recordset object
criteria	String	A search string used to locate a record, similar to the WHERE clause in a SQL statement, but without the word WHERE

Similar to the FindFirst method, for Jet workspaces only, the FindLast method locates the last record in a dynaset or snapshot-type recordset that meets the specified criteria and makes that record the current record. If no matching record is found, the NoMatch property is set to **True**.

VBA Code

```
Private Sub cmdFindLast_Click()

    Dim dbs As Database
```

```
Dim rst As Recordset
Dim strDBName As String
Dim strTable As String
Dim strSearch As String
Dim strName As String

strTable = "Employees"
strDBName = "D:\Documents\Northwind.mdb"
Set dbs = OpenDatabase(strDBName)
Set rst = dbs.OpenRecordset(strTable, dbOpenDynaset)
strName = Chr(39) & "Davolio" & Chr(39)
strSearch = "[LastName] = " & strName
With rst
    .FindLast strSearch
    Debug.Print strName & " found? " & Not .NoMatch
    .Close
End With

End Sub
```

FindNext

recordset.FindNext *criteria*

Argument	Data Type	Description
recordset	Recordset object	An existing dynaset-type or snapshot-type Recordset object
criteria	String	A search string used to locate a record, similar to the WHERE clause in a SQL statement, but without the word WHERE

For Jet workspaces only, the FindNext method locates the next record in a dynaset or snapshot-type recordset that meets the specified criteria and makes that record the current record. If no matching record is found, the NoMatch property is set to **True**, so you can use this property to tell whether the method was successful in locating another match, as shown in the following code sample.

VBA Code

```
Private Sub cmdFindNext_Click()

    Dim dbs As Database
    Dim rst As Recordset
    Dim strDBName As String
    Dim strTable As String
    Dim strSearch As String
    Dim strTitle As String

    strTable = "Employees"
    strDBName = "D:\Documents\Northwind.mdb"
    Set dbs = OpenDatabase(strDBName)
    Set rst = dbs.OpenRecordset(strTable, dbOpenDynaset)
    strTitle = Chr(39) & "Sales Representative" & Chr(39)
```

```
        strSearch = "[Title] = " & strTitle
    With rst
        .FindFirst strSearch
        If .NoMatch = False Then
            Debug.Print "Found a match for " & strTitle & " -- name: " & _
                        !LastName
        End If
        .FindNext strSearch
        If .NoMatch = False Then
            Debug.Print "Found another match for " & strTitle & "--name: " _
                        & !LastName
        End If
        .Close
    End With

End Sub
```

FindPrevious

recordset.FindPrevious *criteria*

Argument	Data Type	Description
recordset	Recordset object	An existing dynaset-type or snapshot-type Recordset object
criteria	String	A search string used to locate a record, similar to the WHERE clause in a SQL statement, but without the word WHERE

FindPrevious works much like FindNext, except that it moves backward through the recordset instead of forward.

VBA Code

```
    Private Sub cmdFindPrevious_Click()

        Dim dbs As Database
        Dim rst As Recordset
        Dim strDBName As String
        Dim strTable As String
        Dim strSearch As String
        Dim strTitle As String

        strTable = "Employees"
        strDBName = "D:\Documents\Northwind.mdb"
        Set dbs = OpenDatabase(strDBName)
        Set rst = dbs.OpenRecordset(strTable, dbOpenDynaset)
        strTitle = Chr(39) & "Sales Representative" & Chr(39)
        strSearch = "[Title] = " & strTitle
        With rst
            .FindFirst strSearch
            If .NoMatch = False Then
                Debug.Print "Found a match for " & strTitle & " -- name: " _
                            & !LastName
            End If
```

```
            .FindNext strSearch
            If .NoMatch = False Then
               Debug.Print "Found another match for " & strTitle & "--name: " _
                           & !LastName
            End If
            .FindPrevious strSearch
            If .NoMatch = False Then
               Debug.Print "Went back to last match for " & strTitle & _
                           " -- name: " & !LastName
            End If
            .Close
         End With

      End Sub
```

GetRows

```
Set varArray = recordset.GetRows(numrows)
```

Argument	Data Type	Description
varArray	Variant	An array that stores the retrieved rows of data
recordset	Recordset object	A Recordset object
numrows	Variant	The number of rows to retrieve (if left blank, all available rows are retrieved)

Retrieves multiple rows from a Recordset object into a two-dimensional array. It is very useful for filling list boxes and combo boxes on Outlook forms or Office UserForms from Access tables since they can't be bound to tables or recordsets, unlike Access controls. See the VBS code sample and the second VBA sample for examples of this usage. If you want to retrieve just one field value from the array, you can specify the array element, as in the first VBA code sample (bear in mind that the array numbering is zero-based).

Access VBA Code

```
      Private Sub cmdGetRows_Click()

         Dim dbs As Database
         Dim rst As Recordset
         Dim strTable As String
         Dim strFieldValue As String
         Dim varRecords As Variant
         Dim intRecord As Integer
         Dim intField As Integer

         strTable = "Employees"
         Set dbs = CurrentDb
         Set rst = dbs.OpenRecordset(strTable, dbOpenSnapshot)
         varRecords = rst.GetRows(10)
         Debug.Print "Fourth field in fifth record: " & varRecords(5, 6)

      End Sub
```

Outlook VBS Code

```
Sub cmdFillListBox_Click

    Dim rst
    Dim dao
    Dim wks
    Dim dbs
    Dim strAccessDir
    Dim objAccess
    Dim CustomerArray(99, 2)

    'Pick up path to Access database directory from Access SysCmd function.
    Set objAccess = Item.Application.CreateObject("Access.Application")
    strAccessDir = objAccess.SysCmd(9)
    strDBName = strAccessDir & "Samples\Northwind.mdb"
    objAccess.Quit

    'Set up reference to Access database.
    Set dao = Application.CreateObject("DAO.DBEngine.35")
    Set wks = dao.Workspaces(0)
    Set dbs = wks.OpenDatabase(strDBName)

    'Retrieve Customer information from table.
    Set rst = dbs.OpenRecordset("Customers")
    Set ctl = Item.GetInspector.ModifiedFormPages("Message"). _
Controls("lstCustomers")

    ctl.ColumnCount = 3
    ctl.ColumnWidths = "50; 150 pt; 75 pt"

    'Assign Access data to an array of 3 columns and 100 rows.
    CustomerArray(99, 2) = rst.GetRows(100)

    ctl.Column() = CustomerArray(99, 2)

End Sub
```

VBA Code Behind an Office UserForm

This code runs from the Initialize event of an Office UserForm, so that the *lstCustomers* listbox is filled with data from Northwind when the form is run. The UserForm could be run from Word 97 or 2000, Excel 97 or 2000, or Outlook 2000:

```
Private Sub UserForm_Initialize()

    Dim dao As Object
    Dim rst As Recordset
    Dim wks As Workspace
    Dim dbs As Database
    Dim strDBName As String
    Dim strAccessDir As String
    Dim objAccess As New Access.Application
```

```
Dim CustomerArray(99, 2)
Dim ctl As ListBox

'Pick up path to Access database directory from Access SysCmd function.
strAccessDir = objAccess.SysCmd(9)
strDBName = strAccessDir & "Samples\Northwind.mdb"
objAccess.Quit

'Set up reference to Access database.
Set dao = CreateObject("DAO.DBEngine.35")
Set wks = dao.Workspaces(0)
Set dbs = wks.OpenDatabase(strDBName)

'Retrieve Customer information from table.
Set rst = dbs.OpenRecordset("Customers")
Set ctl = lstCustomers

ctl.ColumnCount = 3
ctl.ColumnWidths = "50; 150 pt; 75 pt"

'Assign Access data to an array of 3 columns and 100 rows.
CustomerArray(99, 2) = rst.GetRows(100)

ctl.Column() = CustomerArray(99, 2)

End Sub
```

Move

recordset.Move *rows, startbookmark*

Argument	Data Type	Description
recordset	Recordset object	The Recordset object whose current record position is being moved.
rows	Long	The number of rows to move. If *rows* is greater than zero, the movement is forward; if it is negative, the movement is backward.
startbookmark	String	The Bookmark of the record to start movement from. If omitted, Move begins from the current record.

Moves the current position in a recordset, either forward or backward. If you are at the BOF marker and move backward or at the EOF marker and move forward, you will get an error. You will also get a run-time error if you try to use the Move method when either the BOF or EOF property is **True**. (See the BOF and EOF property sections for an explanation of these properties.)

VBA Code

This VBA code moves to the last record in a recordset, then back three records:

```
Private Sub cmdMove_Click()

    Dim dbs As Database
    Dim rst As Recordset
    Dim strDBName As String
    Dim strTable As String

    strTable = "Employees"
    strDBName = "D:\Documents\Northwind.mdb"
    Set dbs = OpenDatabase(strDBName)
    Set rst = dbs.OpenRecordset(strTable, dbOpenDynaset)
    With rst
        .MoveLast
        .Move -3
        Debug.Print "On " & !LastName & " record"
        .Close
    End With

End Sub
```

MoveFirst

recordset.MoveFirst

Moves to the first record in a recordset and makes it the current record. It is often used before a loop that iterates through the records in a recordset to ensure that the loop starts with the first record, as in the code sample in the FillCache section.

If you have edited the current record, before moving to another record, be sure to save the changes with the Update method; otherwise, the changes will be lost with no warning.

MoveLast

recordset.MoveLast

Moves to the last record in a recordset and makes it the current record.

For dynaset- or snapshot-type recordsets, you need to use the Move-Last method before counting the number of records in a recordset in order to get an accurate count.

VBA Code

```
Private Sub cmdMoveLast_Click()

    Dim dbs As Database
    Dim rst As Recordset
    Dim strDBName As String
    Dim strTable As String
    Dim intCount As Integer

    strTable = "Categories"
    strDBName = "D:\Documents\Northwind.mdb"
    Set dbs = OpenDatabase(strDBName)
    Set rst = dbs.OpenRecordset(strTable, dbOpenDynaset)
    intCount = rst.RecordCount
    Debug.Print intCount & " records in recordset (before MoveLast)"

    With rst
        .MoveLast
        intCount = .RecordCount
        .Close
    End With

    Debug.Print intCount & " records in recordset (after MoveLast)"

End Sub
```

MoveNext

recordset.MoveNext

Moves to the next record in a recordset and makes it the current record. It is often used in looping structures in code. See the FillCache section for an example of usage.

MovePrevious

recordset.MovePrevious

Moves to the previous record in a recordset and makes it the current record. Usage is similar to MoveNext, except for the direction of movement.

NextRecordset

Set *boolean* = *recordset*.NextRecordset

Argument	Data Type	Description
boolean	Boolean	True indicates that the next set of records is available in *recordset*; False indicates that there are no more records, and *recordset* is empty.
recordset	Recordset object	An existing Recordset object variable to which you want to return pending records.

This method gets the next set of records (if any) returned by a multipart select query in an OpenRecordset call. It returns a Boolean value indicating whether there are any more additional records pending. The method only applies to ODBC-Direct workspaces.

OpenRecordset

```
Set recordset = object.OpenRecordset(name, type, options, lockedit)
Set recordset = object.OpenRecordset(type, options, lockedit)
```

Argument	Data Type	Description
recordset	Recordset object	The Recordset object to be opened.
object	Connection, Database, Recordset, QueryDef, or TableDef object	The object from which the recordset is to be created.
source	String	The record source for the new Recordset object. May be a table name, a query name, or a SQL statement. For table-type Jet recordsets, only table names are allowable.
name	Integer	A named constant or Integer value defining the type of recordset to open (see Table 8-15).
options	Long	A named constant or Long value (see Table 8-16).
lockedit	Integer	A named constant or Integer value (see Table 8-17).

 A saved query or SQL statement used for the *source* argument must be a query that returns records, not an action query. If you specify an action query, an "Invalid Operation" error occurs.

Table 8-15. The Type Intrinsic Constants

Named Constant	Value	Description
dbOpenTable	1	Opens a table-type Recordset object (Jet workspaces only)
dbOpenDynamic	16	Opens a dynamic-type Recordset object, similar to an ODBC dynamic cursor (ODBCDirect workspaces only)
dbOpenDynaset	2	Opens a dynaset-type Recordset object, similar to an ODBC keyset cursor
dbOpenSnapshot	4	Opens a snapshot-type Recordset object similar to an ODBC static cursor
dbOpenForwardOnly	8	Opens a forward-only-type Recordset object

Table 8-16. The Options Intrinsic Constants

Named Constant	Value	Description
dbAppendOnly	8	Allows users to append new records to the Recordset, but prevents them from editing or deleting existing records (Jet dynaset-type Recordset only).
dbSQLPassThrough	64	Passes a SQL statement to a Jet-connected ODBC data source for processing (Jet snapshot-type Recordset only).
dbSeeChanges	512	Generates a run-time error if one user is changing data that another user is editing (Jet dynaset-type Recordset only). This setting is useful in applications where multiple users have simultaneous read/write access to the same data.
dbDenyWrite	1	Prevents other users from modifying or adding records (Jet Recordset objects only).
dbDenyRead	2	Prevents other users from reading data in a table (Jet table-type Recordset only).
dbForwardOnly	256	Creates a forward-only Recordset (Jet snapshot-type Recordset only). It is provided only for backward compatibility, and you should use the **dbOpenForwardOnly** constant in the *type* argument instead of using this option.
dbReadOnly	4	Prevents users from making changes to the Recordset (Jet only). The **dbReadOnly** constant in the *lockedit* argument replaces this option, which is provided only for backward compatibility.
dbRunAsync	1024	Runs an asynchronous query (ODBCDirect workspaces only).
dbExecDirect	2048	Runs a query by skipping *SQLPrepare* and directly calling *SQLExecDirect* (ODBCDirect workspaces only). Use this option only when you're not opening a Recordset based on a parameter query.
dbInconsistent	16	Allows inconsistent updates (Jet dynaset-type and snapshot-type Recordset objects only).
dbConsistent	32	Allows only consistent updates (Jet dynaset-type and snapshot-type Recordset objects only).

Table 8-17. The LockEdit Intrinsic Constants

Named Constant	Value	Description
dbReadOnly	4	Prevents users from making changes to the Recordset (default for ODBCDirect workspaces). You can use **dbReadOnly** in either the *options* argument or the *lockedit* argument, but not both. If you use it for both arguments, a run-time error occurs.

Table 8-17. The LockEdit Intrinsic Constants (continued)

Named Constant	Value	Description
dbPessimistic	2	Uses pessimistic locking to determine how changes are made to the Recordset in a multiuser environment. The page containing the record you're editing is locked as soon as you use the Edit method (default for Jet workspaces).
dbOptimistic	3	Uses optimistic locking to determine how changes are made to the Recordset in a multiuser environment. The page containing the record is not locked until the Update method is executed.
dbOptimisticValue	1	Uses optimistic concurrency based on row values (ODBCDirect workspaces only).
dbOptimisticBatch	5	Enables batch optimistic updating (ODBCDirect workspaces only).

The OpenRecordset method creates a new recordset and automatically appends it to the Recordsets collection. The first syntax variant for the OpenRecordset method call applies to Connection and Database objects, and the second variant applies to QueryDef, Recordset, and TableDef objects. See the OpenRecordset section in Chapter 5, *Databases Collection and Database Object*, for a number of code samples illustrating use of this method with Database objects in Access VBA, Word VBA, Excel VBA, and Outlook VBS code.

VBA Code

This code opens a filtered recordset based on another recordset and displays the results to the Debug window:

```
Private Sub cmdOpenRecordset_Click()

    Dim dbs As Database
    Dim strDBName As String
    Dim rstEmployees As Recordset
    Dim rstWAEmployees As Recordset
    Dim strSearch As String

    strDBName = "D:\Documents\Northwind.mdb"
    Set dbs = OpenDatabase(strDBName)
    Set rstEmployees = dbs.OpenRecordset("Employees", dbOpenDynaset)

    With rstEmployees
        Debug.Print vbCrLf & "Unfiltered recordset:"
        Do While Not .EOF
            Debug.Print "Name: " & !LastName & ", state: " & !Region
            .MoveNext
        Loop
    End With

    'Create a second, filtered recordset based on the first recordset.
```

```
rstEmployees.Filter = "Region = 'WA'"
Set rstWAEmployees = rstEmployees.OpenRecordset()

With rstWAEmployees
    Debug.Print vbCrLf & "Filtered recordset:"
    Do While Not .EOF
        Debug.Print "Name: " & !LastName & ", state: " & !Region
        .MoveNext
    Loop
End With

End Sub
```

Requery

recordset.Requery *newquerydef*

Argument	Data Type	Description
recordset	Recordset object	An existing Jet dynaset-, snapshot-, or forward-only Recordset object, or an ODBCDirect Recordset object
newquerydef	Variant	(Optional) The Name property of a QueryDef object (Jet workspaces only)

The Requery method updates the data in a recordset by re-executing the query on which it is based. The *newquerydef* argument can be used to specify a new query for the recordset.

When you use the Requery method, the first record in the recordset becomes the current record, which can be a problem on forms. To avoid losing the user's place on a form after requerying, you can set a search string before requerying so you can return to the record you were on, as in the following code sample.

VBA Code

This code runs from a command button on an Access form; it calls a function (*Calcinome*, not reproduced here) that modifies data in the form's record source, so that the form needs requerying:

```
Private Sub cmdRequery_Click()

    Dim strSearch As String
    Dim strContract As String

    'Create search string for current record.
    strContract = Me![ContractNo]
    strSearch = "[ContractNo] = " & strContract
```

```
'Call a function that needs requerying.
Call Calcincome
Me.Requery

'Find the record that matches the control.
Debug.Print "Search string: " & strSearch
Me.RecordsetClone.FindFirst strSearch
Me.Bookmark = Me.RecordsetClone.Bookmark

End Sub
```

Seek

recordset.Seek *comparison, key1, key2...key13*

Argument	Data Type	Description
recordset	Recordset object	An existing table-type Recordset object with an index specified by the Recordset object's Index property
comparison	String	One of the following expressions: <, <=, =, >=, or >
key1, key2..., *key13*		One or more values (up to 13 in number) corresponding to fields in the Recordset object's current index, as specified by its Index property

For indexed table-type recordsets in Jet workspaces, the Seek method locates a record that meets the criteria for the current index and makes it the current record. You must set the Index property to the index you want to use before using Seek. (You can also determine if the index you want is active by retrieving its value beforehand.) If the index identifies a nonunique key field, Seek locates the first record that satisfies the criteria.

For =, >=, and > comparisons, Seek starts at the beginning of the index and seeks forward; for < and <= comparisons, Seek starts at the last record and seeks backward.

You must specify values for all fields defined in the index in order to use Seek.

The *key1* argument must be of the same field data type as the corresponding field in the current index.

Seek can be used even if there is no current record. You can't use Seek on a linked table, because you can't create a table-type recordset on a linked table.

See the Index property section for more information about indexes.

VBA Code

```
Private Sub cmdSeek_Click()

    Dim dbs As Database
    Dim strDBName As String
```

```
Dim rst As Recordset
Dim varBookmark As Variant
Dim intEmployee As Integer

strDBName = "D:\Documents\Northwind.mdb"
Set dbs = OpenDatabase(strDBName)
Set rst = dbs.OpenRecordset("Employees", dbOpenTable)
With rst
    .Index = "PrimaryKey"

    'Bookmark current record so we can return to it later.
    varBookmark = .Bookmark
    intEmployee = InputBox("Enter an Employee ID:")
    .Seek "=", intEmployee

    'Return to current record if Seek fails.
    If .NoMatch Then
        MsgBox "ID " & intEmployee & " not found"
        .Bookmark = varBookmark
    Else
        MsgBox "Found ID at " & !LastName & " record"
    End If
    .Close
End With

End Sub
```

Update

recordset.Update(*updatetype, force*)

Argument	Data Type	Description
recordset	Recordset object	An open, updatable Recordset object.
updatetype	Integer	A named constant or Integer value (see Table 8-18) (for ODBCDirect workspaces only).
force	Boolean	(Optional) If **True**, force changes regardless of whether another user has made any changes. If **False** (default), the update fails if another user has made changes while the update is pending.

Table 8-18. The UpdateType Intrinsic Constants

Named Constant	Value	Description
dbUpdateBatch	4	All pending changes in the update cache are written to disk
dbUpdateCurrentRecord	2	Only the current record's pending changes are written to disk
dbUpdateRegular	1	(Default) Pending changes aren't cached and are written to disk immediately

The Update method is crucial to saving your edits; it must be used for all edits done to a record, after creating a new record with AddNew, or calling the Edit method to edit an existing record. One exception is that you don't need to use Update after deleting a record with Delete. If you don't use Update after making a change (other than a Delete), the changes will be lost in any of the following situations:

- You use Edit or AddNew and move to another record without using Update.

- You use Edit or AddNew then use Edit or AddNew again without first using Update.

- You set the Bookmark property to another record.

- You close the recordset without first using Update.

- You cancel editing by using CancelUpdate.

VBA Code

This example code illustrates a standard use of the Update method after using the Edit method and making some changes to a record, in a looping structure that iterates through an entire recordset:

```
Private Sub cmdUpdate_Click()

    Dim dbs As Database
    Dim strDBName As String
    Dim rst As Recordset

    strDBName = "D:\Documents\Northwind.mdb"
    Set dbs = OpenDatabase(strDBName)
    Set rst = dbs.OpenRecordset("Employees", dbOpenTable)
    With rst
       .MoveFirst
       Do While Not .EOF
          .Edit
          If !Title = "Sales Representative" Then !Title = "Sales Rep"
          .Update
          .MoveNext
       Loop
       .Close
    End With
    dbs.Close

End Sub
```

9

Relations Collection and Relation Object

The Relations collection is a collection of all the Relation objects in a Database object in a Jet workspace. Its position in the DAO object model is shown in Figure 9-1. Each Relation object represents a relationship between fields in tables or queries. Relationships can be created in the user interface by opening the Relationships window and dragging the mouse pointer from a field in one table to a field in another table. They may be created in code using the CreateRelation method of the Database or TableDef objects, as described in the CreateRelation sections of Chapter 5, *Databases Collection and Database Object*, and Chapter 10, *TableDefs Collection and TableDef Object*.

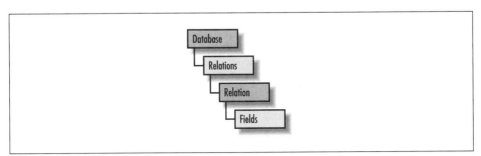

Figure 9-1. The position of the Relations collection in the DAO object model

 Relations created in code may not be viewable in the Relationships window, and relations created in the Relationships window may not be listed when you run the following code.

VBA Code

This code sample lists all the relationships in the Relations object of the North-wind database. (The ListRelations function is called in several other code samples in this chapter.)

```
Private Sub cmdListRelations_Click()

    Call ListRelations

End Sub

Private Function ListRelations()

    Dim dbs As Database
    Dim strDBName As String
    Dim rels As Relations
    Dim rel As Relation

    strDBName = "D:\Documents\Northwind.mdb"
    Set dbs = OpenDatabase(strDBName)
    Set rels = dbs.Relations
    With rels
       Debug.Print "Relationships in Relations Object:"
          For Each rel In rels
             On Error Resume Next
             Debug.Print vbTab & rel.Name
          Next rel
    End With
    dbs.Close

End Function
```

When you create a new relationship in the Relationships window by dragging a field in one table to a field in another table, the Relationships dialog shown in Figure 9-2 pops up, letting you set various properties for the new relationship, such as whether to enforce referential integrity and to cascade updates and deletes.

After clicking the Create button in the Relationships dialog, the new relation appears as a line between the fields in the two tables, as shown in Figure 9-3. Note the 1 and ∞ indicating (respectively) the "one" side and the "many" side of the one-to-many relationship.

In addition to setting properties in the Relationships dialog itself, you can set some more relationship properties by clicking the Join Type button in the Relationships

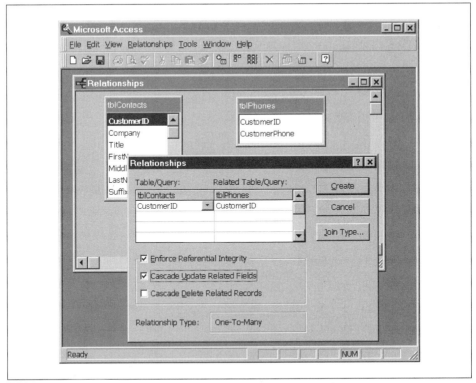

Figure 9-2. Creating a new relationship in the Relationships window

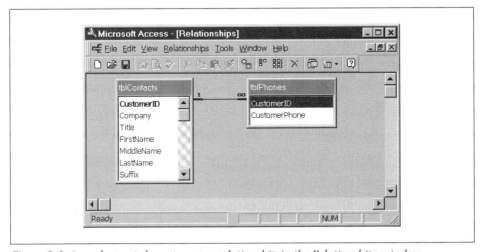

Figure 9-3. A newly created one-to-many relationship in the Relationships window

dialog to open the Join Properties dialog, as shown in Figure 9-4. The three choices correspond to join types, as described in Table 9-1.

Table 9-1. The Relationship Join Types

Number	Description
1	Inner join
2	Left outer join
3	Right outer join

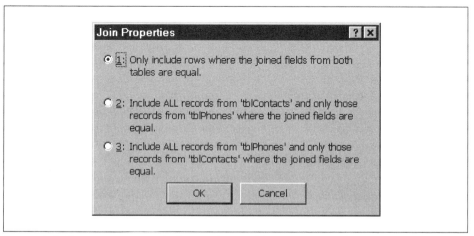

Figure 9-4. The Join Properties dialog, used to modify the join type of a relationship

Relations can be referenced by any of the following syntax variants:

```
Relations(0)
Relations("name")
Relations![name]
```

The Relationships collection has two properties (see Table 9-2) and three methods (shown in Table 9-3). The Relation object has five properties (shown in Table 9-4) and one method (shown in Table 9-5). It also has two collections: the Fields collection, which consists of the Field objects that define the relation, and the Properties object, which contains the Property objects belonging to the Relation object. For more information on the Fields collection, see Chapter 13, *Fields Collection and Field Object.*

Table 9-2. Relations Collection Properties

Property	Description
Count	Indicates the number of items in the collection
Item	(Hidden) Retrieves a Relation object from the collection

Table 9-3. Relations Collection Methods

Method	Description
Append	Adds a relation to the Relations collection
Delete	Removes a relation from the collection
Refresh	Updates the collection to reflect any changes

Table 9-4. Relation Object Properties

Property	Description
Attributes	The flags defining the characteristics of the relation
ForeignTable	The name of the foreign table in a relation
Name	The name of the relation
PartialReplica	Determines whether a relation should be considered in populating a partial replica from a full replica
Table	The name of the primary table in a relation

Table 9-5. Relation Object Method

Method	Description
CreateField	Adds a field to the relation

Access to the Relation Object

Creatable

　Yes

Returned by

　The CreateRelation method of the Database object
　The Relations property of the Database object

Relations Collection Properties

Count   [RO]

Data Type

Integer

Description

Returns the number of objects in the Relations collection. In previous versions of Access, Count was useful for setting up loops to process all the Relation objects in the Relations collection, as in the following code; however, the `For Each...Next` loop is a more efficient way of iterating through the members of a collection.

VBA Code

```
Private Sub cmdCount_Click()

    Dim dbs As Database
    Dim strDBName As String
    Dim rels As Relations
    Dim rel As Relation
    Dim i As Integer
    Dim intCount As Integer

    strDBName = "D:\Documents\Northwind.mdb"
    Set dbs = OpenDatabase(strDBName)
    Set rels = dbs.Relations
    intCount = rels.Count
    For i = 0 To intCount - 1
        Debug.Print "Relation " & i & vbTab & "-- " & rels(i).Name
    Next i
    dbs.Close

End Sub
```

Item   `RO`

```
Relations.Item(Index)
```

Argument	Data Type	Description
Index	Integer	The ordinal position of the Relation object in the Relations collection, or a string containing the name of the Relation object to be retrieved from the collection

Data Type

Relation object

Description

A property hidden in the Object Browser that retrieves a particular Relation object from the Relations collection. A Relation object can be retrieved either based on its ordinal position in the collection or based on its name. Since Relations is a zero-based collection, the following code fragment returns the first Relation:

```
Dim rel As Relation
Set rel = objRelations.Item(0)
```

You can also retrieve a particular Relation object by name. The following code fragment, for instance, retrieves the Relation object named "Customer":

```
Dim rel As Relation
Set rel = objRelations.Item("Customer")
```

Since the Item property is the default member of the Relations collection, it does not need to be explicitly specified to retrieve a particular Relation object. In other words, the following two statements are equivalent; both retrieve the same Relation object:

```
Set rel = objRelations.Item(0)
Set rel = objRelations(0)
```

Similarly, the following three statements all retrieve the same Relation object by name:

```
Set rel = objRelations.Item("Customer")
Set rel = objRelations ("Customer")
Set rel = objRelations![Customer]
```

Relations Collection Methods

Append

```
Relations.Append object
```

After creating a relationship with the CreateRelation method, you must append it to the Relations collection of a database; however, before doing that, you must first set and append the Field objects needed to define the primary and foreign keys. (See the CreateRelation section in Chapter 5 for more details on creating a relationship.) The following VBA code is a segment of a longer code sample, limited to the portion that actually appends the relationship; the full code sample is in the CreateRelation method section of Chapter 5.

VBA Code

```
'Create a relation to join the new Phones table to the
'existing Employees table.
Set rel = .CreateRelation("EmployeePhones", _
    tdfEmp.Name, tdfPhone.Name, dbRelationUpdateCascade)

'Create a Field object for the relation, and set
'its Name and ForeignName properties.
rel.Fields.Append rel.CreateField("EmployeeID")
rel.Fields!EmployeeID.ForeignName = "EmployeeID"
.Relations.Append rel
```

Delete

```
Relations.Delete name
```

Removes a Relation object representing a relationship from the Relations collection.

VBA Code

```
Private Sub cmdDelete_Click()

    Dim dbs As Database
    Dim strDBName As String
```

```
        Debug.Print "List relationships before deleting relationship"
        Call ListRelations

        strDBName = "D:\Documents\Northwind.mdb"
        Set dbs = OpenDatabase(strDBName)
        dbs.Relations.Delete "EmployeePhones"
        dbs.Close

        Debug.Print "List relationships after deleting relationship"
        Call ListRelations

    End Sub
```

Refresh

`Relations.Refresh`

Updates the members of a collection to reflect the current situation. You may need to use this method in multiuser environments where other users may create or delete relationships, but for single-user databases this method appears to be unnecessary, as you can see when running the code in the Delete section earlier in this chapter.

Relation Object Properties

Attributes

Data Type

Long

Description

Indicates one or more characteristics of a Relation object, as listed in Table 9-6. Some of these constants correspond to the selections you can make in the Relationships dialog in the interface (see Figure 9-2). The possible values of the Attributes property are not mutually exclusive. This means that to store multiple values to the property, you add them together, as in:

```
    Relation.Attributes = dbRelationUnique + dbUpdateCascade
```

To determine whether a particular attribute is enabled when you retrieve the value of the Attributes property, logically **And** it with the property value. For example:

```
    lAttrib = Relation.Attributes
    If lAttrib And dbRelationUnique Then
        ' dbRelationUnique attribute is enabled...
```

For an example of usage of the Attributes property, see the code sample in the CreateField section.

Table 9-6. The Relation Attributes Return Values/Settings

Named Constant	Value	Description
dbRelationUnique	1	The relationship is one-to-one.
dbRelationDontEnforce	2	The relationship isn't enforced (no referential integrity).
dbRelationInherited	4	The relationship exists in a noncurrent database that contains the two linked tables.
dbRelationUpdateCascade	256	Updates will cascade.
dbRelationDeleteCascade	4096	Deletions will cascade.

ForeignTable

Data Type

String

Description

Sets or returns the name of the foreign table in a relationship—that is, the other table to which the primary table is related. The ForeignTable property of the Relation object is the Name property of the TableDef or QueryDef object that represents the foreign table or query.

VBA Code

The example VBA code iterates through the relations in the Northwind database, listing their Name, ForeignTable, and Table properties:

```
Private Sub cmdForeignTable_Click()

    Dim dbs As Database
    Dim strDBName As String
    Dim rels As Relations
    Dim rel As Relation

    strDBName = "D:\Documents\Northwind.mdb"
    Set dbs = OpenDatabase(strDBName)
    Set rels = dbs.Relations
    With rels
        Debug.Print "Northwind Relationships:"
            For Each rel In rels
                On Error Resume Next
                Debug.Print vbTab & "Name: " & rel.Name
                Debug.Print vbTab & "ForeignTable: " & rel.ForeignTable
                Debug.Print vbTab & "Table: " & rel.Table & vbCrLf
            Next rel
    End With
    dbs.Close

End Sub
```

Name

Data Type

String

Description

Displays the name of the Relation. Names may be up to 64 characters in length. The property is read-write until the Relation is appended to the Relations collection and read-only after appending.

PartialReplica

`relation.PartialReplica`

Data Type

Boolean

Description

Indicates or determines whether a relation should be considered in populating a partial replica from a full replica. When **True**, the relation should be enforced during synchronization; when **False**, the relation should not be enforced.

The PartialReplica property lets you fine-tune partial replication, going beyond the limitations of the ReplicaFilter property. In particular, it allows you to set criteria based on fields in the primary table, which is not allowed with the ReplicaFilter property.

If you have set the ReplicaFilter property and the PartialReplica property (to different values), they act together with an implicit OR connector.

VBA Code

This code sets the PartialReplica property to **True** to filter tblInterests records prior to populating a partial replica by a ReplicaFilter based on the customer's BusinessState (a field in the relation's primary table, tblCustomers, linked to tblInterests in a one-to-many relationship—see Figure 9-5):

```
Private Sub cmdPartialReplica_Click()

    Dim tdf As TableDef
    Dim strFilter As String
    Dim dbs As Database
    Dim strPartial As String
```

```
Dim strPath As String
Dim rel As Relation

strPath = "D:\Documents\"
strPartial = strPath & "Local Westwind Replica.mdb"

'Open the partial replica
Set dbs = OpenDatabase(strPartial)

With dbs
    Set tdf = .TableDefs("tblContacts")
    Set rel = .Relations("tblContactstblInterests")
    strFilter = "BusinessState = 'MA'"
    tdf.ReplicaFilter = strFilter
    rel.PartialReplica = True
    .Close
End With

End Sub
```

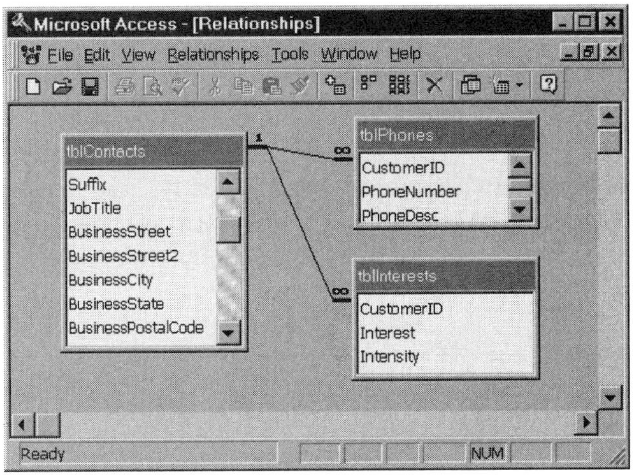

Figure 9-5. A relation used to populate a partial replica

Table

RO

Data Type

String

Description

Returns the name of the primary table in a relationship, which is the Name property of a TableDef or QueryDef object. See the ForeignTable example for usage of this property.

Relation Object Methods

CreateField

```
Set field = relation.CreateField(name, type, size)
```

Argument	Data Type	Description
field	Field object	The field you are creating
relation	Relation object	The relation for which you are creating the new field
name	String	(Optional) The name of the new field; it may be up to 64 characters in length
type	Integer	Ignored for Relation
size	Integer	Ignored for Relation

Use the CreateField method to create a new field for the relationship and specify its name. You can omit *name* when creating a field for a relation and then change it before appending the field to the Fields collection of the Relation object. Some (but not all) field properties can be changed after the field is appended.

Use the Delete method of the Fields collection to remove a field from a Fields collection belonging to a relationship.

You can't delete a field after you create an index that references it, as is likely to be the case when you create a relationship using the field.

You can reference a Field object using any of the following syntax variants:

```
Fields(0)
Fields("name")
Fields![name]
```

VBA Code

The VBA code sample uses the CreateField method in two ways: to append fields to a newly created TableDef object in the Northwind database and to create fields for a new Relation linking the new table to an existing table:

```
Private Sub cmdCreateField_Click()

    Dim wks As Workspace
    Dim dbs As Database
    Dim tdfEmp As TableDef
    Dim tdfPhone As TableDef
    Dim fld As Field
```

```vba
    Dim rel As Relation
    Dim idx As Index

    Set wks = Workspaces(0)
    Set dbs = wks.OpenDatabase("D:\Documents\Northwind.mdb")

    Debug.Print "List relationships before creating new relationship"
    Call ListRelations

    With dbs
        'Create a Tabledef based on an existing table.
        Set tdfEmp = dbs.TableDefs("Employees")

        'Create new table.
        Set tdfPhone = dbs.CreateTableDef("tblPhones")

        'Append fields to new table.
        With tdfPhone
            .Fields.Append .CreateField("EmployeeID", dbLong)
            .Fields.Append .CreateField("PhoneNumber", dbText, 14)
            .Fields.Append .CreateField("PhoneDesc", dbText, 20)

            'Index the new table.
            Set idx = .CreateIndex("EmpIDIndex")

            'Add a field to the index and make it unique.
            idx.Fields.Append idx.CreateField("EmployeeID")
            idx.Unique = True
            .Indexes.Append idx
        End With
        .TableDefs.Append tdfPhone

        'Create a relation to join the new Phones table to the
        'existing Employees table.
        Set rel = .CreateRelation("EmployeePhones", _
            tdfEmp.Name, tdfPhone.Name, dbRelationUpdateCascade)

        'Create a Field object for the relation, and set
        'its Name and ForeignName properties.
        rel.Fields.Append rel.CreateField("EmployeeID")
        rel.Fields!EmployeeID.ForeignName = "EmployeeID"
        .Relations.Append rel
        .Close
    End With

    Debug.Print "List relationships after creating new relationship"
    Call ListRelations

End Sub
```

TableDefs Collection
and TableDef Object

The TableDefs collection is the collection of all the TableDef objects in a Jet database. Its position in the DAO object model is shown in Figure 10-1. This collection is the default collection of a Database object. A TableDef is the table definition (either a base table or a linked table), as opposed to the data in the table. TableDef objects are used to create a new table or examine and possibly modify the structure of an existing base table, including its fields and indexes.

To modify the data in a table, use a recordset based on the table. (See the OpenRecordset section later in this chapter, and Chapter 8, *Recordsets Collection and Recordset Object*, for more details on using recordsets to manipulate data.)

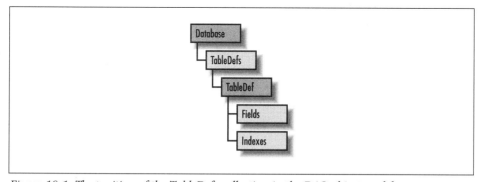

Figure 10-1. The position of the TableDefs collection in the DAO object model

Creating Access Tables

There are several other ways to create tables programmatically in Access, apart from appending a TableDef object to the TableDefs collection:

- Use the CopyObject method of the DoCmd object in the Access object model to create a new table from an existing table.

- Run a make-table query using the OpenQuery method of the DoCmd object to create a new table as the output of a query.

- Use the Jet SQL **CREATE TABLE** statement, as in the following code, which creates a simple two-field table:

```
strSQL = "CREATE TABLE " & "tblForms" & _
    "(FormName TEXT (100), Use YESNO);"
DoCmd.RunSQL strSQL
```

However you create a table, it will be appended to the TableDefs collection. It will also show up in the Tables tab of the database window, although you may need to refresh the Tables view by clicking on another tab and then returning to the Tables tab in order to see it listed.

You can use any of the three following syntax variants to reference a TableDef object in the TableDefs collection:

```
TableDefs(0)
TableDefs("name")
TableDefs![name]
```

The TableDefs object has two properties and three methods; they are listed in Table 10-1. The TableDef object has 14 properties and 5 methods. Its properties are shown in Table 10-2, while its methods appear in Table 10-3. In addition, the TableDef object supports three collections: Fields, the collection of Field objects, each of which represents a single field in the table definition; Indexes, the collection of Index objects, each of which represents one index for the table; and Properties, the collection of Property objects, each of which represents an intrinsic or user-defined property of a TableDef object. For information on the Fields collection, see Chapter 13, *Fields Collection and Field Object*; for information on the Indexes collection, see Chapter 15, *Indexes Collection and Index Object*.

Table 10-1. Members of the TableDefs Collection

Type	Name	Description
Property	Count	Indicates the number of TableDef objects in the collection
Property	Item	(Hidden) Retrieves an individual TableDef object from the collection
Method	Append	Adds a TableDef object to the collection

Table 10-1. Members of the TableDefs Collection (continued)

Type	Name	Description
Method	Delete	Removes a TableDef object from the collection
Method	Refresh	Updates the TableDefs collection to reflect recent changes

Table 10-2. TableDef Object Properties

Property	Description
Attributes	Defines the characteristics of the table
ConflictTable	The name of the table containing the records that had conflicts during synchronization
Connect	Provides information about the source of an open connection
DateCreated	The date and time the TableDef was created
KeepLocal	Custom property that determines whether the table definition should remain local when the database is replicated
LastUpdated	The date and time the TableDef was last updated
Name	The name of the TableDef object
RecordCount	The number of records in the table definition
Replicable	Custom property that determines whether a table definition can be replicated
ReplicableBool	(Jet 3.5 and higher) Custom property that determines whether a table definition can be replicated
ReplicaFilter	Indicates which subset of records is replicated to a table from a full replica
SourceTableName	The name of the source table to which the linked table is linked (for linked tables only)
Updatable	Determines whether a table definition can be changed
ValidationRule	Validation rules to validate data as it is being changed or added to a table field
ValidationText	The message that appears when data for a field fails the validation rule

Table 10-3. TableDef Object Methods

Method	Description
CreateField	Creates a new field to be added to the TableDef
CreateIndex	Creates an index for a TableDef
CreateProperty	Creates a custom property of the TableDef
OpenRecordset	Opens a recordset based on the TableDef
RefreshLink	Updates the connection information for a linked table

VBA Code

This example code lists all the TableDefs in the Northwind database. This is not the same list you will get by listing the members of the Tables container—that container also includes queries (see Chapter 6, *Containers Collection and Container Object*). The *ListTableDefs* function is also called by other code samples in this chapter.

```
Private Sub cmdListTableDefs_Click()

    Call ListTableDefs

End Sub

Private Function ListTableDefs()

    Dim dbs As Database
    Dim strDBName As String
    Dim tdf As TableDef

    strDBName = "D:\Documents\Northwind.mdb"
    Set dbs = OpenDatabase(strDBName)
    Debug.Print "TableDefs in " & dbs.Name
        For Each tdf In dbs.TableDefs
            On Error Resume Next
            Debug.Print vbTab & tdf.Name
        Next tdf
    dbs.Close

End Function
```

Here is a typical listing produced by this code:

```
TableDefs in D:\Documents\Northwind.mdb
    Categories
    Customers
    Employees
    ExtraStuff
    MSysACEs
    MSysCmdbars
    MSysIMEXColumns
    MSysIMEXSpecs
    MSysModules
    MSysModules2
    MSysObjects
    MSysQueries
    MSysRelationships
    Order Details
    Orders
    Phones
    Products
    Shippers
    Suppliers
    tblPhones
```

```
tblRecentOrders
tmakRecentOrders
```

Note the tables starting with MSys. These tables are system tables that contain information about the database structure used internally by Access. If you don't see them in the database window, check the System Objects option on the View page of the Options dialog (on the Tools menu in Access).

Access to the TableDef Object

Creatable

 Yes

Returned by

 The CreateTableDef method of the Database object
 The TableDefs property of the Database object

TableDefs Collection Properties

Count   RO

Data Type

Integer

Description

Returns the number of objects in a database's TableDefs collection. You can count the number of TableDefs using this property. In previous versions of Access it was used to iterate through a collection, but it is now more efficient to use the `For Each...Next` construct for this purpose.

Item   RO

```
TableDefs.Item(Index)
```

Argument	Data Type	Description
Index	Integer	The ordinal position of the TableDef object in the TableDefs collection, or a string containing the name of the TableDef object to be retrieved from the collection

Data Type

TableDef object

Description

A hidden property in the Object Browser, the Item property retrieves a particular TableDef object from the TableDefs collection. A TableDef object can be retrieved either based on its ordinal position in the collection or based on its name. Since TableDefs is a zero-based collection, the following code fragment returns the first TableDef object:

```
Dim tdf As TableDef
Set tdf = tdfs.Item(0)
```

You can also retrieve a particular TableDef object by name. The following code fragment, for instance, retrieves the TableDef object named "Orders":

```
Dim tdf As TableDef
Set tdf = tdfs.Item("Orders")
```

Since the Item property is the default member of the TableDefs collection, it does not need to be explicitly specified to retrieve a particular TableDef object. In other words, the following two statements are equivalent; both retrieve the same Table-Def object:

```
Set tdf = tdfs.Item(0)
Set tdf = tdfs(0)
```

Similarly, the following three statements all retrieve the same TableDef object by name:

```
Set tdf = tdfs.Item("Customer")
Set tdf = tdfs("Customer")
Set tdf = tdfs![Customer]
```

TableDefs Collection Methods

Append

tabledefs.Append *object*

Argument	Data Type	Description
object	TableDef object	A reference to the TableDef to be added to the collection

Appends a new TableDef object represented by *object* to the TableDefs collection. After creating a TableDef object from code (using the CreateTableDef method of a Database object), you need to append the new TableDef object to the Table-Defs collection in order to save it, as in the following code sample. If you attempt to append a table that already exists in the TableDefs collection, runtime error 3010, "Table already exists," is generated. To deal with this possibility, the example code has an error handler that displays an appropriate message and cancels the Append operation if the table name has already been used.

VBA Code

```vba
Private Sub cmdAppend_Click()

On Error GoTo cmdAppend_ClickError

    Dim dbs As Database
    Dim tdf As TableDef
    Dim tdfNew As TableDef

    Set dbs = OpenDatabase("D:\Documents\Northwind.mdb")

    Debug.Print "List of TableDefs before appending new table" & vbCrLf
    Call ListTableDefs

    With dbs
        'Create new table
        Set tdfNew = dbs.CreateTableDef("tblNew")

        'Append fields to new table
        With tdfNew
            .Fields.Append .CreateField("EmployeeID", dbLong)
            .Fields.Append .CreateField("Hobbies", dbText, 14)
            .Fields.Append .CreateField("VacationPreference", dbText, 20)
            .Fields.Append .CreateField("AnnualBonus", dbCurrency)
        End With

        .TableDefs.Append tdfNew
        .Close
    End With

    Debug.Print vbCrLf & "List of TableDefs after appending new table" & _
                vbCrLf
    Call ListTableDefs

cmdAppend_ClickExit:
    Exit Sub

cmdAppend_ClickError:
    If err.Number = 3010 Then
        MsgBox "Table name already used; canceling Append"
    Else
        MsgBox "Error No: " & err.Number & "; Description: " & _
                err.Description
    End If

    Resume cmdAppend_ClickExit

End Sub
```

Delete

tabledefs.Delete name

Argument	Data Type	Description
name	String	Name of the TableDef to be deleted

Deletes a TableDef from the TableDefs collection. If the table contains any records, the data is also deleted. The following code sample first uses the Access VBA *DCount* function to check whether there are any records in a table in the current database, then deletes its TableDef only if the table contains no data. An error handler takes care of the situation in which the specified table is not found in the database.

VBA Code

```
Private Sub cmdDelete_Click()

On Error GoTo cmdDelete_ClickError

    Dim dbs As Database
    Dim lngCount As Long
    Dim strTable As String

    Set dbs = CurrentDb
    strTable = "tblNew"
    lngCount = DCount("*", strTable)

    If lngCount > 0 Then
       MsgBox strTable & " has " & lngCount & " records; not deleting it"
       Exit Sub
    Else
       dbs.TableDefs.Delete strTable
    End If

    dbs.Close

cmdDelete_ClickExit:
    Exit Sub

cmdDelete_ClickError:
    If err.Number = 64231 Then
       MsgBox "Table " & strTable & " not found; canceling Delete"
    Else
       MsgBox "Error No: " & err.Number & "; Description: " & _
              err.Description
    End If

    Resume cmdDelete_ClickExit

End Sub
```

Refresh

`tabledefs.Refresh`

The Refresh method updates the members of the TableDefs collection to reflect the current situation. You may need to use this method in multiuser environments where other users may create or delete tables or modify table definitions. It may not be needed in a single-user database, and in any case using the Refresh method often appears to have no effect. Try running the code for the CreateIndex method later in this chapter several times with different table names; when I did that, sometimes the newly created table showed up the first time (before the Refresh line), sometimes after the Refresh line, and sometimes in neither listing. However, the new table was always visible in the database window, at least after clicking on another tab and then clicking back on the Tables tab.

TableDef Object Properties

Attributes

Data Type

Long

Description

Specifies the characteristics of the table represented by the TableDef object. It is the sum of a combination of the Long constants in Table 10-4.

Table 10-4. The TableDef Attributes Intrinsic Constants

Named Constant	Value	Description
dbAttachExclusive	65536	For databases that use the Microsoft Jet database engine, the table is a linked table opened for exclusive use. You can set this constant on an appended TableDef object for a local table, but not on a remote table.
dbAttachSavePWD	131072	For databases that use the Microsoft Jet database engine, the user ID and password for the remotely linked table are saved with the connection information. You can set this constant on an appended TableDef object for a remote table, but not on a local table.
dbSystemObject	-2147483646	The table is a system table provided by the Microsoft Jet database engine. This constant can be set for an appended TableDef object.

Table 10-4. The TableDef Attributes Intrinsic Constants (continued)

Named Constant	Value	Description
dbHiddenObject	1	The table is a hidden table provided by the Microsoft Jet database engine. This constant can be set on an appended TableDef object.
dbAttachedTable	1073741824	The table is a linked table from a non-ODBC data source such as a Microsoft Jet or Paradox database (read-only).
dbAttachedODBC	536870912	The table is a linked table from an ODBC data source, such as Microsoft SQL Server (read-only).

VBA Code

The code lists the attributes of the Northwind tables to the Debug window:

```
Private Sub cmdAttributes_Click()

    Dim dbs As Database
    Dim strDBName As String
    Dim tdf As TableDef

    strDBName = "D:\Documents\Northwind.mdb"
    Set dbs = OpenDatabase(strDBName)
    Debug.Print "TableDefs in " & dbs.Name
            For Each tdf In dbs.TableDefs
                On Error Resume Next
                Debug.Print vbTab & tdf.Name & " Attributes: " & _
                            tdf.Attributes
            Next tdf
    dbs.Close

End Sub
```

ConflictTable   [RO]

Data Type

String

Description

Returns the name of a conflict table containing the records that had conflicts during synchronization. If there is no conflict table, or the database is not replicated, the return value is a zero-length string ("").

VBA Code

The code checks each table in a replicated database for a conflict table and prints the names of the tables that had conflicts:

```
Private Sub cmdConflictTable_Click()

    Dim dbs As Database
    Dim strDBName As String
    Dim tdf As TableDef

    strDBName = InputBox("Name and path of replicated database")
    Set dbs = OpenDatabase(strDBName)
    Debug.Print "TableDefs in " & dbs.Name
            For Each tdf In dbs.TableDefs
                On Error Resume Next
                Debug.Print vbTab & tdf.Name & " Conflict Table: " & _
                            tdf.ConflictTable
            Next tdf
    dbs.Close

End Sub
```

Connect

tabledef.Connect = *databasetype;parameters;*

Data Type

String

Description

Displays a string providing information about the source of an open connection, a database used in a pass-though query, or a linked table. It is read-write for new TableDefs not yet appended to the TableDefs collection and read-only after appending. It is read-only at all times for base tables. The connect string consists of two parts, each of which is terminated with a semicolon, as shown in Table 10-5.

Table 10-5. The Connect Property Arguments

Argument	Data Type	Description
tabledef	TableDef object	The TableDef whose Connect property is being returned.
databasetype	String	Optional; see Table 10-6 for settings. Omit this argument for Jet databases, but include a semicolon (;) as a placeholder.
parameters	String	Additional parameters to pass to ODBC or install-able ISAM drivers. Use semicolons to separate parameters.

Table 10-6. The Databasetype Argument Settings

Database type	Specifier	Example
Microsoft Jet Database	`[database];`	*drive:\path\filename.mdb*
dBASE III	`dBASE III;`	*drive:\path*
dBASE IV	`dBASE IV;`	*drive:\path*
dBASE 5	`dBASE 5.0;`	*drive:\path*
Paradox 3.x	`Paradox 3.x;`	*drive:\path*
Paradox 4.x	`Paradox 4.x;`	*drive:\path*
Paradox 5.x	`Paradox 5.x;`	*drive:\path*
FoxPro 2.0	`FoxPro 2.0;`	*drive:\path*
FoxPro 2.5	`FoxPro 2.5;`	*drive:\path*
FoxPro 2.6	`FoxPro 2.6;`	*drive:\path*
Excel 3.0	`Excel 3.0;`	*drive:\path\filename.xls*
Excel 4.0	`Excel 4.0;`	*drive:\path\filename.xls*
Excel 5.0 or Excel 95	`Excel 5.0;`	*drive:\path\filename.xls*
Excel 97	`Excel 97;`	*drive:\path\filename.xls*
HTML Import	`HTML Import;`	*drive:\path\filename*
HTML Export	`HTML Export;`	*drive:\path*
Text	`Text;`	*drive:\path*

ODBC	`ODBC; DATABASE=database;`
	`UID=user; PWD=password;`
	`DSN= datasourcename;`
	`[LOGINTIMEOUT= seconds;]`
		None

Exchange	`Exchange;` `MAPILEVEL=folderpath;` `[TABLETYPE={ 0	1 }];` `[PROFILE=profile;]` `[PWD=password;]` `[DATABASE=database;]`	*drive:\path\filename.mdb*

VBA Code

The code sets the Connect string for a linked Access table and refreshes the link:

```
Private Sub cmdConnect_Click()

    Dim dbs As Database
    Dim strDBName As String
    Dim tdf As TableDef

    strDBName = CurrentDb.Name
    Set dbs = OpenDatabase(strDBName)
    Set tdf = dbs.TableDefs("Shippers")
    tdf.Connect = ";DATABASE=D:\Documents\Northwind.mdb"
```

```
        tdf.RefreshLink
        Debug.Print "Connect string: " & tdf.Connect & _
            " for " & tdf.Name
    End Sub
```

DateCreated

Data Type

Date/Time

Description

Returns the date and time the TableDef was created.

VBA Code

The code lists the DateCreated value for each table in the Northwind database:

```
    Private Sub cmdDateCreated_Click()

        Dim dbs As Database
        Dim strDBName As String
        Dim tdf As TableDef

        strDBName = "D:\Documents\Northwind.mdb"
        Set dbs = OpenDatabase(strDBName)
        Debug.Print "TableDefs in " & dbs.Name
            For Each tdf In dbs.TableDefs
                On Error Resume Next
                Debug.Print vbTab & tdf.Name & " created on " & _
                        tdf.DateCreated
            Next tdf
        dbs.Close

    End Sub
```

KeepLocal

`tabledef`.Properties("KeepLocal")

Data Type

String

Description

The KeepLocal property, when set to "T", keeps the TableDef local when the database is replicated. The property must be set before replication; it can't be changed after the TableDef has been replicated.

The KeepLocal property is not a built-in property; it must be created using the CreateProperty method and appended to the TableDef's Properties collection before it can be set.

VBA Code

The VBA code creates a new TableDef, appends some fields to it, saves it, and sets its KeepLocal property to "T":

```
Private Sub cmdKeepLocal_Click()

    Dim dbs As Database
    Dim strDBName As String
    Dim tdfNew As TableDef
    Dim prp As Property

    strDBName = "D:\Documents\Northwind.mdb"
    Set dbs = OpenDatabase(strDBName)

    'Create new table.
    Set tdfNew = dbs.CreateTableDef("tblTest")

    'Append fields to new table.
    With tdfNew
        .Fields.Append .CreateField("EmployeeID", dbLong)
        .Fields.Append .CreateField("Hobbies", dbText, 14)
        .Fields.Append .CreateField("VacationPreference", dbText, 20)
        .Fields.Append .CreateField("AnnualBonus", dbCurrency)
    End With

    dbs.TableDefs.Append tdfNew

    'Create KeepLocal property and append it.
    With tdfNew
        Set prp = .CreateProperty("KeepLocal", dbText, "T")
        'On Error Resume Next
        .Properties.Append prp
        .Properties("KeepLocal") = "T"
        Debug.Print "KeepLocal property: " & .Properties("KeepLocal") _
            & " for " & .Name
    End With

End Sub
```

LastUpdated   `R0`

Data Type

Date/Time

Description

Returns the date and time the TableDef was last updated, in other words, when the data in the table was last changed.

Access VBA Code

The code lists the DateCreated and LastUpdated values for the tables in the current database. Note that the code uses the CurrentDb method from the Access object model:

```
Private Sub cmdLastUpdated_Click()

    Dim dbs As Database
    Dim tdf As TableDef

    Set dbs = CurrentDb
    Debug.Print "TableDefs in " & dbs.Name
        For Each tdf In dbs.TableDefs
            On Error Resume Next
            Debug.Print vbTab & "Date created: " & tdf.DateCreated
            Debug.Print vbTab & "Last updated: " & tdf.LastUpdated
        Next tdf
    dbs.Close

End Sub
```

Name

Data Type

String

Description

The name of a TableDef; this property of a TableDef can be set when you create a table in the interface, or when you create a TableDef in code using the CreateTableDef method. In the latter case the *name* argument of the CreateTableDef method becomes the TableDef's Name property.

VBA Code

The code uses the Name property to list the names of all the TableDef objects in the current database:

```
Private Sub cmdName_Click()

    Dim dbs As Database
    Dim tdf As TableDef

    Set dbs = CurrentDb
    Debug.Print "TableDefs in " & dbs.Name
```

```
        For Each tdf In dbs.TableDefs
            On Error Resume Next
            Debug.Print vbTab & tdf.Name
        Next tdf
    dbs.Close

End Sub
```

RecordCount   `RO`

Data Type

Long

Description

Returns the number of records in a TableDef object. If the table has no records, the RecordCount value is 0.

 For linked TableDef objects, the RecordCount is always −1.

VBA Code

This code lists the number of records in each table of the Northwind database:

```
    Private Sub cmdRecordCount_Click()

        Dim dbs As Database
        Dim strDBName As String
        Dim tdf As TableDef

        strDBName = "D:\Documents\Northwind.mdb"
        Set dbs = OpenDatabase(strDBName)
        Debug.Print "TableDefs in " & dbs.Name
            For Each tdf In dbs.TableDefs
                On Error Resume Next
                Debug.Print vbTab & tdf.Name & " has " & tdf.RecordCount & _
                            " records"
            Next tdf
        dbs.Close

    End Sub
```

Replicable

Data Type

String

Description

Sets or returns a value indicating whether a TableDef object in a Jet workspace can be replicated. Making a TableDef replicable means that it can be replicated when you synchronize a Design Master or replica.

This property does not exist by default; in order to use it, you must first create it using the CreateProperty method and then append it to the TableDef's Properties collection.

The "T" setting is the only one that is usable; if you try to set the Replicable property to "F" after initially setting it to "T", you will get runtime error 3459.

The standard `tabledef.Replicable` syntax won't work with this property; if you use it, you will get a "Method or data member not found" error.

When you create a table in a replicated database, you have the choice of making it replicable or not (see Figure 10-2); the default is that it is set as Local (its Replicable property is set to "F"). However, you can set its value to "T" to make it replicable in code, as in the tdfExisting segment of the following code sample. After making a TableDef replicable, when you next open the database, it has the Replicable icon next to it in the database window.

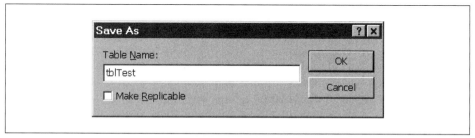

Figure 10-2. The Replicable choice when creating a new table in the interface (for a replicated database)

Figure 10-3 shows nine replicated tables and one local table in a replicated database.

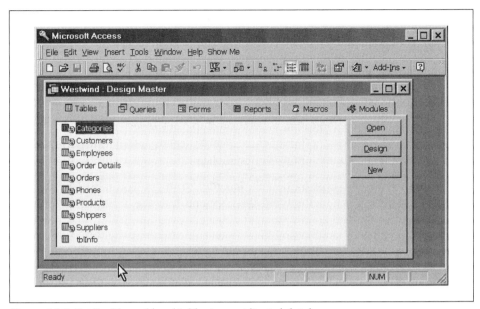

Figure 10-3. Replicable and local tables in a replicated database

VBA Code

```
Private Sub cmdReplicable_Click()

    Dim dbs As Database
    Dim strDBName As String
    Dim tdfNew As TableDef
    Dim tdfExisting As TableDef
    Dim prp As Property

    'Open a replicated database.
    strDBName = "D:\Documents\Westwind.mdb"
    Set dbs = OpenDatabase(strDBName, True)

    'Create new table.
    Set tdfNew = dbs.CreateTableDef("tblNew")

    'Append fields to new table and append table.
    With tdfNew
        .Fields.Append .CreateField("EmployeeID", dbLong)
        .Fields.Append .CreateField("Hobbies", dbText, 14)
        .Fields.Append .CreateField("VacationPreference", dbText, 20)
        .Fields.Append .CreateField("AnnualBonus", dbCurrency)
        dbs.TableDefs.Append tdfNew
        'On Error Resume Next.

        'Create Replicable property for new table.
        Set prp = .CreateProperty("Replicable", dbText, "T")
        .Properties.Append prp
        .Properties("Replicable") = "T"
```

```
            Debug.Print "Table name: " & .Name
            Debug.Print "Replicable: " & .Properties("Replicable")
        End With

        'Modify Replicable property for existing table
        'created in the interface, and thus initially local.
        Set tdfExisting = dbs.TableDefs("tblInfo")
        With tdfExisting
            'Create Replicable property for existing table.
            Set prp = .CreateProperty("Replicable", dbText, "T")
            .Properties.Append prp
            .Properties("Replicable") = "T"
            Debug.Print "Table name: " & .Name
            Debug.Print "Replicable: " & .Properties("Replicable")
        End With

    End Sub
```

ReplicableBool

Data Type

Boolean

Description

If you are using Jet 3.5 or higher, you can use the ReplicableBool property (which is not listed in either Help or the Object Browser) instead of the Replicable property. ReplicableBool takes a Boolean value rather than requiring creation of a custom property. Otherwise, its functionality is identical to that of the Replicable property.

ReplicaFilter

Data Type

String or Boolean

Description

Sets or returns a value indicating which subset of records is replicated to a table from a full replica, as specified in Table 10-7.

Table 10-7. The ReplicaFilter Return Value/Settings

Value	Description
A string	A criterion that a record in the partial replica table must satisfy in order to be replicated from the full replica. The syntax is like a SQL WHERE clause without the WHERE keyword.

Table 10-7. The ReplicaFilter Return Value/Settings (continued)

Value	Description
True	Replicates all records.
False	(Default) Doesn't replicate any records.

To remove a filter, set the ReplicaFilter property to False.

If you change the replica filter and try to synchronize a database without first invoking PopulatePartial, a trappable error occurs.

VBA Code

```
Private Sub cmdReplicaFilter_Click()

    Dim tdf As TableDef
    Dim strFilter As String
    Dim dbs As Database
    Dim strPartial As String
    Dim strFull As String

    strPartial = "F:\DATA\Boston Replica.mdb"
    strFull = "C:\DATA\Full Replica.mdb"

    'Open the partial replica in exclusive mode.
    Set dbs = OpenDatabase(strPartial, True)

    With dbs
        Set tdf = .TableDefs("Contacts")

        'Synchronize with full replica
        'before setting replica filter.
        .Synchronize strFull

        strFilter = "AreaCode = '914'"
        tdf.ReplicaFilter = strFilter

    'Repopulate records from the full replica.
        .PopulatePartial strFull

        .Close
    End With

End Sub
```

SourceTableName

Data Type

String

Description

For a linked table the SourceTableName property returns the name of the source table to which the linked table is linked; for a base table it is a zero-length string. The property is read-only for base tables and read/write for linked tables or unappended TableDefs.

 Although the linked table name is usually the same as the source table name, you can change it if desired—for example, to conform to a naming convention. Changing the linked table name does not affect the original table in any way.

VBA Code

The example code assigns a Connect string to a linked table, refreshes the connection, and then lists the Connect string, the source table name, and the linked table name to the Debug window:

```
Private Sub cmdSourceTableName_Click()

    Dim dbs As Database
    Dim strDBName As String
    Dim tdf As TableDef

    Set dbs = CurrentDb
    Set tdf = dbs.TableDefs("Shippers")
    tdf.Connect = ";DATABASE=D:\Documents\Northwind.mdb"
    tdf.RefreshLink
    Debug.Print "Connect string: " & tdf.Connect & _
        " for " & tdf.Name
    Debug.Print "Source table name: " & tdf.SourceTableName
    Debug.Print "Linked table name: " & tdf.Name

End Sub
```

Updatable   `RO`

Data Type

Boolean

Description

Indicates whether a TableDef can be changed. The Updatable value is always **True** for a newly created TableDef object and always **False** for a linked Table-Def (you can only change the data in a linked table, not the structure). If all the fields in a table are not updatable, the table itself is not updatable.

VBA Code

The example code lists the Updatable property for all the Northwind tables:

```
Private Sub cmdUpdatable_Click()

    Dim dbs As Database
    Dim strDBName As String
    Dim tdf As TableDef

    strDBName = "D:\Documents\Northwind.mdb"
    Set dbs = OpenDatabase(strDBName)
    Debug.Print "TableDefs in " & dbs.Name
        For Each tdf In dbs.TableDefs
            On Error Resume Next
            Debug.Print vbTab & tdf.Name & " updatable? " & tdf.Updatable
        Next tdf
    dbs.Close

End Sub
```

ValidationRule

Data Type

String

Description

Used to validate data as it is being changed or added to a table field. The ValidationRule phrase describes a comparison in the form of a SQL **WHERE** clause without the **WHERE** keyword. If the data does not meet the validation criteria, a trappable run-time error is generated. The error message contains the text of the ValidationText property, if specified, or else the text of the expression specified by the ValidationRule property:

- For a base table the ValidationRule property is read/write; for a linked table, it is read-only. Validation is only supported for Jet databases.

- The ValidationRule property of a TableDef can refer to multiple fields.

- For a linked table the ValidationRule property is inherited from the same property as the source table. If the source table has no validation rule, the property is a zero-length string.

ValidationRule comparison strings are limited to referencing the field being validated; they can't contain references to user-defined functions or queries.

VBA Code

The example code lists the fields in the Northwind Employees table and their validation rules and validation text, if any:

```
Private Sub cmdValidationRule_Click()

    Dim dbs As Database
    Dim tdf As TableDef
    Dim strDBName As String
    Dim strTable As String
    Dim fld As Field

    strTable = "Employees"
    strDBName = "D:\Documents\Northwind.mdb"
    Set dbs = OpenDatabase(strDBName)
    Set tdf = dbs.TableDefs(strTable)
    With tdf
        Debug.Print "Table validation rule: " & .ValidationRule
        For Each fld In .Fields
            Debug.Print fld.Name
            If fld.ValidationRule <> "" Then
                Debug.Print "Validation Rule: " & fld.ValidationRule
                Debug.Print "Validation Text: " & fld.ValidationText
            End If
        Next fld
    End With

End Sub
```

ValidationText

Data Type

String

Description

The ValidationText property (read-write for a base table and read-only for linked tables) returns a value specifying the text of the message that appears when data for a field fails the validation rule specified by the ValidationRule property. It applies only to Jet workspaces. See the code sample in the ValidationRule section for an example that uses this property.

TableDef Object Methods

CreateField

`Set field = tabledef.CreateField(name, type, size)`

Argument	Data Type	Description
field	Field object	The field you are creating.
tabledef	TableDef object	The TableDef for which you are creating the new field.
name	String	(Optional) The name of the new field. It may be up to 64 characters in length.
type	Integer	(Optional) A named constant or Integer value specifying the field's data type (see Table 10-8).
size	Integer	(Optional) The size, in bytes, of a text field. (This parameter is ignored for numeric and fixed-width fields.)

Table 10-8. The Type Intrinsic Constants with the Equivalent Access Data Types

Named Constant	Value	Description	Access Table Data Type
dbBigInt	16	Big Integer	If used, causes Error #3259, "Invalid field data type"
dbBinary	9	Binary	Binary[a]
dbBoolean	1	Boolean	Yes/No
dbByte	2	Byte	Number (Byte)
dbChar	18	Char	If used, causes Error #3259, "Invalid field data type"
dbCurrency	5	Currency	Currency
dbDate	8	Date/Time	Date/Time
dbDecimal	20	Decimal	If used, causes Error #3259, "Invalid field data type"
dbDouble	7	Double	Number (Double)
dbFloat	21	Float	If used, causes Error #3259, "Invalid field data type"
dbGUID	15	GUID	Number (Replication ID)
dbInteger	3	Integer	Number (Integer)
dbLong	4	Long	Number (Long Integer), AutoNumber
dbLongBinary	11	Long Binary	OLE Object
dbMemo	12	Memo	Memo, Hyperlink
dbNumeric	19	Numeric	If used, causes Error #3259, "Invalid field data type"
dbSingle	6	Single	Number (Single)
dbText	10	Text	Text

Table 10-8. The Type Intrinsic Constants with the Equivalent Access Data Types (continued)

Named Constant	Value	Description	Access Table Data Type
dbTime	22	Time	If used, causes Error #3259, "Invalid field data type"
dbTimeStamp	23	Time Stamp	If used, causes Error #3259, "Invalid field data type"
dbVarBinary	17	VarBinary (VBA Code)	If used, causes Error #3259, "Invalid field data type"

a Creates an Access table field displayed as Binary, although this is not one of the available choices.

Creates a new field and specifies its name, data type, and size. You can omit one or more of the optional parts when creating a field then change it before appending the field to the Fields collection of the appropriate object. Some (but not all) field properties can be changed after they are appended. See the Append section for an example that uses this method.

You may wonder why there are 21 data types in Table 10-8 while there are only 14 data types for fields in Access tables. The extra ones are available for use when linking to other databases or for compatibility with field types in other database languages. The Access data types, which correspond to the DAO data type constants, are listed in the fourth column in Table 10-8. The other constants can't be used to create TableDef fields.

CreateIndex

```
Set index = tabledef.CreateIndex(name)
```

Argument	Data Type	Description
index	Index object	The index you are creating.
tabledef	TableDef object	The TableDef for which you are creating the index.
name	String	The name of the index. It can be up to 64 characters in length.

Creates an index for a TableDef object. It can be used to create an index for an existing table or for a new TableDef object as it is being created. The index's *name* argument must be unique in the TableDef object's Indexes collection; if it is not, a run-time error will occur when you try to append the index. Note that the existing index is overwritten if the index specified by *name* already exists; a syntax error does not result. To remove an index from a collection, use the Delete method with the Indexes collection of a TableDef object, as in the second code sample following, which has a **Select Case** error handling structure to take care of either the specified table or index not being found.

VBA Code

The code sample creates a new table, appends some fields to it, and creates an index for the new table:

```
Private Sub cmdCreateIndex_Click()

On Error GoTo cmdCreateIndex_ClickError

    Dim dbs As Database
    Dim tdf As TableDef
    Dim fld As Field
    Dim idx As Index
    Dim strTable As String

    Set dbs = CurrentDb

    With dbs
        'Create a new table.
        strTable = InputBox("Name of new table:")
        Set tdf = dbs.CreateTableDef(strTable)

        'Append fields to new table.
        With tdf
            .Fields.Append .CreateField("EmployeeID", dbLong)
            .Fields.Append .CreateField("PhoneNumber", dbText, 14)
            .Fields.Append .CreateField("PhoneDesc", dbText, 20)

            'Index the new table.
            Set idx = .CreateIndex("EmpIDIndex")

            'Add a field to the index and make it unique.
            idx.Fields.Append idx.CreateField("EmployeeID")
            idx.Unique = True
            .Indexes.Append idx
        End With
        .TableDefs.Append tdf
    End With

    Debug.Print "List of TableDefs before refreshing" & vbCrLf
    Call ListTableDefs
    dbs.TableDefs.Refresh
    Debug.Print vbCrLf & "List of TableDefs after refreshing" & vbCrLf
    Call ListTableDefs
    dbs.Close

cmdCreateIndex_ClickExit:
    Exit Sub

cmdCreateIndex_ClickError:
    If err.Number = 3010 Then
        MsgBox "Table name already used; canceling table creation"
    Else
        MsgBox "Error No:" & err.Number & "; Description:" & _
```

```
                    err.Description
        End If

        Resume cmdCreateIndex_ClickExit
    End Sub


    Private Sub cmdDeleteIndex_Click()

    On Error GoTo cmdDeleteIndex_ClickError

        Dim dbs As Database
        Dim tdf As TableDef
        Dim idx As Index

        Set dbs = CurrentDb
        Set tdf = dbs.TableDefs("tblHourlyWorkers")
        'Set idx = tdf.Indexes("EmpIDIndex")
        tdf.Indexes.Delete "EmpIDIndex"
        MsgBox "EmpIDIndex index deleted from tblHourlyWorkers"


    cmdDeleteIndex_ClickExit:
        Exit Sub

    cmdDeleteIndex_ClickError:
        Select Case err.Number
            Case 64231
                MsgBox "tblHourlyWorkers not found; canceling Delete Index"
            Case 3265
                MsgBox "EmpIDIndex not found; canceling Delete Index"
            Case Else
                MsgBox "Error No:" & err.Number & "; Description:" & _
                        err.Description
        End Select

        Resume cmdDeleteIndex_ClickExit
    End Sub
```

CreateProperty

```
Set property = tabledef.CreateProperty(name, type, value, DDL)
```

Argument	Data Type	Description
property	Property object	The property you are creating.
tabledef	TableDef object	A TableDef object variable used to create the new property.
name	String	(Optional) The name of the new property. Property names can be up to 64 characters in length.
type	Integer	(Optional) A named constant or Integer value indicating the property's data type (see Table 10-9).
value	Variant	(Optional) The initial property value.

Argument	Data Type	Description
DDL	Boolean	(Optional) If `True`, the property is a DDL Object and users can't change or delete it unless they have `dbSecWriteDef` permission. If `False`, it is not a DDL object and can be changed or deleted by users.

Creates a new user-defined Property object in the Properties collection of a Table-Def object, for Jet workspaces only. See the Replicable section later in this chapter for an important use for this method. This allows you to supplement the basic properties of a TableDef object (which are listed in the section "TableDefs Collection Properties") with properties that you define, such as an "Internal" property to mark tables of data for internal use only. See Table 10-8 to match the DAO data type constants with the Access table data type equivalents (not all of the DAO constants match Access table data types).

You don't have to assign values to all the arguments when you create a property; you can set them later, before you append the Property to the TableDef object. After appending, some (but not all) of the property settings can be altered.

If you try to create a property with a name that already exists in the Properties collection (such as the name of a built-in property), an error occurs.

Table 10-9. The Type Intrinsic Constants

Named Constant	Value	Description
`dbBigInt`	16	Big Integer
`dbBinary`	9	Binary
`dbBoolean`	1	Boolean
`dbByte`	2	Byte
`dbChar`	18	Char
`dbCurrency`	5	Currency
`dbDate`	8	Date/Time
`dbDecimal`	20	Decimal
`dbDouble`	7	Double
`dbFloat`	21	Float
`dbGUID`	15	GUID

Table 10-9. The Type Intrinsic Constants (continued)

Named Constant	Value	Description
dbInteger	3	Integer
dbLong	4	Long
dbLongBinary	11	Long Binary (OLE Object)
dbMemo	12	Memo
dbNumeric	19	Numeric
dbSingle	6	Single
dbText	10	Text
dbTime	22	Time
dbTimeStamp	23	Time Stamp
dbVarBinary	17	VarBinary (VBA Code)

VBA Code

The code example creates a new property for the Northwind Employees table, then lists the names and values of any nonempty properties for that table (including the newly created one) to the Debug window:

```
Private Sub cmdCreateProperty_Click()

    Dim dbs As Database
    Dim tdf As TableDef
    Dim prp As Property
    Dim prpNew As Property

    Set dbs = OpenDatabase("D:\Documents\Northwind.mdb")
    Set tdf = dbs.TableDefs("Employees")
    Set prpNew = tdf.CreateProperty("Internal", dbBoolean, False)
    tdf.Properties.Append prpNew

    'Enumerate TableDef properties.
    For Each prp In tdf.Properties
       If prp <> "" Then
          Debug.Print prp.Name & " = " & prp
       End If
    Next prp

    dbs.Close

End Sub
```

OpenRecordset

```
Set recordset = tabledef.OpenRecordset(type, options, lockedit)
```

Argument	Data Type	Description
recordset	Recordset object	The recordset to be opened
tabledef	TableDef object	The TableDef from which to create the recordset

Argument	Data Type	Description
type	Integer	(Optional) A named constant or Integer value (see Table 10-10)
options	Long	(Optional) A named constant or Long value (see Table 10-11)
lockedit	Integer	(Optional) A named constant or Integer value (see Table 10-12)

The OpenRecordset method can be used to work with data in both base and attached tables. The *type* settings let you determine what type of recordset to create from the table. You can use the same method with a QueryDef (as described in Chapter 7, *QueryDefs Collection and QueryDef Object*) and generally the Open-Recordset method is used with QueryDefs, since they are more flexible than TableDefs.

Table 10-10. The Type Intrinsic Constants

Named Constant	Value	Description
dbOpenTable	1	Opens a table-type Recordset object (Jet workspaces only). In this case the TableDef object cannot represent a linked table.
dbOpenDynamic	16	Opens a dynamic-type Recordset object similar to an ODBC dynamic cursor (ODBCDirect workspaces only).
dbOpenDynaset	2	Opens a dynaset-type Recordset object similar to an ODBC keyset cursor.
dbOpenSnapshot	4	Opens a snapshot-type Recordset object similar to an ODBC static cursor.
dbOpenForwardOnly	8	Opens a forward-only-type Recordset object.

Table 10-11. The Options Intrinsic Constants

Named Constant	Value	Description
dbAppendOnly	8	Allows users to append new records to the Recordset, but prevents them from editing or deleting existing records (Jet dynaset-type Recordset only).
dbSQLPassThrough	64	Passes a SQL statement to a Jet-connected ODBC data source for processing (Jet snapshot-type Recordset only).
dbSeeChanges	512	Generates a run-time error if one user changes data that another user is editing (Jet dynaset-type Recordset only). This setting is useful in applications where multiple users have simultaneous read/write access to the same data.
dbDenyWrite	1	Prevents other users from modifying or adding records (Jet Recordset objects only).
dbDenyRead	2	Prevents other users from reading data in a table (Jet table-type Recordset only).

Table 10-11. The Options Intrinsic Constants (continued)

Named Constant	Value	Description
dbForwardOnly	256	Creates a forward-only Recordset (Jet snapshot-type Recordset only). It is provided only for backward compatibility; you should use the **dbOpenForwardOnly** constant in the *type* argument instead of this option.
dbReadOnly	4	Prevents users from making changes to the Recordset (Jet only). The **dbReadOnly** constant in the *lockedits* argument replaces this option, which is provided only for backward compatibility.
dbRunAsync	1024	Runs an asynchronous query (ODBCDirect workspaces only).
dbExecDirect	2048	Runs a query by skipping SQLPrepare and directly calling SQLExecDirect (ODBCDirect workspaces only). Use this option only when you're not opening a Recordset based on a parameter query.
dbInconsistent	16	Allows inconsistent updates (Jet dynaset-type and snapshot-type Recordset objects only).
dbConsistent	32	Allows only consistent updates (Jet dynaset-type and snapshot-type Recordset objects only).

Table 10-12. The LockEdit Intrinsic Constants

Named Constant	Value	Description
dbReadOnly	4	Prevents users from making changes to the Recordset (default for ODBCDirect workspaces). You can use **dbReadOnly** in either the *options* argument or the *lockedit* argument, but not both. If you use it for both arguments, a run-time error occurs.
dbPessimistic	2	Uses pessimistic locking to determine how changes are made to the Recordset in a multiuser environment. The page containing the record you're editing is locked as soon as you use the Edit method (default for Jet workspaces).
dbOptimistic	3	Uses optimistic locking to determine how changes are made to the Recordset in a multiuser environment. The page containing the record is not locked until the Update method is executed.
dbOptimisticValue	1	Uses optimistic concurrency based on row values (ODBCDirect workspaces only).
dbOptimisticBatch	5	Enables batch optimistic updating (ODBCDirect workspaces only).

VBA Code

The Access VBA code opens a recordset based on a table and lists its fields and first record values to the Immediate window:

```
Private Sub cmdOpenRecordset_Click()
```

```
Dim dbs As Database
Dim rstTable As Recordset
Dim strTable As String
Dim fld As Field
Dim flds As Fields
Dim tdf As TableDef

Set dbs = OpenDatabase("D:\Documents\Northwind.mdb")
strTable = "Orders"
Set tdf = dbs.TableDefs(strTable)
Set rstTable = tdf.OpenRecordset(dbOpenTable)

'List fields from the recordset to the Debug window.
Set flds = rstTable.Fields
Debug.Print strTable & " fields:" & vbCrLf
Debug.Print "Recordset type:" & rstTable.Type
For Each fld In flds
    Debug.Print "Field name:" & fld.Name & vbTab & " = " & fld.Value
Next fld

End Sub
```

RefreshLink

tabledef.RefreshLink

Updates the connection information for a linked table. To change the connection information for a linked table, first reset the TableDef's Connect property, then use RefreshLink to update the information. See the Connect section for an example of usage of this property.

11

Groups Collection and Group Object

The Groups collection is a collection of the Group objects in a workspace or user account, for secured Jet workspaces only. Groups and Users (see Chapter 12, *Users Collection and User Object*) are used to manage access to data and interface objects in an Access database. The relationship between User and Group objects is rather peculiar (see Figure 11-1). Users can belong to groups, as you would expect, but they can also belong directly to workspaces. You can create a user first, and then create a group and add the user to it.

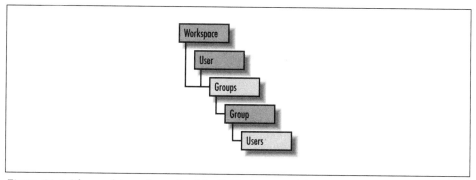

Figure 11-1. The workspace branch of the DAO object model with the Groups and Users collections

There are two ways you can make a user a member of a group:

- You can append a Group object to the Groups collection belonging to a User object to make that user a member of the Group.

- You can append a User object to the Users collection belonging to a Group object, which gives the user the global permissions of that group.

For either method, the Group object must already be a member of the Groups collection of the current Workspace object (see Chapter 4, *Workspaces Collection and Workspace Object*).

A Group object is a group of user accounts with common access permission to database objects and/or data. Once you have set up a group, you can use its name to set and enforce access permissions for databases, tables, and queries, using the database's Document objects that represent the TableDef and QueryDef objects you want to work with.

 The Jet engine automatically creates three Group objects for a workspace: Admins, Users, and Guests.

You can reference a Group object by any of the following syntax variants:

```
Groups(0)
Groups("name")
Groups![name]
```

The Groups collection supports two properties (shown in Table 11-1) and three methods (shown in Table 11-2). The Group object has two collections: Properties, the collection of all intrinsic and user-defined properties supported by the Group object; and Users, the collection of all User objects in the group. In addition, it has two properties and one method, which are shown in Table 11-3.

Table 11-1. Groups Collection Properties

Property	Description
Count	Number of Group objects in the collection
Item	(Hidden) Returns a reference to a particular Group object

Table 11-2. Groups Collection Methods

Method	Description
Append	Adds a new Group object to the collection
Delete	Removes a Group object from the collection
Refresh	Updates the Groups collection

Table 11-3. Group Object Members

Type	Name	Description
Property	Name	The name of the group
Property	PID	The group's personal identifier
Method	CreateUser	Creates a new user account

Access to the Group Object

Creatable

Yes

Returned by

The CreateGroup method of the User object
The Groups property of the User object
The CreateGroup method of the Workspace object
The Groups property of the Workspace object

Groups Collection Properties

Count `RO`

Data Type

Integer

Description

Indicates the number of Group objects in the Groups collection, as in the example code.

VBA Code

```
Private Sub cmdCount_Click()

    Dim wks As Workspace

    Set wks = Workspaces(0)
    MsgBox "There are " & wks.Groups.Count & _
           " groups in the Groups collection"

End Sub
```

Item `RO`

Groups.Item(*Index*)

Argument	Data Type	Description
Index	Integer	The ordinal position of the Group object in the Groups collection, or a string containing the name of the Group object to be retrieved from the collection

Data Type

Group object

Description

A hidden property in the Object Browser, the Item property retrieves a particular Group object from the Groups collection. A Group object can be retrieved either based on its ordinal position in the collection or based on its name. Since Groups is a zero-based collection, the following code fragment returns the first Group object:

```
Dim grp As Group
Set grp = Groups.Item(0)
```

You can also retrieve a particular Group object by name. The following code fragment, for instance, retrieves the Group object named "PowerUsers":

```
Dim grp As Group
Set grp = Groups.Item("PowerUsers")
```

Since the Item property is the default member of the Groups collection, it does not need to be explicitly specified to retrieve a particular Group object. In other words, the following two statements are equivalent; both retrieve the same Group object:

```
Set grp = Groups.Item(0)
Set grp = Groups(0)
```

Similarly, the following three statements all retrieve the same Group object by name:

```
Set grp = Groups.Item("Customer")
Set grp = Groups("Customer")
Set grp = Groups![Customer]
```

Groups Collection Methods

Append

```
Groups.Append object
```

Appends a new Group object to the Groups collection, as in the example code. Before trying this code, first join a secured workgroup using the Workgroup Administrator, as described in the sidebar, "Joining a Workgroup."

 You can drag the Workgroup Administrator executable (*wrkgadm.exe*) from its location in the *\Windows\System* folder to the ODE program group as a shortcut for easier access.

Joining a Workgroup

To change from the default workgroup to another workgroup, you need to use the Workgroup Administrator utility, which for some unaccountable reason no longer has an icon in the ODE program group for Access 97 or the Microsoft Office 2000 Developer group for Access 2000. Here is how to change to a secure workgroup:

1. Open an Explorer pane to the *Windows**System* folder.

2. Locate the *wrkgadm.exe* file and double-click it.

3. The Workgroup Administrator opens, displaying the workgroup (.*mdw*) file you are currently using; the default file is *System.mdw*, as Figure 11-2 shows.

4. Click the Join button to join an existing workgroup (most likely a secured workgroup set up to support a secured database). Alternatively, you can create one from this dialog by clicking the Create button and following the Wizard's instructions.

5. The Workgroup Information File dialog opens, showing the filename of the current workgroup, as Figure 11-3 illustrates; click the Browse button to select another file.

6. The next dialog, shown in Figure 11-4, is a standard File Open dialog from which you can select the file for the secure workgroup.

7. After clicking the OK button, you are returned to the previous dialog with the new filename selected; after clicking the OK button there, you will get a message confirming that you have joined the workgroup, as shown in Figure 11-5.

8. Click the OK button then the Exit button on the original dialog.

9. If any Access databases are open, close and reopen them; now you are ready to work with the secured workgroup.

VBA Code

The following code creates a new group called Group 1, makes the Admin a member of the group, then lists the group's members to the Debug window. The error handler has a special case for the group name already in use:

```
Private Sub cmdAppend_Click()

On Error GoTo ErrorHandler

    Dim wks As Workspace
    Dim grp As Group
    Dim grpTemp As Group
```

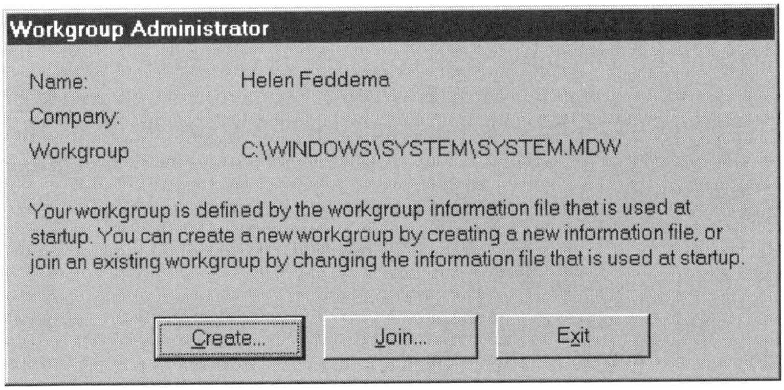

Figure 11-2. The initial Workgroup Administrator dialog

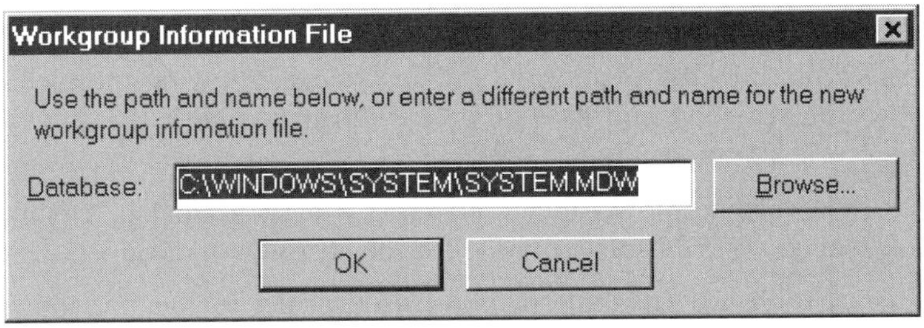

Figure 11-3. The currently selected workgroup filename

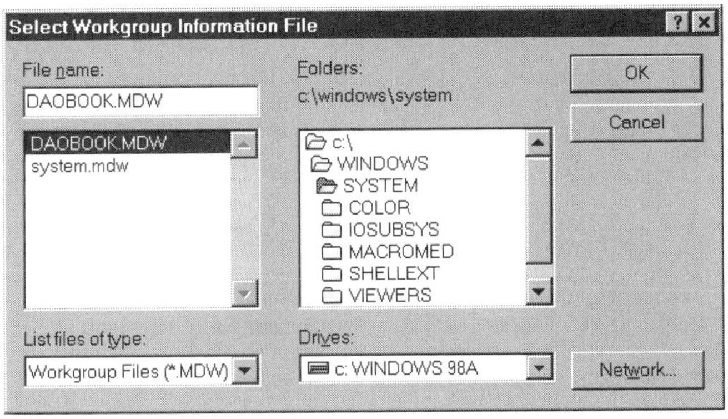

Figure 11-4. Selecting another workgroup file

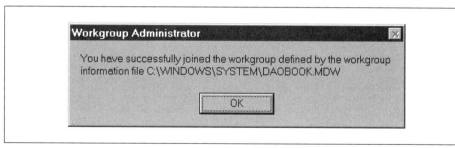

Figure 11-5. Confirmation message on joining a new workgroup

```
    Dim prp As Property
    Dim usr As User

    Set wks = DBEngine.Workspaces(0)

    With wks
        'Create and append new group.
        Set grp = .CreateGroup("Group 1", "WWILC82935XKSI3")
        .Groups.Append grp

        'Make the Admin user a member of the new group.
        Set grpTemp = .Users("admin").CreateGroup("Group 1")
        .Users("admin").Groups.Append grpTemp

        Debug.Print grp.Name & " Users collection"

        For Each usr In grp.Users
            Debug.Print vbTab & "Users group member: " & usr.Name
        Next usr

        'Delete the new Group object.
        .Groups.Delete "Group 1"
    End With

ErrorHandlerExit:
    Exit Sub

ErrorHandler:
    Select Case err.Number
        Case 3390
            MsgBox "Group name already in use; canceling Group Append"
        Case Else
            MsgBox "Error No: " & err.Number & "; Description: " & _
                    err.Description
    End Select

    Resume ErrorHandlerExit

End Sub
```

Delete

```
Groups.Delete name
```

Deletes a group from the Groups collection, as in the code in the Append section.

Refresh

```
Groups.Refresh
```

Updates the members of the Groups collection to reflect the current situation. You can use this method in case you are working in a multiuser environment where another user might modify groups.

Group Object Properties

Name

Data Type

String

Description

The name of a group. A Group name can be up to 20 characters in length. It is a read-write property until the group is appended and read-only after appending.

VBA Code

The example code lists the names of the groups in the current workspace:

```
Private Sub cmdName_Click()

    Dim wks As Workspace
    Dim grp As Group

    Set wks = DBEngine.Workspaces(0)
    Debug.Print wks.Name & " groups:" & vbCrLf

    For Each grp In wks.Groups
        Debug.Print grp.Name
    Next grp

End Sub
```

PID   [WO]

Data Type

String

Description

The PID (personal identifier) is a case-sensitive alphanumeric string from four to 20 characters in length that (together with the Name property) identifies a Group. The property is write-only for unappended Groups and is not available at all for appended Groups.

 The PID is not a password; the password is a separate property of User objects.

See the code in the CreateUser section for an example of usage of the PID property.

Group Object Methods

CreateUser

```
Set user = group.CreateUser(name, pid, password)
```

Argument	Data Type	Description
user	User object	The user you are creating.
object	Group or Workspace object	A Group or Workspace object for which you want to create the new user.
name	String	The name of the new user.
pid	String	The PID (Personal ID) of a user account; it must contain from 4 to 20 alphanumeric characters.
password	String	The new user's password; it can be up to 14 characters long and may contain any character except ASCII character 0 (null). If not set, the password is a zero-length string ("").

Creates a user account for a group in a secured workgroup. The user will inherit the permissions of the Group.

You can reference a User object by any of the following syntax variants:

```
[workspace | group].Users(0)
[workspace | group].Users("name")
[workspace | group].Users![name]
```

VBA Code

This code creates a new user, appends the new user to an existing group (getting the group and user names from input boxes), and lists the new user properties. The error handler has a special case for the group or user name already in use:

```
Private Sub cmdCreateUser_Click()

On Error GoTo ErrorHandler

    Dim wks As Workspace
    Dim grp As Group
    Dim grpTemp As Group
    Dim prp As Property
    Dim usr As User
    Dim usrTemp As User
    Dim strGroup As String
    Dim strUser As String

    strUser = InputBox("New user name:")
    Set wks = DBEngine.Workspaces(0)
    strGroup = InputBox("Enter group name:")

    With wks
        'Create and append new user.
        Set usr = .CreateUser(strUser)
        usr.PID = "US82PECLWPWLO90"
        usr.Password = "OpenSesame"
        .Users.Append usr

        'Make the new user a member of an existing group.
        Set usrTemp = .Groups(strGroup).CreateUser(strUser)
        .Groups(strGroup).Users.Append usrTemp

        'List the properties of the new user.
        Debug.Print usr.Name & " Properties"
        For Each prp In usr.Properties
            On Error Resume Next
            If prp <> "" Then Debug.Print vbTab & prp.Name & " = " & prp
            On Error GoTo 0
        Next prp

    End With

ErrorHandlerExit:
    Exit Sub

ErrorHandler:
    Select Case err.Number
        Case 3390
            MsgBox "User or group name already taken; canceling Create User"
        Case Else
            MsgBox "Error No: " & err.Number & "; Description: " & _
                    err.Description
    End Select

    Resume ErrorHandlerExit

End Sub
```

12

Users Collection and User Object

The Users collection contains all the User objects in a Workspace or Group object. Its position in the DAO object model is shown in Figure 12-1. Each User object represents a user account with specific permissions to access database objects and data in a secure workgroup. You can append a User object to a Group object, which gives the user the same access permissions as the Group, or you can append a Group object to a User object's Groups collection to give that user membership in that group.

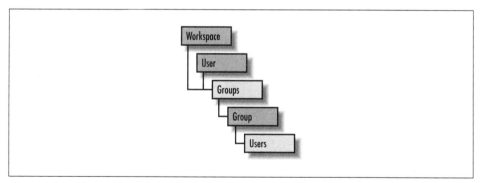

Figure 12-1. The position of the Users collection in the DAO object model

The Users collection (and User objects) have some characteristics that need to be taken into account when writing code to manipulate them:

- Each user's identity depends on the User object's Name, PID, and Password properties. If no password is assigned, the Password property is a zero-length string ("").

- You can read the Name property of a User object but not the PID or Password properties.

- The Jet engine predefines two User objects: Admin and Guest. Admin belongs to both the Admins and Users groups; Guest belongs only to the Guests group.

- To create a new user, you can use the Append method of the Users collection, or the CreateUser method of the Group object. (See Chapter 11, *Groups Collection and Group Object*, for a code sample for the CreateUser method.)

You can reference a User object by any of the following syntax variants:

```
[workspace | group].Users(0)
[workspace | group].Users("name")
[workspace | group].Users![name]
```

The Users collection has two properties (see Table 12-1) and three methods (see Table 12-2). The User object has two collections: the Groups collection, which consists of Group objects, and the Properties collection, which is a collection of Property objects representing intrinsic and user-defined properties supported by a User object. In addition, the User object has three properties (shown in Table 12-3) and two methods (shown in Table 12-4).

Table 12-1. Users Collection Properties

Property	Description
Count	The number of User objects in the collection
Item	(Hidden) Returns a reference to an individual User object in the collection

Table 12-2. Users Collection Methods

Method	Description
Append	Adds a User object to the collection
Delete	Removes a User object from the collection
Refresh	Updates the collection to reflect recent changes

Table 12-3. User Object Properties

Property	Description
Name	The name of the User object
Password	The password assigned to the user account
PID	The personal ID for the user account

Table 12-4. User Object Methods

Method	Description
CreateGroup	Gives the user membership in a group
NewPassword	Changes the password for a user account

Access to the User Object

Creatable

Yes

Returned by

The CreateUser method of the Group object
The Users property of the Group object
The CreateUser method of the Workspace object
The Users property of the Workspace object

Users Collection Properties

Count `RO`

Data Type

Integer

Description

Indicates the number of Users in the Users collection of a workspace or Group, as in the code example, which counts the users in the current workspace.

VBA Code

```
Private Sub cmdCount_Click()

    Dim wks As Workspace

    Set wks = Workspaces(0)
    MsgBox "There are " & wks.Users.Count & _
           " users in the current workspace"

End Sub
```

Item `RO`

Users.Item(*Index*)

Argument	Data Type	Description
Index	Integer	The ordinal position of the User object in the Users collection or a string containing the name of the User object to be retrieved from the collection

Data Type

User object

Description

A hidden property in the Object Browser, the Item property retrieves a particular User object from the Users collection. A User object can be retrieved either based on its ordinal position in the collection or based on its name. Since Users is a zero-based collection, the following code fragment returns the first User object:

```
Dim usr As User
Set usr = Users.Item(0)
```

You can also retrieve a particular User object by name. The following code fragment, for instance, retrieves the User object named "JohnDoe":

```
Dim usr As User
Set usr = Users.Item("JohnDoe")
```

Since the Item property is the default member of the Users collection, it does not need to be explicitly specified to retrieve a particular User object. In other words, the following two statements are equivalent; both retrieve the same User object:

```
Set usr = Users.Item(0)
Set usr = Users(0)
```

Similarly, the following three statements all retrieve the same User object by name:

```
Set usr = Users.Item("Customer")
Set usr = Users("Customer")
Set usr = Users![Customer]
```

Users Collection Methods

Append

```
Users.Append object
```

Appends a new User object, *object*, to the Users collection of a Group or Workspace object, as in the code example.

VBA Code

The code example creates a new User object in a workspace and lists its properties. Before trying this code, first join a secured workgroup using the Workgroup Administrator, as described in the sidebar in Chapter 11. The error handler takes care of the situation where the user name has already been assigned:

```
Private Sub cmdAppend_Click()

On Error GoTo ErrorHandler

    Dim wks As Workspace
    Dim prp As Property
```

```
        Dim usr As User
        Dim strUser As String
        Dim usrTemp As User

        Set wks = DBEngine.Workspaces(0)
        strUser = "Abigail"

        With wks
            'Create and append new user.
            Set usr = .CreateUser(strUser)
            usr.PID = "US82PELWPWLO90"
            usr.Password = "OpenSesame"
            .Users.Append usr

            'List the properties of the new user.
            Debug.Print usr.Name & " Properties"
            For Each prp In usr.Properties
                On Error Resume Next
                If prp <> "" Then Debug.Print vbTab & prp.Name & " = " & prp
                On Error GoTo 0
            Next prp

        'Delete temporary user.
        .Users.Delete strUser

        End With

    ErrorHandlerExit:
        Exit Sub

    ErrorHandler:
        Select Case err.Number
            Case 3265
                MsgBox "User name already taken; canceling Create User"
            Case Else
                MsgBox "Error No: " & err.Number & "; Description: " & _
                        err.Description
        End Select

        Resume ErrorHandlerExit

    End Sub
```

Delete

```
Users.Delete objectname
```

Deletes a User object, **objectname**, from the Users collection, as in the code in
the Append section.

Refresh

```
Users.Refresh
```

Updates the members of the Users collection to reflect the current situation. You can use this method if you are working in a multiuser environment where another user might modify group or user accounts.

User Object Properties

Name

Data Type

String

Description

The name of a user. Like a group name, a user name can be up to 20 characters in length. It is a read-write property until the user is appended and read-only after appending.

VBA Code

The example code lists the names of the users in the current workspace:

```
Private Sub cmdName_Click()

    Dim wks As Workspace
    Dim usr As User

    Set wks = DBEngine.Workspaces(0)
    Debug.Print wks.Name & " groups:" & vbCrLf

    For Each usr In wks.Users
        Debug.Print "User: " & usr.Name
    Next usr

End Sub
```

Password   `WO`

Data Type

String

Description

The Password property of a User account can be up to 14 characters long and can include any characters except ASCII 0 (null). Passwords are case-sensitive. The property is write-only for new Users not yet appended to a Users collection, and it is not available after appending. You should set the Password property (and the PID property) when creating a new User account.

To clear a password, set the NewPassword argument of the New-Password method to a zero-length string. See the NewPassword method section (earlier in this chapter) for details.

You can't change another user's password unless you have access permission to that account.

VBA Code

```vba
Private Sub cmdPassword_Click()

On Error GoTo ErrorHandler

    Dim wks As Workspace
    Dim usr As User
    Dim strUser As String
    Dim usrTemp As User

    Set wks = DBEngine.Workspaces(0)
    strUser = "Lenore"

    With wks
        'Create and append new user.
        Set usr = .CreateUser(strUser)
        usr.PID = "US82WI1EP87270"
        usr.Password = "BackDoor"
        .Users.Append usr

        'List the users in the workspace.
        Debug.Print wks.Name & " groups:" & vbCrLf

        For Each usr In wks.Users
            Debug.Print "User: " & usr.Name
        Next usr

        'Delete temporary user and group.
        .Users.Delete strUser

    End With

ErrorHandlerExit:
    Exit Sub
```

```
ErrorHandler:
    Select Case err.Number
        Case 3265
            MsgBox "User name already taken; canceling Create User"
        Case Else
            MsgBox "Error No: " & err.Number & "; Description: " & _
                    err.Description
    End Select

    Resume ErrorHandlerExit

End Sub
```

PID   `WO`

Data Type

String

Description

Sets the PID (personal ID) for a user account. PIDs can be from 4 to 20 alphanumeric characters. The property is write-only for new users not yet appended to a Users collection and is not available for appended Users. The property should be set (along with the Name property) when you create a new user account. See the code sample in the Password section for an example of usage.

User Object Methods

CreateGroup

```
Set group = user.CreateGroup(name, pid)
```

Argument	Data Type	Description
group	Group object	A group
user	User object	A user for which you want to create the new group
name	String	The name of the new group
pid	String	The PID (Personal ID) of a group account; must contain from 4 to 20 alphanumeric characters

The CreateGroup method, when used with a User object, gives that user membership in the group, as in the code example.

VBA Code

```
Private Sub cmdCreateGroup_Click()

On Error GoTo ErrorHandler
```

```
    Dim wks As Workspace
    Dim prp As Property
    Dim usr As User
    Dim strUser As String
    Dim usrTemp As User
    Dim strGroup As String
    Dim grp As Group
    Dim grpTemp As Group

    Set wks = DBEngine.Workspaces(0)
    strUser = "Zachary"
    strGroup = "Group 9"

    With wks
        'Create and append new user.
        Set usr = .CreateUser(strUser)
        usr.PID = "US82WI1EP87270"
        usr.Password = "BackDoor"
        .Users.Append usr

        'Create a new group and append it to the User
        'so the user now has the group's permissions.
        Set grp = .CreateGroup(strGroup, "WWksuwi92304ml8")
        .Groups.Append grp

        'Make the new user a member of the new group.
        Set grpTemp = .Users("admin").CreateGroup(strGroup)
        .Users(strUser).Groups.Append grpTemp

        'List user's group memberships.
        Debug.Print "User: " & usr.Name & vbCrLf

        For Each grp In usr.Groups
            Debug.Print "Group: " & grp.Name
        Next grp

        'Delete temporary user and group.
        .Users.Delete strUser
        .Groups.Delete strGroup

    End With

ErrorHandlerExit:
    Exit Sub

ErrorHandler:
    Select Case err.Number
        Case 3265
            MsgBox "User name already taken; canceling Create User"
        Case 3390
            MsgBox "Group name already taken; canceling Create Group"
        Case Else
            MsgBox "Error No: " & err.Number & "; Description: " & _
                    err.Description
```

```
    End Select

    Resume ErrorHandlerExit

End Sub
```

NewPassword

user.NewPassword *bstrold, bstrnew*

Argument	Data Type	Description
user	User Object	The user whose password you want to change.
bstrold	String	The current password of the user account. The password is a case-sensitive string up to 14 characters long and can include any characters except ASCII 0 (null).
bstrnew	String	The new password for the database. It can be up to 14 characters long and can include any characters except ASCII 0 (null).

Changes the password for an existing user account (for Jet workspaces only). You can only change the user password if the database is secured.

To clear a password, set the *bstrnew* argument to a zero-length string.

VBA Code

The code example assigns a new password to a user account that has a default zero-length string password. The error handler takes care of the situation where the specified user is not found:

```
Private Sub cmdNewPassword_Click()

On Error GoTo ErrorHandler

    Dim wks As Workspace
    Dim strPW As String
    Dim strUser As String
    Dim usr As User

    Set wks = Workspaces(0)
    strUser = "Jane"
    Set usr = wks.Users(strUser)
    usr.NewPassword "", "Nicky"
    MsgBox strUser & "'s password successfully changed!"

ErrorHandlerExit:
```

```
     Exit Sub

ErrorHandler:
   Select Case err.Number
      Case 3265
         MsgBox "User name not found; canceling Change Password"
      Case Else
         MsgBox "Error No: " & err.Number & "; Description: " & _
                err.Description
   End Select

   Resume ErrorHandlerExit

End Sub
```

13

Fields Collection
and Field Object

There is a Fields collection in each TableDef, QueryDef, Recordset, Relation, or Index object, as shown in Figure 13-1. The collection contains the definitions of the fields contained in these objects. The most widely used Fields collection is the one in a Recordset object that represents the Field objects in a data record. These Field objects can be used to read and write values to the current record in a Recordset object.

A Field object can be referenced by any of the following syntax variants:

```
Fields(0)
Fields("name")
Fields![name]
```

The same syntax is used to reference the Field object or its default Value property; to ensure that your code works as you intend, it is best to explicitly use the Value property if you want to work with a field's value.

The Fields collection has only two properties (shown in Table 13-1) and three methods (shown in Table 13-2). The Field object contains 1 collection (Properties), 20 properties, and 3 methods. (The Properties collection of the Field object is covered in the Field properties section.)

Some of the properties only apply to fields in specific Fields collections, as noted in the sections. Field object properties are listed in Table 13-3 and methods in Table 13-4.

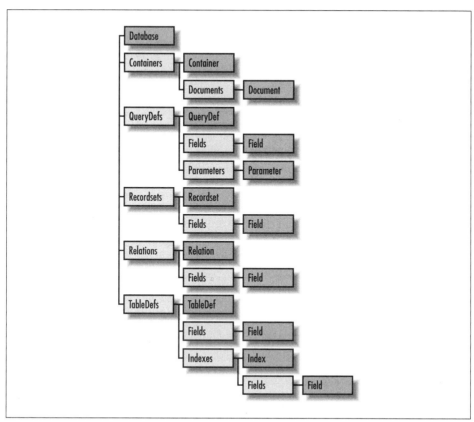

Figure 13-1. The Fields collections of various objects in the DAO object model

Table 13-1. Fields Collection Properties

Property	Description
Count	Indicates the number of Field objects in the Fields collection.
Item	Returns a particular member of the Fields collection. Although hidden in the DAO type library, it is the default member of the Fields collection.

Table 13-2. Fields Collection Methods

Method	Description
Append	Adds a new Field object to the Fields collection
Delete	Deletes a Field object from the Fields collection
Refresh	Refreshes the Fields collection

Table 13-3. Field Object Properties

Property	Description
AllowZeroLength	Indicates whether a zero-length string can be stored in a field
Attributes	Characteristics of a field
CollatingOrder	Text sorting order
DataUpdatable	Indicates whether field value can be updated
DefaultValue	The default value of a field
FieldSize	The size of a Memo or Long Binary field
ForeignName	The name of the field in a foreign table that links to a primary table
Name	The name of the field
OrdinalPosition	The relative position of the field in the Fields collection
OriginalValue	The value of a field when the last batch update began
Required	Indicates whether the field must have a non-Null value
Size	The size of a field (other than Memo or Long Binary fields)
SourceField	The source field for field data in a recordset
SourceTable	The source table for a field in a recordset
Type	The data type of a field
ValidateOnSet	Indicates whether to validate a field when its value is set
ValidationRule	The rule for validating a field's data
ValidationText	The text to display when invalid data is entered into a field
Value	(Default) The data in a field
VisibleValue	A value newer than OriginalValue

Table 13-4. Field Object Methods

Method	Description
AppendChunk	Appends chunks of data to a Memo or Long Binary field
CreateProperty	Creates a user-defined property for a field
GetChunk	Retrieves chunks of data from a Memo or Long Binary field

Access to the Field Object

Creatable

Yes

Returned by

The CreateField method of the Index object
The Fields property of the Index object
The Fields property of the QueryDef object
The Fields property of the Recordset object
The CreateField method of the Relation object
The Fields property of the Relation object

The CreateField method of the TableDef object
The Fields property of the TableDef object

Fields Collection Properties

Count   `RO`

Data Type

Integer

Description

The number of objects in the Fields collection. In previous versions of Access, Count was useful for setting up loops to process all objects in a collection; however, the **For Each...Next** loop is a more efficient way of iterating through the members of a collection. (See the Append section for an example of using **For Each...Next** to process all members of the Fields collection.) The example opens a recordset based on the Northwind Employees table and reports on the number of fields it contains.

VBA Code

```
Private Sub cmdCount_Click()

On Error GoTo ErrorHandler

    Dim dbs As Database
    Dim strDBName As String
    Dim rst As Recordset

    strDBName = "D:\Documents\Northwind.mdb"
    Set dbs = OpenDatabase(strDBName)
    Set rst = dbs.OpenRecordset("Employees", dbOpenSnapshot)
    Debug.Print "There are " & rst.Fields.Count & " fields in " _
        & rst.Name
    dbs.Close

ErrorHandlerExit:
    Exit Sub

ErrorHandler:
    MsgBox "Error No: " & err.Number & "; Description: " & err.Description
    Resume ErrorHandlerExit

End Sub
```

Item   `RO`

```
Fields.Item(Index)
```

Argument	Data Type	Description
Index	Integer	Represents the ordinal position of the Field object in the Fields collection or a string containing the name of the Field object to be retrieved from the Fields collection

Data Type

Field object

Description

Retrieves a particular Field object from the Fields collection, using the index number or the field's name. Item is the default property, so it may be omitted; the following two code fragments are equivalent:

```
Fields.Item(0)
Fields(0)
```

Fields Collection Methods

Append

```
Fields.Append object
```

Adds a new Field object to the Fields collection of a TableDef, QueryDef, Recordset, Relation, or Index object.

 You don't have to save a newly appended field or close the object to which the field has been appended.

VBA Code

The code adds three new fields of different data types to a TableDef object representing an existing table in the current database:

```
Private Sub cmdAppend_Click()

    Dim dbs As Database
    Dim strTable As String
    Dim tdf As TableDef
    Dim fld As Field
```

```
        Set dbs = CurrentDb

        'Append custom fields to an existing table.
        strTable = "tblNewFields"
        Set tdf = dbs.TableDefs(strTable)
        Set fld = tdf.CreateField("Name", dbText)
        fld.AllowZeroLength = True
        tdf.Fields.Append fld
        Set fld = tdf.CreateField("Date", dbDate)
        tdf.Fields.Append fld
        Set fld = tdf.CreateField("Cost", dbCurrency)
        tdf.Fields.Append fld
        DoCmd.OpenTable strTable

On Error GoTo ErrorHandler

ErrorHandlerExit:
    Exit Sub

ErrorHandler:
    MsgBox "Error No: " & err.Number & "; Description: " & err.Description
    Resume ErrorHandlerExit

End Sub
```

Delete

```
Fields.Delete name
```

Removes a Field object from the Fields collection of a TableDef, QueryDef, Recordset, Relation, or Index object.

VBA Code

This code deletes the three fields added in the Append section code sample:

```
Private Sub cmdDelete_Click()

On Error GoTo ErrorHandler

    Dim dbs As Database
    Dim strTable As String
    Dim tdf As TableDef
    Dim fld As Field

    Set dbs = CurrentDb

    'Delete three fields from an existing table.
    strTable = "tblNewFields"
    Set tdf = dbs.TableDefs(strTable)
    tdf.Fields.Delete "Name"
    tdf.Fields.Delete "Date"
    tdf.Fields.Delete "Cost"
    DoCmd.OpenTable strTable
```

```
ErrorHandlerExit:
    Exit Sub

ErrorHandler:
    MsgBox "Error No: " & err.Number & "; Description: " & err.Description
    Resume ErrorHandlerExit

End Sub
```

Refresh

```
Fields.Refresh
```

Updates the Fields collection to reflect recent changes. Normally, you don't need to refresh the Fields collection, but in some cases it may be desirable to use this method, particularly in multiuser environments where other users may add or delete fields.

 If you change the OrdinalPosition property of a Field object, the order of Field objects in the collection may not change until you use the Refresh method.

Field Object Properties

AllowZeroLength

Data Type

Boolean

Description

Indicates whether a Field object's Value property can accept a zero-length string for a text or memo field. The property is read/write if a field has not yet been appended to the Fields collection. For appended fields, its read-write status depends on the Field object's parent object, as shown in Table 13-5.

Table 13-5. Read/Write Characteristics of the AllowZeroLength Property for Various Objects

Object Type of Fields Collection	Read/Write Status
Index object	Not supported
QueryDef object	Read-only
Recordset object	Read-only
Relation object	Not supported
TableDef object	Read/write

The Append section code sample illustrates setting this property for a text field.

Attributes

Data Type

Long

Description

One or more characteristics of a Field object; it can be a combination of the constants listed in Table 13-6. The property is read-write for fields that have not been appended to a Fields collection; for appended fields, see Table 13-7.

Table 13-6. The Attributes Intrinsic Constants for Field Objects

Named Constant	Value	Description
dbAutoIncrField	16	The field value for new records is automatically incremented to a new Long value (only supported for Jet database tables).
dbDescending	1	Sorted in descending order. It only applies to Field objects in a Fields collection of an Index object. If omitted, the records are sorted in ascending order.
dbFixedField	1	The field size is fixed (default for Numeric fields).
dbHyperlinkField	32768	The field contains hyperlink information (memo fields only).
dbSystemField	8192	The field stores replication information for replicas. It can't be deleted (Jet workspaces only).
dbUpdatableField	32	The field value can be changed.
dbVariableField	2	The field size is variable (text fields only).

Two members of the `FieldAttributeEnum` enumeration in Table 13-6 have the same value. I tested them in the Immediate window, and got the value 1 for both.

Table 13-7. Read/Write Characteristics of the Attributes Property for Various Objects

Object Type of Fields Collection	Read/Write Status
Index object	Read-write until the Index object's parent TableDef object is appended to a Database object
QueryDef object	Read-only
Recordset object	Read-only
Relation object	Not supported
TableDef object	Read/write

VBA Code

This example lists the attributes (as a Long number) of all the tables in the sample Northwind database to the Debug window:

```
Private Sub cmdAttributes_Click()

On Error GoTo ErrorHandler

    Dim dbs As Database
    Dim tdf As TableDef

    Set dbs = OpenDatabase("D:\Documents\Northwind.mdb")
    For Each tdf In dbs.TableDefs
        Debug.Print "Attributes of " & tdf.Name & ":" & vbCrLf _
            & tdf.Attributes
    Next tdf

ErrorHandlerExit:
    Exit Sub

ErrorHandler:
    MsgBox "Error No: " & err.Number & "; Description: " & err.Description
    Resume ErrorHandlerExit

End Sub
```

CollatingOrder

Data Type

Long

Description

Specifies the sequence of text sorting order, using the constants listed in Table 13-8. The read/write characteristics of the property are listed in Table 13-9.

 Curiously, the default sort order is Paradox International.

Table 13-8. The CollatingOrder Property Intrinsic Constants

Named Constant	Value	Description
dbSortGeneral	1033	General (English, French, German, Portuguese, Italian, and Modern Spanish)
dbSortArabic	1025	Arabic

Table 13-8. The CollatingOrder Property Intrinsic Constants (continued)

Named Constant	Value	Description
dbSortChineseSimplified	2052	Simplified Chinese
dbSortChineseTraditional	1028	Traditional Chinese
dbSortCyrillic	1049	Russian
dbSortCzech	1029	Czech
dbSortDutch	1043	Dutch
dbSortGreek	1032	Greek
dbSortHebrew	1037	Hebrew
dbSortHungarian	1038	Hungarian
dbSortIcelandic	1039	Icelandic
dbSortJapanese	1041	Japanese
dbSortKorean	1042	Korean
dbSortNeutral	1024	Neutral
dbSortNorwDan	1030	Norwegian or Danish
dbSortPDXIntl	1033	Paradox International
dbSortPDXNor	1030	Paradox Norwegian or Danish
dbSortPDXSwe	1053	Paradox Swedish or Finnish
dbSortPolish	1045	Polish
dbSortSlovenian	1060	Slovenian
dbSortSpanish	1034	Spanish
dbSortSwedFin	1053	Swedish or Finnish
dbSortThai	1054	Thai
dbSortTurkish	1055	Turkish
dbSortUndefined	-1	Undefined or unknown

Table 13-9. Read/Write Characteristics of the CollatingOrder Property for Various Objects

Object Type of Fields Collection	Read/Write Status
Index object	Not supported
QueryDef object	Read-only
Recordset object	Read-only
Relation object	Not supported
TableDef object	Read-only

VBA Code

The example lists the CollatingOrder property (as a Long integer) of all the tables in the sample Northwind database to the Immediate window:

```
Private Sub cmdCollatingOrder_Click()

On Error GoTo ErrorHandler
```

```
      Dim dbs As Database
      Dim tdf As TableDef

      Set dbs = OpenDatabase("D:\Documents\Northwind.mdb")
      For Each tdf In dbs.TableDefs
         Debug.Print "Collating order of " & tdf.Name & ":" & vbCrLf _
            & tdf.Attributes
      Next tdf

   ErrorHandlerExit:
      Exit Sub

   ErrorHandler:
      MsgBox "Error No: " & err.Number & "; Description: " & err.Description
      Resume ErrorHandlerExit

   End Sub
```

DataUpdatable   `RO`

Data Type

Boolean

Description

Indicates whether field data can be updated by using the Value property of a Field
object. This property is always **False** if the Field object's Attributes property is
dbAutoIncrField. The property only applies to Field objects belonging to Fields
collections of QueryDef, Recordset, and Relation objects.

DefaultValue

Data Type

String

Description

The default value of a field. It is written to the field automatically when a new
record is created. This property doesn't apply to AutoNumber or Long Binary
fields. Default values are specified by the user, either in the interface or in code. If
no default value is specified, a field contains a Null. When you create a numeric
field in table design view, it has a default value of 0; other fields don't have default
values unless you set them.

The read/write characteristics of the property are listed in Table 13-10.

Table 13-10. Read/Write Characteristics of the DefaultValue Property for Various Objects

Object Type of Fields Collection	Read/Write Status
Index object	Not supported
QueryDef object	Read-only
Recordset object	Read-only
Relation object	Not supported
TableDef object	Read/write

The DefaultValue property of a Long data type field belonging to a TableDef object can be set to a special value, `GenUniqueID()`. This setting causes a random number to be written to the field when a new record is created.

FieldSize   `RO`

Data Type

Long

Description

Indicates the number of characters for a Memo field or the number of Bytes for a Long Binary field belonging to a Recordset object. An attempt to retrieve the value of the FieldSize property for a field of any other data type generates runtime error 3259, "Invalid field data type." An attempt to retrieve the FieldSize property of a Field object that is not a member of the Fields collection of a DAO Recordset object raises runtime error 3267, "Property can be set only when the Field is part of a Recordset object's Fields collection."

To determine the size of fields of other data types, use the Size property.

ForeignName

Data Type

String

Description

The name of a field in a foreign table that corresponds to a field in the primary table for a relationship (usually a one-to-many relationship, as depicted in Figure 13-2). Only fields belonging to a Relation object have a ForeignName property.

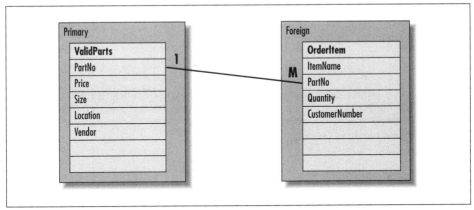

Figure 13-2. A one-to-many relationship showing the name of the linking field

VBA Code

The example code lists several properties of the Relation objects in the sample Northwind database, including the ForeignName property:

```
Private Sub cmdForeignName_Click()

On Error GoTo ErrorHandler

    Dim dbs As Database
    Dim tdf As TableDef
    Dim rel As Relation

    Set dbs = OpenDatabase("D:\Documents\Northwind.mdb")
    For Each rel In dbs.Relations
        With rel
            Debug.Print .Name & " Relation"
            Debug.Print "                    Table - Field"
            Debug.Print "    Primary (One)    ";
            Debug.Print .Table & " - " & .Fields(0).Name
            Debug.Print "    Foreign (Many)    ";
            Debug.Print .ForeignTable & " - " & _
                .Fields(0).ForeignName
        End With
    Next rel

ErrorHandlerExit:
    Exit Sub

ErrorHandler:
```

```
          MsgBox "Error No: " & err.Number & "; Description: " & err.Description
          Resume ErrorHandlerExit

      End Sub
```

Name

Data Type

String

Description

The name of a Field object. The name can be provided as an argument to the Item property to retrieve Field objects from the Fields collection. The read/write characteristics of the Name property are listed in Table 13-11.

Table 13-11. Read/Write Characteristics of the Name Property for a Field Object

Appended State	Read/Write Status
Unappended	Read/write
Appended to Index object	Read-only
Appended to QueryDef object	Read-only
Appended to Recordset object	Read-only
Appended to native TableDef object	Read-only
Appended to linked TableDef object	Read-only
Appended to Relation object	Read-only

VBA Code

This code lists the names of all fields in all tables in the sample Northwind database:

```
    Private Sub cmdName_Click()

    On Error GoTo ErrorHandler

        Dim dbs As Database
        Dim tdf As TableDef
        Dim fld As Field

        Set dbs = OpenDatabase("D:\Documents\Northwind.mdb")
        For Each tdf In dbs.TableDefs
           Debug.Print tdf.Name & " fields:"
           For Each fld In tdf.Fields
              Debug.Print vbTab & fld.Name
           Next fld
        Next tdf

    ErrorHandlerExit:
        Exit Sub
```

```
ErrorHandler:
    MsgBox "Error No: " & err.Number & "; Description: " & err.Description
    Resume ErrorHandlerExit

End Sub
```

OrdinalPosition

Data Type

Integer

Description

Indicates the relative position of a Field object in a Fields collection. The default value is 0. Two or more fields in a Fields collection can have the same Ordinal-Position property, in which case they are ordered alphabetically.

The read/write characteristics of the property (for unappended fields) are listed in Table 13-12. Appended fields are read-only.

Table 13-12. Read/Write Characteristics of the OrdinalPosition Property for Various Objects

Object Type of Fields Collection	Read/Write Status
Index object	Not supported
QueryDef object	Read-only
Recordset object	Read-only
Relation object	Not supported
TableDef object	Read/write

OriginalValue　　　　　　　　　　　　　　　　　　　　　　　`RO`

Data Type

Variant

Description

The value of a field in the database that existed when the last batch update began (for ODBCDirect workspaces only).

Properties

Data Type

Properties collection

Description

Returns a collection containing all the properties of a Field object, including both built-in and user-defined properties. User-defined properties are created using the CreateProperty method and added to the Properties collection with its Append method. They are deleted using the Delete method. Although user-defined properties are more commonly used with objects higher in the object hierarchy (databases, tables, and queries), you can create user-defined properties for fields too.

VBA Code

The sample code creates a new property for a field in the Northwind Employees table and then lists all the properties of that field to the Debug window:

```
Private Sub cmdPropertiesCollection_Click()

    Dim dbs As Database
    Dim prp As Property
    Dim prpNew As Property
    Dim tdf As TableDef
    Dim strDBName As String
    Dim fld As Field

    strDBName = "D:\Documents\Northwind.mdb"
    Set dbs = OpenDatabase(strDBName)
    Set tdf = dbs.TableDefs("Employees")
    Set fld = tdf.Fields("LastName")
    Set prpNew = fld.CreateProperty("UserProp", dbBoolean, False)
    fld.Properties.Append prpNew

    'Enumerate field properties
    Debug.Print "Properties of the " & fld.Name & " field:"
    For Each prp In fld.Properties
        If prp.Name <> "" Then
            On Error Resume Next
            Debug.Print prp.Name & " = " & prp
        End If
    Next prp

End Sub
```

Required

Data Type

Boolean

Description

Indicates whether the field must have a non-Null value. The Required property can be used in combination with the AllowZeroLength, ValidateOnSet, or ValidationRule properties to validate the field's Value property setting. If Required is set to

`False`, the field can contain Null values, as well as values that meet the Allow-ZeroLength and ValidationRule property settings.

 If there is a choice of setting the Required property for a Field object or an Index object, it is best to select the Field object, as its validity is checked before the Index object's.

The read/write characteristics of the property are listed in Table 13-13.

Table 13-13. Read/Write Characteristics of the Required Property for Various Objects

Object Type of Fields Collection	Read/Write Status
Index object	Not supported
QueryDef object	Read-only
Recordset object	Read-only
Relation object	Not supported
TableDef object	Read/write

Size

Data Type

Byte

Description

The maximum size of a Field object. For fields (other than Memo fields) that contain character data, the Size property indicates the maximum number of characters the field can hold (up to 255 characters for text fields). For numeric fields the Size property indicates how many bytes of storage are required. For Long Binary and Memo fields, Size is always set to 0, and the maximum size of these fields is determined by system resources or database constraints. For other fields with other data types, the Type property setting automatically determines the size of the field.

The read/write characteristics of the Size property are listed in Table 13-14.

Table 13-14. Read/Write Characteristics of the Size Property for Various Objects

Object Type of Fields Collection	Read/Write Status
Index object	Not supported
QueryDef object	Read-only
Recordset object	Read-only
Relation object	Not supported
TableDef object	Read-only

VBA Code

The sample illustrates creating a new text field in a Northwind table and setting its Size property to 25:

```
Private Sub cmdSize_Click()

On Error GoTo ErrorHandler

    Dim dbs As Database
    Dim tdf As TableDef
    Dim fld As Field

    Set dbs = OpenDatabase("D:\Documents\Northwind.mdb")
    Set tdf = dbs.TableDefs("Employees")
    Set fld = tdf.CreateField("FaxPhone")
    fld.Type = dbText
    fld.Size = 25
    tdf.Fields.Append fld
    Debug.Print tdf.Name & " fields:"
       For Each fld In tdf.Fields
          Debug.Print vbTab & fld.Name
       Next fld

ErrorHandlerExit:
    Exit Sub

ErrorHandler:
    MsgBox "Error No: " & err.Number & "; Description: " & err.Description
    Resume ErrorHandlerExit

End Sub
```

SourceField

Data Type

String

Description

The name of the field that is the original source of a Field object's data. See Table 13-15 for a listing of read/write properties for Field objects appended to various collections.

Table 13-15. Read/Write Characteristics of SourceField and SourceTable

Object Type of Fields Collection	Read/Write Status
Index object	Not supported
QueryDef object	Read-only
Recordset object	Read-only

Table 13-15. Read/Write Characteristics of SourceField and SourceTable (continued)

Object Type of Fields Collection	Read/Write Status
Relation object	Not supported
TableDef object	Read-only

VBA Code

The code sample lists the SourceField and SourceTable properties for a recordset based on two tables in the Northwind sample database. Note that the source fields for the EmployeeName concatenated field are not listed:

```
Private Sub cmdSourceField_Click()

On Error GoTo ErrorHandler

    Dim dbs As Database
    Dim rst As Recordset
    Dim strSQL As String
    Dim fld As Field

    strSQL = "SELECT [FirstName] & ' ' & [LastName] AS EmployeeName, " _
        & "Orders.OrderID, Orders.OrderDate FROM Employees INNER JOIN " _
        & "Orders ON Employees.EmployeeID = Orders.EmployeeID;"

    Set dbs = OpenDatabase("D:\Documents\Northwind.mdb")
    Set rst = dbs.OpenRecordset(strSQL)

    Debug.Print "Field name - SourceTable - SourceField"
    For Each fld In rst.Fields
        Debug.Print "     " & fld.Name & " - " & _
            fld.SourceTable & " - " & fld.SourceField
    Next fld

    rst.Close
    dbs.Close

ErrorHandlerExit:
    Exit Sub

ErrorHandler:
    MsgBox "Error No: " & err.Number & "; Description: " & err.Description
    Resume ErrorHandlerExit

End Sub
```

SourceTable

Data Type

String

Description

The name of the table that is the original source of a Field object's data. See Table 13-15 for a listing of read/write properties for Field objects appended to various collections. The code sample for the SourceField property also illustrates use of the SourceTable property.

Type

Data Type

Integer

Description

Indicates the data type of a field. The Type value settings are listed in Table 13-16.

Table 13-16. The Type Property Intrinsic Constants

Named Constant	Value	Description
dbBigInt	16	Big Integer
dbBinary	9	Binary
dbBoolean	1	Boolean
dbByte	2	Byte
dbChar	18	Character
dbCurrency	5	Currency
dbDate	8	Date/Time
dbDecimal	20	Decimal
dbDouble	7	Double
dbFloat	21	Float
dbGUID	15	GUID
dbInteger	3	Integer
dbLong	4	Long
dbLongBinary	11	Long Binary (OLE Object)
dbMemo	12	Memo
dbNumeric	19	Numeric
dbSingle	6	Single
dbText	10	Text
dbTime	22	Time
dbTimeStamp	23	Time Stamp
dbVarBinary	17	VarBinary

VBA Code

The code sample (a portion of a longer function in my Outlook Automation add-in) illustrates the use of the Type property, in this case when converting Outlook field data types (represented by the *lngDataType* variable) to the nearest equivalent Access field data types:

```
For Each prp In itm.UserProperties
    strFieldName = prp.Name
    lngDataType = prp.Type

    'Convert Outlook data types to closest Access data types.
    Select Case lngDataType

        Case 1
        lngDataType = dbText

        Case 3
        lngDataType = dbLong

        Case 5
        lngDataType = dbDate

        Case 6
        lngDataType = dbBoolean

        Case 7
        lngDataType = dbLong

        Case 11
        lngDataType = dbText

        Case 12
        lngDataType = dbSingle

        Case 14
        lngDataType = dbCurrency

        Case 18
        lngDataType = dbText

        Case 19
        lngDataType = dbText

    End Select
    Debug.Print "Access Data Type: " & lngDataType

    Set fld = tdf.CreateField(strFieldName, lngDataType)
    fld.AllowZeroLength = True
    tdf.Fields.Append fld
Next prp
```

ValidateOnSet

Data Type

Boolean

Description

Indicates whether the value of a Field object is immediately validated when the Value property is set (Jet workspaces only). If **True**, the value is checked when the Value property is set; if **False**, it is validated when the record is updated. Only Field objects in Recordset objects support this property as read/write.

 Setting ValidateOnSet to **True** can be useful when records include large amounts of data in Memo fields, since it saves time in writing lengthy Memo data when the validation rule has been broken in another field.

ValidationRule

Data Type

String

Description

An expression used to validate data in a field as it is changed or added to a table (Jet workspaces only). The expression has the form of a SQL **WHERE** clause without the **WHERE** reserved word. Field validation rules can only refer to the field itself, not to user-defined functions, SQL aggregate functions, or queries. If the ValidateOnSet property for the field is **False**, the ValidationRule property setting is ignored.

For unappended fields this property is read/write. The read/write characteristics of the property for appended fields are shown in Table 13-17.

Table 13-17. Read/Write Characteristics of the ValidationRule Property for Various Objects

Object Type of Fields Collection	Read/Write Status
Index object	Not supported
QueryDef object	Read-only
Recordset object	Read-only
Relation object	Not supported
TableDef object	Read/write

VBA Code

The code sample lists the ValidationRule and ValidationText properties of all fields in all tables in the sample Northwind database (skipping fields with no validation rules):

```
Private Sub cmdValidationRule_Click()

On Error GoTo ErrorHandler

    Dim dbs As Database
    Dim tdf As TableDef
    Dim fld As Field

    Set dbs = OpenDatabase("D:\Documents\Northwind.mdb")
    For Each tdf In dbs.TableDefs
       Debug.Print tdf.Name & " fields:"
       For Each fld In tdf.Fields
          If fld.ValidationRule <> "" Then
             Debug.Print fld.Name
             Debug.Print vbTab & "Validation rule: " & fld.ValidationRule
             Debug.Print vbTab & "Validation text: " & fld.ValidationText
          End If
       Next fld
    Next tdf

ErrorHandlerExit:
    Exit Sub

ErrorHandler:
    MsgBox "Error No: " & err.Number & "; Description: " & err.Description
    Resume ErrorHandlerExit

End Sub
```

ValidationText

Data Type

String

Description

The text of the message displayed when a Field object fails to pass the Validation-Rule test. This property is read/write for unappended fields; for appended fields, see Table 13-18.

Table 13-18. Read/Write Characteristics of the ValidationText Property

Object Type of Fields Collection	Read/Write Status
Index object	Not supported
QueryDef object	Read-only

Table 13-18. Read/Write Characteristics of the ValidationText Property (continued)

Object Type of Fields Collection	Read/Write Status
Recordset object	Read-only
Relation object	Not supported
TableDef object	Read/write

See the code sample for the ValidationRule property for usage of the Validation-
Text property as well.

Value

Data Type

Variant

Description

The value of a Field object; this property is most commonly used to retrieve or
edit data in Recordset fields. Value is the default property of Field objects, so it can
be omitted in code, though it is advisable to use it in order to avoid possible confusion. For example, the following two statements appear to be more or less
identical:

```
strCustomer = rst.Fields("ContactName")
Set fld = rst.Fields("ContactName")
```

However, the first line uses the default Value property to retrieve the value of the
ContactName field for the current record. The second line, on the other hand, uses
the default Item property to retrieve the Field object that represents the Contact-
Name column. Changing the first line of code to:

```
strCustomer = rst.Fields("ContactName").Value
```

would remove the ambiguity.

VisibleValue   `RO`

Data Type

Variant

Description

For ODBCDirect workspaces only, returns a value currently in the database that is
newer than the OriginalValue property, as determined by a batch update conflict.

Field Object Methods

AppendChunk

recordset!field.AppendChunk *val*

Argument	Data Type	Description
recordset	Recordset object	The Recordset object containing the Fields collection
field	Field object	A Field object whose Type property is dbMemo or dbLongBinary
val	String	An expression or variable containing the data to append to *field*

Appends data from a String expression to a Memo or Long Binary field in a recordset. This method is used to move data when working with large amounts of data in Memo or Long Binary fields. The first time you use AppendChunk (after an Edit or AddNew call), the data is placed in the field, overwriting any existing data. Thereafter, AppendChunk calls in the same Edit or AddNew session append the new data to the existing data in the field.

VBA Code

The code sample uses the AppendChunk and GetChunk methods to copy bitmap images from one table to another:

```
Private Sub cmdAppendChunk_Click()

On Error GoTo ErrorHandler

    Dim dbs As Database
    Dim rstSource As Recordset
    Dim rstTarget As Recordset

    Set dbs = CurrentDb
    Set rstSource = dbs.OpenRecordset("tblImages")
    Set rstTarget = dbs.OpenRecordset("tblPictures")

    'Add records to target table, using GetChunk and AppendChunk
    'to copy images in chunks.

    Do While Not rstSource.EOF
        rstTarget.AddNew
        Call CopyImage(rstSource![Image], rstTarget![Image])
        rstTarget.Update
        rstSource.MoveNext
        rstTarget.MoveNext
    Loop

ErrorHandlerExit:
```

```
    Exit Sub

ErrorHandler:
    MsgBox "Error No: " & err.Number & "; Description: " & _
        err.Description
    Resume ErrorHandlerExit

End Sub

Function CopyImage(fldSource As Field, fldTarget As Field)

On Error GoTo ErrorHandler

    'Set size of chunk in bytes.
    Const conChunkSize = 32768

    Dim lngOffset As Long
    Dim lngTotalSize As Long
    Dim strChunk As String

    'Copy an image from one Recordset to the other in 32K
    'chunks until the entire field is copied.
    lngTotalSize = fldSource.FieldSize
    Do While lngOffset < lngTotalSize
        strChunk = fldSource.GetChunk(lngOffset, conChunkSize)
        fldTarget.AppendChunk strChunk
        lngOffset = lngOffset + conChunkSize
    Loop

ErrorHandlerExit:
    Exit Function

ErrorHandler:
    MsgBox "Error No: " & err.Number & "; Description: " & _
        err.Description
    Resume ErrorHandlerExit

End Function
```

CreateProperty

```
Set property = object.CreateProperty(name, type, value, DDL)
```

Argument	Data Type	Description
property	Property object	The Property object you want to create.
object	A Database, Field, Index, QueryDef, Document, or TableDef object	The object for which you want to create a new property.
name	String	The name of the new Property object.
type	Variant	A named constant or Integer value (see Table 13-16).

Argument	Data Type	Description
value	Variant	The initial property value (see the Value property section for details).
DDL	Boolean	Indicates whether or not the Property is a DDL (Dynamic Data Language) object. The default value is False. If DDL is True, the Property object can't be changed or deleted unless users have dbSecWriteDef permission.

See the example in the Properties Collection section for usage of this method.

GetChunk

```
variable = recordset!field.GetChunk(offset, bytes)
```

Argument	Data Type	Description
variable	String	Receives the data from field
recordset	Recordset object	The recordset containing the Fields collection
field	Field object	A field whose Type property is set to dbMemo or dbLongBinary
offset	Long	The number of bytes to skip before copying begins
bytes	Long	The number of bytes to return

Like AppendChunk, the GetChunk method is used when working with large amounts of data in Memo or Long Binary fields. GetChunk retrieves data from fields in portions of the specified size.

The syntax in the Help example for GetChunk is incorrect; GetChunk returns a variable, not an object.

To prevent problems, put text data in Memo fields and binary data in Long Binary fields.

See the example for the AppendChunk method for usage of this method.

14

Parameters Collection and Parameter Object

The Parameters collection contains all the Parameter objects in a QueryDef object. The position of the Parameters collection in the DAO object model is shown in Figure 14-1.

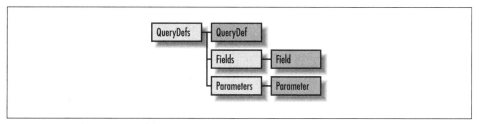

Figure 14-1. The position of the Parameters collection in the DAO object model

A Parameter object represents a value supplied to a query. In the Query Designer interface, parameters are entered into the criteria row of a field, and they may also be entered as specific data types in the Parameters dialog, which is opened from the Query Parameters dialog. To open the Query Parameters dialog, select Parameters from the Query menu of a query open in the Query Designer. Figure 14-2 shows a query with parameters in the Query Designer.

You can use parameters to change the arguments in a QueryDef object without having to recompile the query. The Parameters collection has two properties (see Table 14-1) and one method (see Table 14-2), and the Parameter object has one collection (Properties), four properties (see Table 14-3), and no methods.

A Parameter object can be referenced by any of the following syntax variants:

```
Parameters(0)
Parameters("name")
Parameters![name]
```

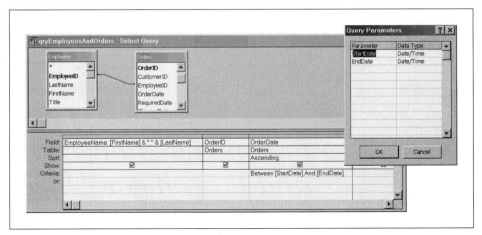

Figure 14-2. A query with parameters in design view

Table 14-1. The Parameters Collection Properties

Property	Description
Count	Indicates the number of Parameter objects in a Parameters collection.
Item	Returns a particular member of the Parameters collection. Although hidden in the DAO type library, it is the default member of the Parameters collection.

Table 14-2. The Parameters Collection Method

Method	Description
Refresh	Refreshes the Parameters collection

Table 14-3. The Parameter Object Properties

Property	Description
Direction	Determines whether the parameter is an input or output parameter (or both)
Name	The name of the parameter
Properties	Returns the Parameter object's Properties collection
Type	The data type of a parameter
Value	The value the parameter will pass to the query

VBA Code

The sample code illustrates using parameters to change a query's arguments based on user input:

```
Private Sub cmdParameters_Click()

On Error GoTo ErrorHandler
```

```
      Dim dbs As Database
      Dim qdf As QueryDef
      Dim prmBegin As Parameter
      Dim prmEnd As Parameter
      Dim dteFirst As Date
      Dim dteLast As Date
      Dim rst As Recordset

      Set dbs = OpenDatabase("D:\Documents\Northwind.mdb")
      Set qdf = dbs.CreateQueryDef("", "PARAMETERS dteStartDate DateTime, " _
         & "dteEndDate DateTime; SELECT [FirstName] & ' ' & [LastName] " _
         & "AS EmployeeName, Orders.OrderID, Orders.OrderDate " _
         & "FROM Orders INNER JOIN Employees ON Orders.EmployeeID = " _
         & "Employees.EmployeeID WHERE Orders.OrderDate Between " _
         & "[dteStartDate] And [dteEndDate] ORDER BY Orders.OrderDate;")
      Set prmBegin = qdf.Parameters!dteStartDate
      Set prmEnd = qdf.Parameters!dteEndDate
      dteFirst = CDate(InputBox("Start date"))
      dteLast = CDate(InputBox("End date"))

      'Feed new parameter values to recordset and print
      'values to the Debug window.
      prmBegin = dteFirst
      prmEnd = dteLast
      Set rst = qdf.OpenRecordset(dbOpenForwardOnly)
      Debug.Print "Printing records from " & prmBegin & " to " & prmEnd

      Do While Not rst.EOF
         Debug.Print "Employee: " & rst!EmployeeName
         Debug.Print "Order date: " & rst!OrderDate
         rst.MoveNext
      Loop

      rst.Close

   ErrorHandlerExit:
      Exit Sub

   ErrorHandler:
      MsgBox "Error No: " & err.Number & "; Description: " & err.Description
      Resume ErrorHandlerExit

   End Sub
```

Access to the Parameter Object
Creatable
No

Returned by
The Parameters property of the QueryDef object

Parameters Collection Properties

Count

Data Type

Integer

Description

Gives the number of Parameter objects in a Parameters collection. In previous versions of Access, Count was useful for setting up loops to process all objects in a collection; however, the `For Each...Next` loop is a more efficient way of iterating through the members of a collection.

Item

```
Parameters.Item(Index)
```

Argument	Data Type	Description
Index	Integer	The ordinal position of the Parameter object in the Parameters collection, or a string containing the name of the Parameter object to be retrieved from the collection

Data Type

Parameter object

Description

A hidden property in the Object Browser, the Item property retrieves a particular Parameter object from the Parameters collection. A Parameter object can be retrieved either based on its ordinal position in the collection or based on its name. Since Parameters is a zero-based collection, the following code fragment returns the first Parameter object:

```
Dim prm As Parameter
Set prm = prms.Item(0)
```

You can also retrieve a particular Parameter object by name. The following code fragment, for instance, retrieves the Parameter object named `"dteBegin"`:

```
Dim prm As Parameter
Set prm = prms.Item("dteBegin")
```

Since the Item property is the default member of the Parameters collection, it does not need to be explicitly specified to retrieve a particular Parameter object. In other words, the following two statements retrieve the same Parameter object:

```
Set prm = prms.Item(0)
Set prm = prms(0)
```

Similarly, the following three statements all retrieve the same Parameter object by name:

```
Set prm = prms.Item("dteBegin")
Set prm = prms("dteBegin")
Set prm = prms![dteBegin]
```

Parameters Collection Methods

Refresh

```
Parameters.Refresh
```

As with the Fields collection, this method is not generally needed, but in some cases it may be desirable to use it, particularly in multiuser environments where other users may add or delete parameters.

Parameter Object Properties

Direction

Data Type

Long

Description

For ODBCDirect workspaces, indicates whether a Parameter object represents an input parameter, an output parameter, both, or the return value from the procedure. It can be any of the constants shown in Table 14-4.

Table 14-4. The Direction Intrinsic Constants

Named Constant	Value	Description
dbParamInput	1	Passes information to the procedure
dbParamInputOutput	3	Passes information both to and from the procedure
dbParamOutput	2	Returns information from the procedure as in an output parameter in SQL
dbParamReturnValue	4	Passes the return value from a procedure

Name `RO`

Data Type

String

Description

The name of a Parameter object.

Properties

Data Type

Properties Collection

Description

Returns a collection that contains all the built-in properties of a Parameter object. (The Parameter object does not support user-defined properties.) The sample code lists the properties of the two parameters from the Parameters code sample.

VBA Code

```
Private Sub cmdProperties_Click()

    Dim dbs As Database
    Dim qdf As QueryDef
    Dim prmBegin As Parameter
    Dim prmEnd As Parameter
    Dim prp As Property

    Set dbs = OpenDatabase("D:\Documents\Northwind.mdb")
    Set qdf = dbs.CreateQueryDef("", "PARAMETERS dteStartDate DateTime, " _
        & "dteEndDate DateTime; SELECT [FirstName] & ' ' & [LastName] " _
        & "AS EmployeeName, Orders.OrderID, Orders.OrderDate " _
        & "FROM Orders INNER JOIN Employees ON Orders.EmployeeID = " _
        & "Employees.EmployeeID WHERE Orders.OrderDate Between " _
        & "[dteStartDate] And [dteEndDate] ORDER BY Orders.OrderDate;")
    Set prmBegin = qdf.Parameters!dteStartDate
    Set prmEnd = qdf.Parameters!dteEndDate

    Debug.Print "prmBegin properties:"
    For Each prp In prmBegin.Properties
        Debug.Print prp.Name
    Next prp

    Debug.Print "prmEnd properties:"
    For Each prp In prmEnd.Properties
        Debug.Print prp.Name
    Next prp
```

```
On Error GoTo ErrorHandler

ErrorHandlerExit:
   Exit Sub

ErrorHandler:
   MsgBox "Error No: " & err.Number & "; Description: " & err.Description
   Resume ErrorHandlerExit

End Sub
```

Type

RO

Data Type

Integer

Description

The data type of a parameter. The Type value settings are listed in Table 14-5.

Table 14-5. The Type Property Intrinsic Constants

Named Constant	Value	Description
dbBigInt	16	Big Integer
dbBinary	9	Binary
dbBoolean	1	Boolean
dbByte	2	Byte
dbChar	18	Character
dbCurrency	5	Currency
dbDate	8	Date/Time
dbDecimal	20	Decimal
dbDouble	7	Double
dbFloat	21	Float
dbGUID	15	GUID
dbInteger	3	Integer
dbLong	4	Long
dbLongBinary	11	Long Binary (OLE Object)
dbMemo	12	Memo
dbNumeric	19	Numeric
dbSingle	6	Single
dbText	10	Text
dbTime	22	Time
dbTimeStamp	23	Time Stamp
dbVarBinary	17	VarBinary

VBA Code

The code sample lists the Name, Type, and Value properties of the two parameters from the Parameters code sample to the Debug window:

```
Private Sub cmdType_Click()

    Dim dbs As Database
    Dim qdf As QueryDef
    Dim prmBegin As Parameter
    Dim prmEnd As Parameter
    Dim dteFirst As Date
    Dim dteLast As Date

    Set dbs = OpenDatabase("D:\Documents\Northwind.mdb")
    Set qdf = dbs.CreateQueryDef("", "PARAMETERS dteStartDate DateTime, " _
        & "dteEndDate DateTime; SELECT [FirstName] & ' ' & [LastName] " _
        & "AS EmployeeName, Orders.OrderID, Orders.OrderDate " _
        & "FROM Orders INNER JOIN Employees ON Orders.EmployeeID = " _
        & "Employees.EmployeeID WHERE Orders.OrderDate Between " _
        & "[dteStartDate] And [dteEndDate] ORDER BY Orders.OrderDate;")
    Set prmBegin = qdf.Parameters!dteStartDate
    Set prmEnd = qdf.Parameters!dteEndDate
    dteFirst = CDate(InputBox("Start date"))
    dteLast = CDate(InputBox("End date"))
    prmBegin = dteFirst
    prmEnd = dteLast

    Debug.Print "Parameter information:"
    Debug.Print vbTab & prmBegin.Name
    Debug.Print vbTab & prmBegin.Type
    Debug.Print vbTab & prmBegin.Value
    Debug.Print vbCrLf
    Debug.Print vbTab & prmEnd.Name
    Debug.Print vbTab & prmEnd.Type
    Debug.Print vbTab & prmEnd.Value

On Error GoTo ErrorHandler

ErrorHandlerExit:
    Exit Sub

ErrorHandler:
    MsgBox "Error No: " & err.Number & "; Description: " & err.Description
    Resume ErrorHandlerExit

End Sub
```

Value

Data Type

Variant

Description

The value of a Parameter object. Value is the default property of Parameter objects, so it can be omitted in code, though it is advisable to use it in order to avoid possible confusion. See the example in the Type section for usage.

15

Indexes Collection and Index Object

Each TableDef object has an Indexes collection that contains all the stored Index objects for that TableDef object (for Jet workspaces only). When using a table-type recordset, the recordset's Index property can be used to specify the order of records by setting it to the name of a stored index belonging to the underlying TableDef object, as in the code sample.

 The Append or Delete method can be used for an index only if the TableDef object's Updatable property is set to **True**.

The position of the Indexes collection and the Index object in the DAO object model is shown in Figure 15-1. The Indexes collection has two properties and three methods, which are shown in Table 15-1 and Table 15-2, respectively. The Index object has 10 properties (shown in Table 15-3) and 2 methods (shown in Table 15-4).

Table 15-1. Indexes Collection Properties

Property	Description
Count	Indicates the number of Index objects in an Indexes collection
Item	Returns a particular member of the Indexes collection. Although hidden in the DAO type library, it is the default member of the Indexes collection.

Table 15-2. Indexes Collection Methods

Method	Description
Append	Adds a newly created Index to an Indexes collection

Table 15-2. Indexes Collection Methods (continued)

Method	Description
Delete	Deletes an Index from an Indexes collection
Refresh	Refreshes an Indexes collection

Table 15-3. Index Object Properties

Property	Description
Clustered	Indicates whether the index is a clustered index
DistinctCount	The number of records with a unique key value
Fields	The collection of Fields in an Index
Foreign	Indicates whether the index is a foreign index
IgnoreNulls	Indicates whether to index records with Nulls
Name	The name of an Index
Primary	Indicates whether the index is a primary index
Properties	The collection of Properties in an Index
Required	Indicates whether all records must have a non-Null value in the index field
Unique	Indicates whether an index is a unique (key) index

Table 15-4. Index Object Methods

Method	Description
CreateField	Creates a new field for an index
CreateProperty	Creates a user-defined property for an index

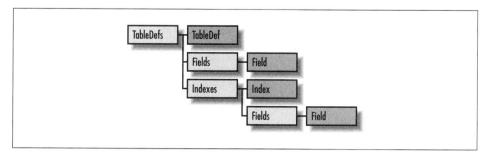

Figure 15-1. The position of the Indexes collection in the DAO object model

VBA Code

```
Private Sub cmdRecordsetIndex_Click()

On Error GoTo ErrorHandler

    Dim dbs As Database
    Dim tdf As TableDef
    Dim idx As Index
```

```
    Dim rst As Recordset

    Set dbs = OpenDatabase("D:\Documents\Northwind.mdb")
    Set tdf = dbs.TableDefs("Suppliers")
    Set rst = tdf.OpenRecordset(dbOpenTable)
    rst.Index = "CompanyName"

    With rst
       Do While Not .EOF
          Debug.Print !CompanyName
          .MoveNext
       Loop
    End With

ErrorHandlerExit:
    Exit Sub

ErrorHandler:
    MsgBox "Error No: " & err.Number & "; Description: " & err.Description
    Resume ErrorHandlerExit

End Sub
```

Access to the Index Object

Creatable

Yes

Returned by

The Indexes property of the Recordset object

The CreateIndex method of the TableDef object

The Indexes property of the TableDef object

Indexes Collection Properties

Count   `RO`

Data Type

Integer

Description

Gives the number of Index objects in an Indexes collection. In previous versions of Access, Count was useful for setting up loops to process all objects in a collection; however, the `For Each...Next` loop is a more efficient way of iterating through the members of a collection.

Item

```
Indexes.Item(Index)
```

Argument	Data Type	Description
Index	Integer	Represents the ordinal position of the Index object in the Indexes collection or a string containing the name of the Index object to be retrieved from the Fields collection

Data Type

Index object

Description

Retrieves a particular Index object from the Indexes collection using the Index number. Item is the default property, so it may be omitted; the following two code fragments are equivalent:

```
Indexes.Item(0)
Indexes(0)
```

Indexes Collection Methods

Append

```
Indexes.Append object
```

This method adds a new Index object designated by the *object* reference to the Indexes collection of a TableDef object, after it has been created using the CreateIndex method. Unlike some other collections, it is necessary to use the Append method after creating an index in order to save the index and add it to the Indexes collection of a TableDef.

VBA Code

The sample code creates a new table and then creates and appends an index for the new table. The table and its index are shown in Figure 15-2.

```
Private Sub cmdAppend_Click()

On Error GoTo ErrorHandler

    Dim dbs As Database
    Dim tdf As TableDef
    Dim idx As Index
    Dim strSQL As String
    Dim strTable As String

    Set dbs = CurrentDb
```

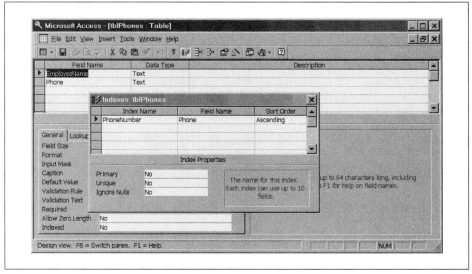

Figure 15-2. A newly created table and index

```
strTable = "tblPhones"
strSQL = "CREATE TABLE " & strTable & _
    "(EmployeeName TEXT (100), Phone TEXT (20));"
DoCmd.RunSQL strSQL
Set tdf = dbs.TableDefs(strTable)
Set idx = tdf.CreateIndex("PhoneNumber")
idx.Fields.Append idx.CreateField("Phone")
tdf.Indexes.Append idx

ErrorHandlerExit:
    Exit Sub

ErrorHandler:
    MsgBox "Error No: " & err.Number & "; Description: " & err.Description
    Resume ErrorHandlerExit

End Sub
```

Delete

```
Indexes.Delete name
```

Deletes an Index object from an Indexes collection, but only if it is a new index belonging to the Indexes collection of a TableDef object that hasn't yet been appended to the database.

VBA Code

```
Private Sub cmdDelete_Click()

On Error GoTo ErrorHandler
```

```
      Dim dbs As Database
      Dim tdf As TableDef
      Dim strTable As String

      Set dbs = CurrentDb
      strTable = "tblPhones"
      dbs.TableDefs(strTable).Indexes.Delete ("PhoneNumber")

   ErrorHandlerExit:
      Exit Sub

   ErrorHandler:
      MsgBox "Error No: " & err.Number & "; Description: " & err.Description
      Resume ErrorHandlerExit

   End Sub
```

Refresh

```
Indexes.Refresh
```

As with the Fields collection, this method is not generally needed, but in some cases it may be desirable to use it, particularly in multiuser environments where other users may add or delete fields.

Index Object Properties

Clustered

Data Type

Boolean

Description

For Jet workspaces only, the Clustered property indicates whether an Index object represents a clustered index or not. By default, its value is **False** for newly created indexes.

A *clustered index* is one in which the physical order of rows is the same as the indexed order; clustered indexes are used by some IISAM (Installable Indexed Sequential Access Method) database formats, such as dBASE, Paradox, and Excel. The property is read/write for unappended indexes and read-only for an index that has been appended to an Indexes collection.

Jet databases ignore the Clustered property since the Jet database engine doesn't support clustered indexes. The Clustered property is always **False** for ODBC data sources.

DistinctCount `RO`

Data Type

Long

Description

For Jet workspaces, DistinctCount gives the number of unique values (or unique keys) for the Index object in the associated table. Basically, it only counts each key once, no matter how many records with that value are in the table (of course, this is only meaningful for an index that allows duplicate values).

 The DistinctCount property may not reflect changes caused by rolled-back transactions or deletion of records with unique keys.

VBA Code

The sample code gives the number of records in the Northwind Customers table and then the number of distinct City records, using the City index of that table:

```
Private Sub cmdDistinctCount_Click()

On Error GoTo ErrorHandler

    Dim dbs As Database
    Dim tdf As TableDef
    Dim rst As Recordset

    Set dbs = OpenDatabase("D:\Documents\Northwind.mdb")
    Set tdf = dbs.TableDefs("Customers")
    Set rst = dbs.OpenRecordset("Customers", dbOpenTable)

    Debug.Print "Number of records in recordset: " _
        & rst.RecordCount
    Debug.Print "Number of distinct records (by city) in recordset:" _
        & tdf.Indexes("City").DistinctCount

ErrorHandlerExit:
    Exit Sub

ErrorHandler:
    MsgBox "Error No: " & err.Number & "; Description: " & err.Description
    Resume ErrorHandlerExit

End Sub
```

Fields

Data Type

Fields Collection

Description

Returns a collection containing the Fields that make up the index. For details on working with the Fields collection object, see Chapter 13, *Fields Collection and Field Object.*

Foreign   `RO`

Data Type

Boolean

Description

Indicates whether an index represents a foreign key in a table, for Jet workspaces only. A *foreign key* consists of one or more fields in a foreign table that uniquely identify all rows in a primary table.

VBA Code

The example lists whether each Northwind table index is a foreign index (skipping system tables, which start with "Msys"):

```
Private Sub cmdForeign_Click()

On Error GoTo ErrorHandler

    Dim dbs As Database
    Dim tdf As TableDef
    Dim idx As Index

    Set dbs = OpenDatabase("D:\Documents\Northwind.mdb")
    For Each tdf In dbs.TableDefs
        If left(tdf.Name, 4) <> "MSys" Then
            Debug.Print vbCrLf & tdf.Name & " indexes:"
            For Each idx In tdf.Indexes
                Debug.Print "Index: " & idx.Name
                Debug.Print "Foreign index? " & idx.Foreign
            Next idx
        End If
    Next tdf

ErrorHandlerExit:
    Exit Sub

ErrorHandler:
```

```
        MsgBox "Error No: " & err.Number & "; Description: " & err.Description
        Resume ErrorHandlerExit

    End Sub
```

IgnoreNulls

Data Type

Boolean

Description

Indicates whether records with Null values in their index fields have index entries (Jet workspaces only). The property is read/write for a new, unappended index and read-only for an index that has been appended to an Indexes collection. Whether a record with a Null index value has an index entry is determined by the settings of the IgnoreNulls and Required properties, as shown in Table 15-5.

Table 15-5. Treatment of Records with Nulls in Index Fields

If IgnoreNulls is	And Required is	Then
True	False	A Null value is allowed in the index field; no index entry is added.
False	False	A Null value is allowed in the index field; an index entry is added.
True or False	True	A Null value isn't allowed in the index field; no index entry added.

Name

Data Type

String

Description

The name of the Index object.

VBA Code

The sample code lists the Name property of all Northwind table indexes (skipping system tables, which start with "MSys"):

```
    Private Sub cmdIndexes_Click()

    On Error GoTo ErrorHandler

        Dim dbs As Database
        Dim tdf As TableDef
```

```
    Dim idx As Index

    Set dbs = OpenDatabase("D:\Documents\Northwind.mdb")
    For Each tdf In dbs.TableDefs
        If left(tdf.Name, 4) <> "MSys" Then
            Debug.Print vbCrLf & tdf.Name & " indexes:"
            For Each idx In tdf.Indexes
                Debug.Print idx.Name
                Debug.Print "Required? " & idx.Required
            Next idx
        End If
    Next tdf

ErrorHandlerExit:
    Exit Sub

ErrorHandler:
    MsgBox "Error No: " & err.Number & "; Description: " & err.Description
    Resume ErrorHandlerExit

End Sub
```

Primary

Data Type

Boolean

Description

Indicates whether an index is a primary index for a table (Jet workspaces only). (A *primary index* has unique values for each record in the table.) The property is read/write for a new, unappended index and read-only for an index that has been appended to an Indexes collection. If the index has been appended to a TableDef object that hasn't been appended to the TableDefs collection, the Index property is read/write.

Setting the Primary property to **True** also causes the index's Unique property to be set to **True**.

When you set a primary key for a table, it becomes the primary index for the table.

VBA Code

For Northwind tables (other than system tables), the example lists whether each index is a primary index:

```
Private Sub cmdPrimary_Click()

On Error GoTo ErrorHandler

    Dim dbs As Database
    Dim tdf As TableDef
    Dim idx As Index

    Set dbs = OpenDatabase("D:\Documents\Northwind.mdb")
    For Each tdf In dbs.TableDefs
       If left(tdf.Name, 4) <> "MSys" Then
          Debug.Print vbCrLf & tdf.Name & " indexes:"
          For Each idx In tdf.Indexes
             Debug.Print "Index: " & idx.Name
             Debug.Print "Primary index? " & idx.Primary
          Next idx
       End If
    Next tdf

ErrorHandlerExit:
    Exit Sub

ErrorHandler:
    MsgBox "Error No: " & err.Number & "; Description: " & err.Description
    Resume ErrorHandlerExit

End Sub
```

Required

Data Type

Boolean

Description

For an Index object, the Required property indicates whether all index fields must have a non-Null value. The property is read/write for a new, unappended index and read-only for an index that has been appended to an Indexes collection in a Recordset or TableDef object.

 There is a table in the Help topic that incorrectly lists the Required property as not supported for Indexes. (See the Name section for code using this property, which definitely is supported.)

If you have a choice of setting the Required property for a field or an index, set it for the field, as a field will be checked before an index.

Unique

Data Type

Boolean

Description

For Jet workspaces only, indicates whether an index is a unique (key) index for a table. This property is read/write until the index is appended to a collection, and read-only after it is appended. A unique index arranges all records in a table in a unique, predefined order. If the index has only one field, each record must have a unique value in that field; if it is a multifield index, each combination of the index fields must be unique.

Index Object Methods

CreateField

```
Set field = index.CreateField(name, type, size)
```

Argument	Data Type	Description
field	Field object	The field you are creating
index	Index object	The index for which you are creating the new field
name	String	(Optional) The name of the new field; it may be up to 64 characters in length
type	Integer	Ignored when creating index fields
size	Integer	Ignored when creating index fields

 You can't delete a field from a TableDef object's Fields collection after you create an index that uses the field, until you have first deleted the index.

Creates a new Field object for an Index (for Jet workspaces only). You can change the name before appending the field to the Fields collection of the Index object. See the Append section for an example that uses this method.

CreateProperty

```
Set property = index.CreateProperty(name, type, value, DDL)
```

Argument	Data Type	Description
property	Property object	An object variable representing the property you are creating.
index	Index object	An index object variable used to create the new property.
name	String	(Optional) The name of the new property. Property names can be up to 64 characters in length.
type	Integer	(Optional) A named constant or Integer value indicating the property's data type (see the entry for the Type property in Chapter 16, *Properties Collection and Property Object*).
value	Variant	(Optional) The initial property value.
DDL	Boolean	(Optional) If **True**, the Property is a DDL object, and users can't change or delete it unless they have **dbSecWriteDef** permission. If **False**, it is not a DDL object and can be changed or deleted by users.

Creates a new user-defined Property object in the Properties collection of an Index object, for Jet workspaces only.

You don't have to assign values to all the arguments when you create a property; you can set them later, before you append the Property to the Index object. After appending, some (but not all) of the property settings can be altered.

If you try to create a property with a name that already exists in the index's Properties collection (such as the name of a built-in property), an error occurs.

16

Properties Collection and Property Object

Except for the Connection and Error objects, there is a Properties collection in every DAO object. Even a Property object (a member of a Properties collection) itself includes a Properties collection. The Properties collection automatically includes built-in Property objects (usually just called properties). Additionally, you can create user-defined properties with the CreateProperty and Append methods of the object that contains the collection, as in the code sample for the Append method.

A property can be referenced using any of the following syntax variants (the syntax is the same for built-in and user-defined properties):

```
object.Properties(0)
object.Properties("name")
object.Properties![name]
```

For built-in properties (only), the following short syntax can also be used:

```
object.name
```

 If you try to read a write-only property (such as the Password or PID property of a Workspace object) or if you try to read or write a property in an inappropriate context, you will get an error.

The same syntax is used to reference a Property object or its default Value property, depending on the context of the reference.

The Properties collection has two properties and three methods, shown in Table 16-1; the Property object has one collection (Properties) and four properties, shown in Table 16-2.

Table 16-1. Members of the Properties Collection

Type	Name	Description
Property	Count	The number of Property objects in the Properties collection.
Property	Item	Returns a particular member of the Properties collection. Although hidden in the DAO type library, it is the default member of the Properties collection.
Method	Append	Adds a new user-defined Property to the Properties collection.
Method	Delete	Deletes a user-defined Property from the Properties collection.
Method	Refresh	Refreshes the Properties collection.

Table 16-2. Members of the Property Object

Type	Name	Description
Property	Inherited	Whether the property is inherited from an underlying object
Property	Name	The property's name
Collection	Properties	The property's Properties collection
Property	Type	The data type of the property
Property	Value	The value stored in the property

Access to the Property Object

Creatable

No

Returned by

The Properties property of the Container object
The CreateProperty method of the Database object
The Properties property of the Database object
The Properties property of the DBEngine object
The CreateProperty method of the Document object
The Properties property of the Document object
The CreateProperty method of the Field object
The Properties property of the Field object
The Properties property of the Group object
The CreateProperty method of the Index object
The Properties property of the Index object
The Properties property of the Parameter object
The Properties property of the Property object
The CreateProperty method of the QueryDef object
The Properties property of the QueryDef object

The Properties property of the Recordset object
The Properties property of the Relation object
The CreateProperty method of the TableDef object
The Properties property of the TableDef object
The Properties property of the User object
The Properties property of the Workspace object

Properties Collection Properties

Count `RO`

Data Type

Integer

Description

The number of properties in a Properties collection. In previous versions of Access, Count was useful for setting up loops to process all objects in a collection; however, the `For Each...Next` loop is a more efficient way of iterating through the members of a collection (see the Append section for an example of using `For Each...Next` to process all members of the Properties collection).

Item `RO`

```
Properties.Item(Index)
```

Argument	Data Type	Description
Index	Integer	Represents the ordinal position of the property in the Properties collection or a string containing the name of the property to be retrieved from the Properties collection

Data Type

Property object

Description

Retrieves a particular Property object from the Properties collection, using the index number or the property name. Item is the default property, so it may be omitted; the following two code fragments are equivalent:

```
Properties.Item(0)
Properties(0)
```

Properties Collection Methods

Append

```
Properties.Append object
```

Argument	Data Type	Description
object	String	A reference to the Property object being added to the collection

Adds a new user-defined property to the Properties collection of an object (for Jet workspaces only).

VBA Code

The sample code creates a new property for a field in the Northwind Employees table then lists all the properties of that field to the Debug window:

```
Private Sub cmdAppend_Click()

    Dim dbs As Database
    Dim prp As Property
    Dim prpNew As Property
    Dim tdf As TableDef
    Dim strDBName As String
    Dim fld As Field

    strDBName = "D:\Documents\Northwind.mdb"
    Set dbs = OpenDatabase(strDBName)
    Set tdf = dbs.TableDefs("Employees")
    Set fld = tdf.Fields("LastName")
    Set prpNew = fld.CreateProperty("NewUserProp", dbBoolean, False)
    fld.Properties.Append prpNew

    'Enumerate field properties.
    Debug.Print "Properties of the " & fld.Name & " field:"
    For Each prp In fld.Properties
        If prp.Name <> "" Then
            On Error Resume Next
            Debug.Print prp.Name & " = " & prp
        End If
    Next prp

End Sub
```

Delete

`collection.Properties.Delete name`

Argument	Data Type	Description
`collection`	Any type of DAO object except a Connection or Error object	The object the Properties collection belongs to
`name`	String	The name of the user-defined property to delete

Deletes a user-defined property from a Properties collection. Built-in properties can't be deleted from a Properties collection.

VBA Code

The code deletes the user-defined property added in the Append section code:

```
Private Sub cmdDelete_Click()

    Dim dbs As Database
    Dim prp As Property
    Dim prpNew As Property
    Dim tdf As TableDef
    Dim strDBName As String
    Dim fld As Field

    strDBName = "D:\Documents\Northwind.mdb"
    Set dbs = OpenDatabase(strDBName)
    Set tdf = dbs.TableDefs("Employees")
    Set fld = tdf.Fields("LastName")
    fld.Properties.Delete "NewUserProp"

    'Enumerate field properties.
    Debug.Print "Properties of the " & fld.Name & " field:"
    For Each prp In fld.Properties
        If prp.Name <> "" Then
            On Error Resume Next
            Debug.Print prp.Name & " = " & prp
        End If
    Next prp

End Sub
```

Refresh

`Properties.Refresh`

Updates a Properties collection to reflect recent changes. Normally, you don't need to refresh the Properties collection, but in some cases it may be desirable to use this method, particularly in multiuser environments where other users may add or delete user-defined properties.

Property Object Properties

Inherited

Data Type

Boolean

Description

Indicates whether a property is inherited from an underlying object. For built-in properties, Inherited is always **False**; for user-defined properties, it can be **True**. For example, if a user-defined property is created for a TableDef object, and a recordset is created based on the TableDef, the property will be inherited by the Recordset object.

 This property appears to be buggy. Running the following code reveals that the new user-defined property that the recordset inherited from the TableDef actually has its inherited property set to **False**; it should be **True**.

VBA Code

This code illustrates creating a user-defined property for a table, then creating a recordset based on the table, and listing its properties, noting whether they are inherited:

```
Private Sub cmdInherited_Click()

    Dim dbs As Database
    Dim tdf As TableDef
    Dim rst As Recordset
    Dim prp As Property
    Dim prpNew As Property

    Set dbs = OpenDatabase("D:\Documents\Northwind.mdb")
    Set tdf = dbs.TableDefs("Employees")
    Set prpNew = tdf.CreateProperty("Special", dbBoolean, False)
    tdf.Properties.Append prpNew
    Set rst = tdf.OpenRecordset

    'Enumerate recordset properties.
    For Each prp In rst.Properties
        Debug.Print prp.Name & " = " & prp.Name
        Debug.Print "Inherited? " & prp.Inherited
    Next prp
```

```
        rst.Close
        dbs.Close

    End Sub
```

Name

Data Type

String

Description

The name of the property. The Name property is read-write so long as the property has not yet been appended to a Properties collection; it is read-only after the property has been appended. The name must start with a letter and can include numbers and underscore characters, but not punctuation or spaces. It can be up to 64 characters in length. See the code sample in the Append section for usage of this property.

Type

Data Type

Integer

Description

The data type of a property. The Type value settings are listed in Table 16-3. See the code sample in the Append section for usage of the Type property when creating a user-defined property.

Table 16-3. The Type Property Intrinsic Constants

Named Constant	Value	Description
dbBigInt	16	Big Integer
dbBinary	9	Binary
dbBoolean	1	Boolean
dbByte	2	Byte
dbChar	18	Character
dbCurrency	5	Currency
dbDate	8	Date/Time
dbDecimal	20	Decimal
dbDouble	7	Double
dbFloat	21	Float
dbGUID	15	GUID

Table 16-3. The Type Property Intrinsic Constants (continued)

Named Constant	Value	Description
dbInteger	3	Integer
dbLong	4	Long
dbLongBinary	11	Long Binary (OLE Object)
dbMemo	12	Memo
dbNumeric	19	Numeric
dbSingle	6	Single
dbText	10	Text
dbTime	22	Time
dbTimeStamp	23	Time Stamp
dbVarBinary	17	VarBinary

Value

Data Type

Variant

Description

The data stored in the property; its data type corresponds to the Type property of the property. Value is the default property of Property objects, so it is not necessary to specify it, although it is advisable to do so to avoid ambiguity in code. For example, the following two statements appear to be more or less identical:

```
blnSpecialCustomer = tdf.Properties("Special")
Set prp = tdf.Properties("Special")
```

However, the first line uses the default Value property to retrieve the value of the Special user-defined Boolean property. The second line, on the other hand, uses the default Item property to retrieve the Property object itself. Changing the first line of code to:

```
blnSpecialCustomer = tdf.Properties("Special").Value
```

would remove the ambiguity.

VBA Code

```
Private Sub cmdValue_Click()

    Dim dbs As Database
    Dim tdf As TableDef
    Dim prp As Property
    Dim blnSpecialCustomer As Boolean

    Set dbs = OpenDatabase("D:\Documents\Northwind.mdb")
```

```
    Set tdf = dbs.TableDefs("Employees")

    'Enumerate recordset properties.
    blnSpecialCustomer = tdf.Properties("Special")
    Set prp = tdf.Properties("Special")
    Debug.Print "Special customer? " & blnSpecialCustomer
    Debug.Print "Property name: " & prp.Name
    dbs.Close

End Sub
```

Object Model Browser

For most Visual Basic programmers, two tools for browsing type libraries are readily available:

- The Object Browser*, which is included both in Visual Basic and in the Visual Basic Editor provided with hosted versions of VBA. The Object Browser can be accessed by pressing the F2 key or by selecting the Object Browser option from the View menu. Figure A-1 shows the Object Browser displaying information about the objects of the VB library in the left pane and the members of the Label control in the right.

- The OLE/COM Object Viewer (commonly known as OLEView), which is a more low-level tool suitable for viewing interface information and registry information, and for examining type libraries directly. Figure A-2 shows OLE-View displaying the type library information for the Visual Basic Library in the left pane and for the _Label interface (which defines the members of the Label control) in the right.

Notice that, to the degree that both tools offer a graphical view of type libraries (though in the case of OLEView, that degree is rather limited), they depict objects in a linear way. That is, their graphical interfaces make it fairly easy to determine what objects exist and to find out what the members (i.e., the properties, methods, and events) of those objects are. But because their focus is on an object and its members, they make it very difficult to determine how a particular object and its members fit into an object model. Yet, this information is very important when instantiating an object, as well as in those cases where it is necessary to navigate from one object to another object in a particular model.

---

* This is a special version of the Object Model Browser, which was developed by Dr. Steven Roman and is Copyright 1999 The Roman Press, Inc.

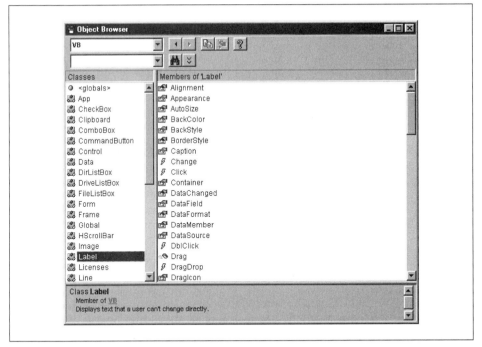

Figure A-1. The Object Browser

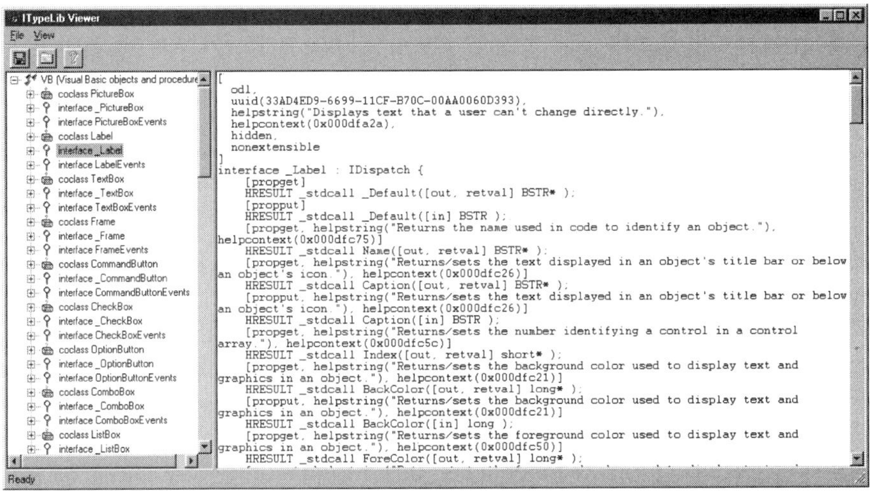

Figure A-2. OLEView

Imagine, for instance, that you want your code to retrieve a reference to an open database named MyDB. The Object Browser simply tells you that the Database object exists in DAO; it doesn't tell you how to navigate to a particular Database object from the top of the hierarchy. How, then, might you do it? The following seems possible:

```
Dim dbs As Database
Set dbs = DBEngine.Databases("MyDB")
```

This, however, doesn't work, since the Databases collection is returned by the Databases property of the Workspace object. In other words, if you start at the DBEngine object at the top of the DAO object hierarchy, you'd need a code fragment like the following to retrieve the reference to the MyDB Database object:

```
Dim dbs As Database
Set dbs = DBEngine.Workspaces(0).Databases("MyDB")
```

Object Model Browser, on the other hand, was designed to depict object hierarchies and therefore successfully depicts the path to a Database object within the DAO object model, as Figure A-3 shows.

Object Model Browser has the following system requirements:
— Windows 9x, Windows NT 4.0, or Windows 2000
— A screen resolution of 800 by 600 or higher

Installation

Object Model Browser uses a standard installation program in which a setup program (named *setup.exe*) uncompresses a CAB file. The steps in installing the program are:

1. Run *setup.exe*, located in the root directory of the CD-ROM. You can do this in the usual way using the Start menu's Run command, through the Control Panel's Add/Remove Programs applet, or by double clicking on *setup.exe* in an Explorer window.

2. The program will copy temporary files required for the installation, as well as check a number of system libraries to determine whether they are up-to-date. If it finds that the installation files include any later versions of system DLLs, a dialog like the one shown in Figure A-4 appears. Click the OK button. When all system files have been updated, a dialog will inform you that the system must be rebooted. Click Yes to continue.

3. When the installation program's startup dialog (shown in Figure A-5) appears, select the directory in which the Object Model Browser will be installed by clicking on the Change Directory button. By default the Object Model Browser

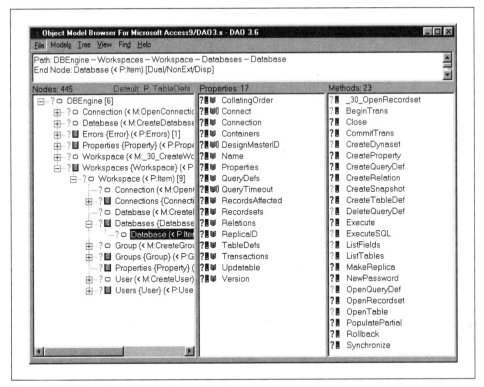

Figure A-3. The path to the Database object

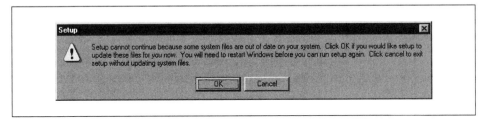

Figure A-4. Updating system files

is installed in *C:\Program Files\Object Model Browser 2\???*, where *???* is the name of the particular version of Object Model Browser that you are installing. For example, it might be *OMB2_DAO3* or *OMB2_Access9*.

4. Click the setup button in the upper-left portion of the dialog to begin the actual installation.

5. The installation program will display a dialog asking which program group on the Start menu you'd like to contain the Object Model Browser's icon. You can select an existing group or enter the name of a new one. When the installa-

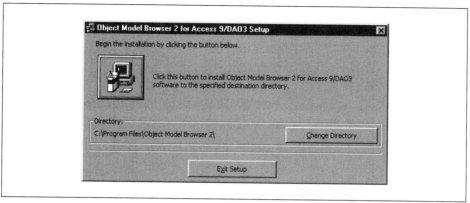

Figure A-5. The installation's startup dialog

tion program finishes, you may also want to create a shortcut to the Object Model Browser on your desktop.

The installation program itself installs the necessary executable files on your system, but doesn't actually collect any object model information. To do this, you must complete the installation by launching the Object Model Browser. The steps are as follows:

1. Start the Object Model Browser. After you close the Welcome window, select the Create Model Wizard option from the File menu. This produces the Create Model Wizard dialog shown in Figure A-6.

2. The easiest way to initialize the DAO object model information is to select the Registry option button, then click on the Read Registry button. Then you can select the Microsoft DAO **x.x** Object Library item from the list box, where **x.x** is the particular version of DAO whose library is available on your system and whose object model is of interest to you. However, there are two other ways to indicate which type library you'd like Object Model Browser configured to display:

   — If you know the physical location of the type library, you can navigate to it directly by making sure the Browse option button is checked (the default) and selecting it from the file list box once you have navigated to the correct directory.

   — You can search for the DAO library that you'd like to install (click on the Search option button, select the drive that you'd like to search for type libraries, and click the Search button) and select the particular version of DAO library that you'd like to access.

3. Click the Make Data File button. Note that the result of this step is a *.DAT* file. If you've already created that *.DAT* file previously, you can also reload it by

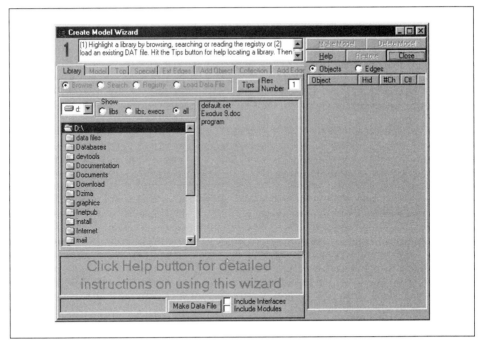

Figure A-6. The Create Model Wizard dialog

selecting the Load Data File option button and selecting the data file containing the object model you'd like to access.

4. Click the Make Model button in the upper-right portion of the window.

Note that you can create object model information for the DAO 3.5, DAO 3.51, and DAO 3.6 object libraries, and that the basic procedure outlined in steps 2 through 4 must be repeated for every object model you wish to make available to the Object Model Browser.

Uninstalling Object Model Browser

To uninstall Object Model Browser, use the Control Panel's Add/Remove Programs applet. Select the application in the list box then click the Add/Remove button. When the program has finished, you will also need to erase any remaining files from the Object Model Browser directories and remove those directories.

DLL Access Violations

If you receive a "???.DLL Access Violation" error message during installation (for example "MSVCRT.DLL Access Violation"), it means that a program currently running on your system is using this DLL, thereby preventing the installation program from overwriting the file with a newer version. You have two choices:

- You can try just hitting the Ignore button and proceeding with the installation. The newer version of *MSVCRT.DLL* (or whatever the filename of the DLL is) will not be copied to your system, but our tests indicate that this *may* still work.

- If you want (or need) to install the new DLL, shut down ALL running programs. Unfortunately, this may include behind-the-scenes programs such as virus checkers or PCMCIA card services. In extreme cases, you may even need to remove all programs from startup folders and reboot, then try the installation again.

If this doesn't work and you are grimly determined, there is another procedure that we have used from time to time in other circumstances, but it is not for the fainthearted (and we cannot help you if you get into trouble, so we recommend it only for experienced PC users):

1. Reboot the computer to Windows Command Prompt Only mode. This should free up the DLL. (If it doesn't, you can also try booting to DOS using a DOS disk.)

2. Copy the offending DLL to a floppy disk. Carefully rename the offending DLL on your hard disk, say by changing its file extension from *.DLL* to *.DLLOld* so you can easily spot the file.

3. Extract the newer DLL from the *ObjectBrowser.CAB* file on the CD to a temporary location on your hard disk. Use the *Extract.exe* program found on the Windows source disk, with the syntax:

   ```
   extract PathandNameToCabFile FileToExtract /l DestinationPath
   ```

   You can use the syntax:

   ```
   extract /?
   ```

   to get the complete syntax for the extract program.

4. Copy the newly extracted DLL to the location of the older DLL (probably the Windows System folder) and reboot to Windows in the normal manner.

5. If for some reason the reboot fails, reboot to Command Prompt only (or to DOS) and replace the newer DLL with the older (original) version.

You should now be able to run Object Model Browser's installation program without problems.

Using the Object Browser

The Object Browser is a complete type library browser that offers a complete set of features, including:

- The ability to display the path to any object, which includes not only that object's place in the object model, but the names of all objects containing members that return that object

- The capability to search for any class or class member

- Integration with the relevant library's help file

- The ability to save and restore views of a particular object model

Although for the most part the interface of the Object Model Browser is quite intuitive, in this section we'll examine some of the more unique features that can be of particular value in your programming.

Accessing an Object Model

Once you've followed the steps outlined in the earlier section, "Installation," to create a browsable object model for Object Model Browser, you can access it by selecting the Models menu option. An Open Object Model dialog like the one shown in Figure A-7 appears, allowing you to choose the object model the viewer should display.

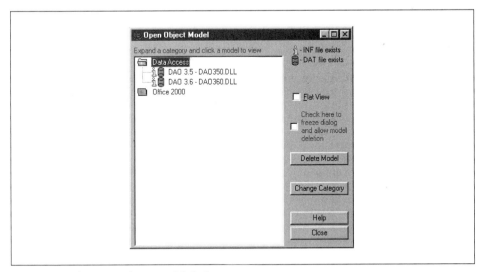

Figure A-7. The Open Object Model dialog

Instantiating a New or Existing Object

One of the questions that always arises when working with an object model is how to instantiate a particular kind of object. This is an area where, unless you already know the answer, Microsoft's Object Browser is not likely to be of much help. This is because, in addition what might be termed the "navigational properties" that return a reference to a contained object or collection, many objects also have methods that return other objects.

To take an example, how do you instantiate a Recordset object using DAO? The most obvious way is to navigate to it. For instance, within the DAO object model, the Recordset object is a member of the Recordsets collection of a particular Database object. So assuming that a Recordset object already exists, you can retrieve a reference to it by simply navigating to it in the object hierarchy, as the following code fragment does:

```
Set rs = DBEngine.Workspaces(0).Databases(0).Recordsets(0)
```

Frequently, however, you want to create a recordset. One of the most common ways to do this uses the **New** keyword either in the object variable declaration or the object assignment. Not all object variables, however, are creatable. The Microsoft Object Browser offers no help here, but the Object Model Browser does. To determine whether an object is externably creatable, you can select the Creatable Objects option from Object Model Browser's View menu. The resulting dialog lists all the externally creatable objects in the DAO object model. As you can see from Figure A-8, the Recordset object is not listed; it cannot be created using the **New** keyword or by calling the VBA *CreateObject* function.

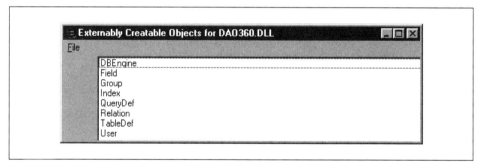

Figure A-8. The Externally Creatable Objects dialog

Since Recordset objects are not creatable, it follows that new recordsets must be returned by one or more recordset creation functions (that is, properties or methods). Graphically, the Object Model Browser depicts this by showing an object returned by the method of another object as the child of that object. For instance, take a look at Figure A-9, which depicts the Database object as a child of the

DBEngine object. This, however, makes no sense if you want to navigate to a Database object from the top of the DAO object model using the properties of the DBEngine object; the statement:

```
Set db = DBEngine.Database
```

generates an error. However, if you toggle the Show Origins option on the Tree menu on, you'll see why the Database object appears as a child of the DBEngine object: it is returned by the DBEngine's CreateDatabase method. Although you can't navigate to it using the properties of each parent object, you can retrieve an object reference by calling a method.

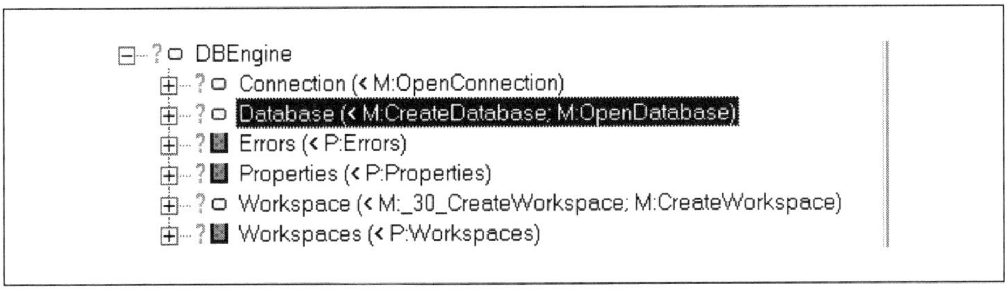

```
⊟··?□ DBEngine
    ⊞··?□ Connection (< M:OpenConnection)
    ⊞··?□ Database (< M:CreateDatabase; M:OpenDatabase)
    ⊞··?▣ Errors (< P:Errors)
    ⊞··?▣ Properties (< P:Properties)
    ⊞··?□ Workspace (< M:_30_CreateWorkspace; M:CreateWorkspace)
    ⊞··?▣ Workspaces (< P:Workspaces)
```

Figure A-9. The Database object as a child of DBEngine

The Object Model Browser also offers some additional facilities to identify how to navigate to, instantiate, or create an object of a particular type. When you select the Find Paths to Object option from the Find menu and enter the name of an object in the resulting dialog, the Object Model Browser opens a window that displays all of the paths to an object of that type. For example, the window shown in Figure A-10 displays each of the 36 possible paths to the Recordset object—that is, each of the 36 possible ways to create a new Recordset object or reference an existing one using the object model's objects, properties, and methods.

If the complete list of paths to a particular object type proves to be overwhelming, an alternative is to select the Find Parents option from the Find menu and to enter the name of the object whose parents you'd like to find in the resulting dialog. The Object Model Browser then opens a window that lists each of the parents of the designated object, along with the property or method that returns or instantiates it. Figure A-11, for example, shows the five parents of the Recordset object, along with the members that return a Recordset object.

Enumerations

Like the Microsoft Object Browser, the Object Model Browser graphically depicts enumerations and their member constants. Unlike the Microsoft Object Browser, enumerations are displayed in a separate window that opens when you select the

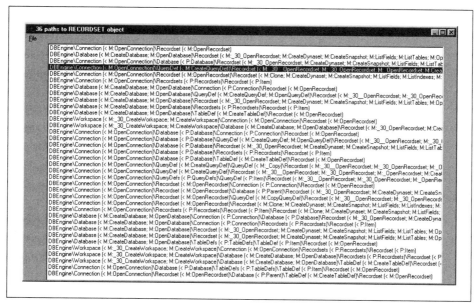

Figure A-10. Paths to the Recordset object

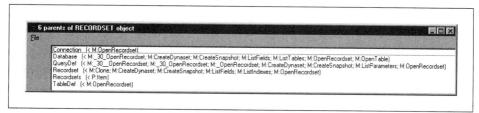

Figure A-11. The parents of the Recordset object

Enums option from the View menu. The enumerations are shown in the window's left pane, while the members of the selected enumeration are shown in the right. Figure A-12 shows the enumerations from the DAO 3.6 type library. Since the `RecordsetTypeEnum` is selected, its member constants (`adOpenTable`, `adOpenDynaset`, etc.) along with their values appear in the right pane.

Along with the enumerations from the type library that you've loaded, the Object Model Browser automatically displays the enumerations defined in the VB library. To display them, select the VB/VBA Enums option from the View menu.

When you select the Create Enum Select Code option from the Enum window's Options menu, the Object Model Browser opens the Enum Select Code window and displays a `Select Case` statement containing the members of a particular

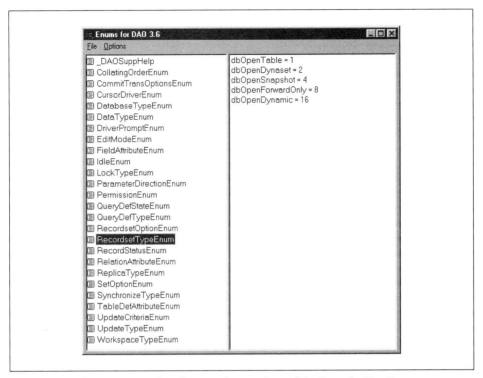

Figure A-12. The Enums window showing the members of the RecordsetTypeEnum enumeration

enumeration. This can be copied to the Clipboard and pasted into your application. For instance, the code produced for the **RecordsetTypeEnum** enumeration is shown in Example A-1.

Example A-1. Code Produced for the Enum Select Code Window

```
Function RecordsetTypeEnumName(lValue As Long) As String
' Returns symbolic name for given value of enum RecordsetTypeEnum.
Dim sName As String
Select case lValue
    Case 1: sName = "dbOpenTable"
    Case 2: sName = "dbOpenDynaset"
    Case 4: sName = "dbOpenSnapshot"
    Case 8: sName = "dbOpenForwardOnly"
    Case 16: sName = "dbOpenDynamic"
    Case Else: sName = "<invalid>"
End Select
RecordsetTypeEnumName = sName
End Function
```

If you're wondering of what practical significance this can be, recall that VBA does absolutely no type or range checking for enumerations. For instance, assuming that your application allows the user to select the recordset type, you might rely on a function like the following to open the recordset:

```
Public Function OpenRS(eRSTypes As RecordsetTypeEnum) As Recordset

Dim rs As Recordset

Set rs = db.OpenRecordset("Employees", eRSTypes)
Set OpenRS = rs

End Function
```

The problem here, though, is that defining *eRSTypes* as a variable of type RecordsetTypeEnum does nothing to guarantee that the value passed to the function will be a member of RecordsetTypeEnum; an invalid value won't be detected until the call to the OpenRecordset method. To guarantee against this, we must check the value of *eRSTypes* to make sure it's a member of RecordSetTypeEnum:

```
Public Function OpenRS(eRSTypes As Long) As Recordset

Dim rs As Recordset

CheckRSTypes eRSTypes

If eRSTypes = 0 Then
    Set rs = Nothing
Else
    Set rs = db.OpenRecordset("Employees", eRSTypes)
End If
Set OpenRS = rs

End Function

Public Sub CheckRSTypes(eRSTypes As Long)

' Test that eRSTypes is a member of RecordSetTypeEnum
Select Case eRSTypes
    Case 1, 2, 4, 8, 16
        ' Do nothing
    Case Else
        eRSTypes = 0
End Select

End Sub
```

In this case, a value of 0 indicates that the original value of *eRSTypes* was not a valid member of the RecordsetTypeEnum enumeration (as does the Recordset object having a value of Nothing). This is perfectly fine, except that it requires a relatively code-intensive approach to each enumeration; you have to hand code each of the values and assign some number that signifies an illegal value (0 in the case of this example) that will be different for each enumeration.

On the other hand, the code produced by the Object Model Browser, like that shown in Example A-1, requires a less code-intensive approach. Whenever the function that performs the validity check returns the string "`<invalid>`" (you could also change this to a null string), the validity check has failed. Because the Object Model Browser generates a complete routine to check whether a value is a valid member of an enumeration, the code that you need to write is extremely simple:

```
Public Function OpenRS(eRSTypes As Long) As Recordset

Dim rs As Recordset

If RecordsetTypeEnumName(eRSTypes) = "<invalid>" Then
    Set rs = Nothing
Else
    Set rs = db.OpenRecordset("Employees", eRSTypes)
End If
Set OpenRS = rs

End Function
```

B

Object Model Browser Reference

Table B-1 documents the menu options available from the Object Model Browser on an item-by-item basis.

Table B-1. Object Model Browser Menu Options

Menu	Menu Item	Description
File	Create Model Wizard	Launches the Create Model Wizard, which generates a data (*.dat*) file for a particular object model.
File	Exit	Closes the Object Model Browser.
Models	—	Opens the Open Object Model dialog, which allows you to select one of the available object models to browse.
Tree	Local View	Provides a more detailed view of a portion of the object model by hiding objects that are not direct parents or children of the selected object. This allows you to see deeper levels under the selected node. Figure B-1 shows an Object pane in local view when the Database object is selected.
Tree	Global View	Provides the fullest view of the object model by displaying objects that are not direct parents or children of the selected object. Figure B-2 shows an Object pane in global view when the Database object is selected.
Tree	Refresh	Reloads the object model but preserves the current local view, if there is one. In addition, it collapses all nodes in the tree.
Tree	Expand All Nodes	Fully expands all nodes in the Objects pane.
Tree	Collapse All Nodes	Fully collapses all nodes in the Objects pane so that only the root node (the DBEngine object) and its children are visible.

Table B-1. Object Model Browser Menu Options (continued)

Menu	Menu Item	Description
Tree	Expand Levels	Opens a dialog that prompts for an integer representing the level to which all nodes should be expanded and optionally for a second integer representing the level beyond which all nodes should be contracted. The root node (i.e., the DBEngine object) is at level 0. For example, entering 2 expands nodes at levels 0–2, while entering 2< expands nodes at levels 0–2 and collapses all higher-level nodes.
Tree	Show Contained Objects	Toggles the display of the name of objects contained in collection objects.
Tree	Show Child Counts	Toggles the display of the number of its child objects beside the name of an object. This information comes from the library itself and thus includes all children, even those not in the current tree.
Tree	Show External Objects	Toggles the display of objects from other libraries that are referenced by the current library.
Tree	Show Hidden Objects	Toggles the display of hidden objects in the current tree.
Tree	Show Flags	Toggles the display of flags for each object in the Object pane. The more common flag settings are shown in Table B-2. Note that most flags are rather technical and not of much direct interest to programmers.
Tree	Show Origins	Toggles the display of the names of the properties and methods of the parent object that return a reference to this (child) object.
Tree	Save View	Saves the current view. The information saved includes the local or global view and the level to which all nodes are expanded.
Tree	Load View	Opens a dialog that allows you either to load or to delete a saved view.
View	Enums	Opens the Enums window, which displays all the enumerations defined in the object model's type library.
View	VB/VBA Enums	Opens the VB/VBA Enums window, which displays all the enumerations defined in the VBA and VB Runtime libraries.
View	Hidden Objects	Opens the Hidden Objects window, which lists the names of objects (not members) that are hidden in the object model. DAO, for instance, includes only one hidden object, IndexFields.
View	Creatable Objects	Opens the Externally Creatable Objects dialog, which lists objects that can be created using the New keyword.
View	Objects and Their Frequencies	Displays a list of all objects in the object library along with the number of times these objects appear in the current tree. (This number could be 0.)
View	All Members	Opens the Members window, which displays an alphabetical list of all the members (properties, methods, enumerated constants) in the current object model.

Table B-1. Object Model Browser Menu Options (continued)

Menu	Menu Item	Description
View	Branch Counts	Displays a list of all objects in the object library and the maximum number of times an object can appear as an *internal* node in the tree. This allows you to change this frequency to "sculpt" the tree.
View	Library Statistics	Opens the Library Statistics window, which displays basic information (such as the name and version) and statistics (such as the number of objects, number of collections, number of readable properties, number of writable properties, number of methods) about the current object model.
View	Options	Opens the Options dialog, which allows customization of the font used by Object Model Browser, as well as the scale factor for the Object Model Browser window in split mode, the object tree indentation value, and a number of other options.
Find	Find Object in Tree	Searches for a designated object in the Object pane.
Find	Find Again	Repeats the previous search.
Find	Find Parents	Opens a dialog listing the parent objects of a designated object. A parent object is any object that has a property or method that returns the designated object.
Find	Find Paths to Object	Prompts for an object name and displays all possible paths to it in the current tree.
Find	Find Objects with Member	Displays a list of the objects having a property or method whose name includes a substring entered by the user.
Help	Help	Opens the Object Model Browser help window with Contents, Index, and Find tabs.
Help	Legend	Opens the Legend window, which explains the icons used in Object Model Browser panes. For a list of icons, see Figure B-2.
Help	Welcome Window	Displays the welcome dialog that typically opens whenever Object Model Browser is launched. (You can suppress this window if desired.)
Help	About	Opens the About dialog, which displays the version number and serial number of Object Model Browser along with contact information for upgrades to OMB.
Help	Upgrade OMB	Upgrades Object Model Browser to the full version of OMB, which can browse virtually any object library.
Help	Library Help File	Opens the help file for the current object library, if one is present on the user's system.
Help	Split mode	Automatically sizes the Object Model Browser window to occupy the top portion of the screen with the precise percentage determined by the Scale Factor for Split Mode value in the Options dialog; the default is 50 percent. The remainder of the screen will be occupied by the Help window of the current object model when help is requested.

Table B-1. Object Model Browser Menu Options (continued)

Menu	Menu Item	Description
Help	AutoHelp	Places the Object Model Browser in split mode (see Help → Split Mode), opens the current object model's help file, keeps the focus on the Object Model Browser window, and automatically opens the appropriate help topic for the object or member selected in the active Object Model Browser pane.
Help	Set Help File Location	Defines the location of the object model's type library.

Table B-2. Flag Values and Their Meanings

Flag	Description
Agg	The object supports aggregation. That is, the object's interfaces are exposed to a container class so that the containing object creates the aggregatable object as part of its creation process and exposes the aggegatable object's interfaces as its own.
AppObj	The object is an application object (not to be confused with an object whose name happens to be Application). The members of Application objects are global.
Auto	The object is fully compatible with Automation and may be displayed in an object browser.
CanCre	Object instances can be created by `ITypeInfo::CreateInstance` (or by Visual Basic's New keyword or *CreateObject* function).
Ctrl	The object is a control from which a container will derive other types. It should not be displayed in object browsers intended for non-visual objects.
Disp	The object's interface derives from `IDispatch`, either directly or indirectly.
Dual	The object supports dual interfaces; that is, it exposes properties and methods through `IDispatch` and directly through the VTBL.
Hid	The object is hidden and should not be displayed to browsers.
Lic	The object is licensed and must be instantiated using `IClassFactory2`.
NonExt	The class' `IDispatch` implementation includes only the properties and methods listed in the interface description; it cannot add additional members at runtime. (By default, Automation supports extending interfaces by adding members at runtime.)
Predef	The object is predefined.
Repl	The object supports `IConnectionPoint` for bidirectional communication.
Rest	The object is restricted and should not be called arbitrarily. Typically, this is a system-level object that should not be accessible from a macro language and that the browser should not display.

Table B-3. Icons Used by Object Model Browser

Icon	Description
	An object.
	A collection object.
	Online help is available.
	Online help is not available.
	The member is not browsable.
	The member is hidden.
	The member is non-browsable and hidden.
	The member is browsable and is not hidden.
	The property is readable.
	The property is writable.

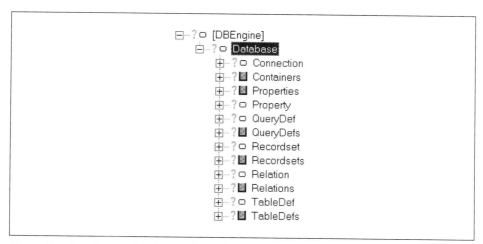

Figure B-1. Local view with the Database object selected

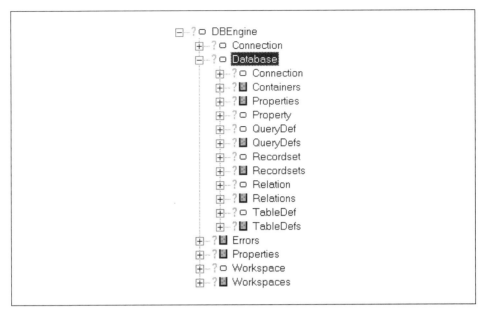

Figure B-2. Global view with the Database object selected

Index

About the Author

Helen Feddema grew up in New York City. She was ready for computers when she was 12, but computers were not ready for her yet, so she got a B.S. in philosophy from Columbia and an M.T.S. in theological studies from Harvard Divinity School, while working at various office jobs. It was at HDS that she got her first computer, an Osborne, and soon computers were her primary interest. She started with word processing and spreadsheets, went on to learn dBASE, and did dBASE development for six years, part of this time as a corporate developer. After being laid off in a flurry of corporate downsizing, she started doing independent consulting and development, using dBASE, ObjectVision, WordPerfect and Paradox.

Always looking for something new and better, Helen beta tested Access 1.0 and soon recognized that this was the database she had been looking for ever since Windows 3.0 was introduced. Since that time, she has worked as a developer of Microsoft Office applications, concentrating on Access, Word, and Outlook.

Helen coauthored *Inside Microsoft Access*, (New Riders, 1992), and wrote two books for Pinnacle's "The Pros Talk Access" series, *Power Forms* and *Power Reports* (1994). She also coauthored *Access How-Tos for the Waite Group Press* (1995), and more recently contributed to *The Microsoft Outlook Handbook* (Osborne-McGraw-Hill), *Que's Special Edition: Using Microsoft Outlook 97* (1997), *Office Annoyances* (O'Reilly & Associates, 1997), and *Outlook Annoyances* (O'Reilly & Associates, 1998). She also contributed chapters to *Que's Special Edition: Using Microsoft Project 98* (1997) and *Teach Yourself Project* (1998). Most recently, Helen coauthored *Sybex' MCSD: Access 95 Study Guide* (1998). She has also been a regular contributor to Pinnacle's *Smart Access* and *Office Developer* journals, *Woody's Underground Office* newsletter, *PC Magazine's Undocumented Office* and the *MS Office and VBA Journal*. She recently contributed articles on Menu Manager and Outlook Automation Access add-ins and Access-Word data merging to *Smart Access*, as well as writing the "Access Archon" column for the *Woody's Office Watch* e-zine.

Helen sometimes beta tests seven or eight products at once, mostly Microsoft, but with some from other vendors as well. She lives in the mid-Hudson area of New York state, with three cats and three computers. Helen maintains a web page (*http://www.ulster.net/~hfeddema*) with a large selection of code samples concentrating on connecting Access, Outlook, Word, and Excel. She is an MVP on the WOPR Lounge, a threaded discussion group devoted to Microsoft Office.

Colophon

Our look is the result of reader comments, our own experimentation, and feedback from distribution channels. Distinctive covers complement our distinctive approach to technical topics, breathing personality and life into potentially dry subjects.

The animal on the cover of *DAO Object Model: The Definitive Reference* is a sparrow hawk (*Accipiter nisus*). "Sparrow hawk" is the common name for several smaller members of the hawk genus. The American kestrel is also commonly called a sparrow hawk, but the kestrel is a falcon that has little in common with the true sparrow hawk except for its small size. The true sparrow hawk is colored a bluish-gray, with brown and white markings. It has a long tail and short wings. The male grows to a length of approximately 11 inches, and the female to 15 inches.

The sparrow hawk is widely distributed throughout Eurasia and North Africa, from Ireland to Japan. As its name implies, this bird of prey feeds on other birds, from the small sparrow to the medium-sized wood pigeon. It will occasionally eat small rodents, but birds make up the majority of its diet. Its preferred habitat is a somewhat open woodland, with plenty of areas of cover from which it can launch surprise attacks on its prey.

Clairemarie Fisher O'Leary was the production editor and the copyeditor for *DAO Object Model: The Definitive Reference*. Maureen Dempsey, Jeff Holcomb, and Nicole Arigo provided quality control. Bruce Tracy wrote the index.

Edie Freedman designed the cover of this book. The cover image is a 19th-century engraving from the Dover Pictorial Archive. Kathleen Wilson produced the cover layout with QuarkXPress 3.32 using Adobe's ITC Garamond font.

Alicia Cech designed the interior layout based on a series design by Nancy Priest. Mike Sierra implemented the design in FrameMaker 5.5. The text and heading fonts are ITC Garamond Light and Garamond Book. The illustrations that appear in the book were produced by Robert Romano and Rhon Porter using Macromedia FreeHand 8 and Adobe Photoshop 5. Kathleen Wilson designed the CD-ROM label. This colophon was written by Clairemarie Fisher O'Leary.

Whenever possible, our books use RepKover™, a durable and flexible lay-flat binding. If the page count exceeds RepKover's limit, perfect binding is used.

How to stay in touch with O'Reilly

1. Visit Our Award-Winning Web Site

http://www.oreilly.com/

★ "Top 100 Sites on the Web" —*PC Magazine*
★ "Top 5% Web sites" —*Point Communications*
★ "3-Star site" —*The McKinley Group*

Our web site contains a library of comprehensive product information (including book excerpts and tables of contents), downloadable software, background articles, interviews with technology leaders, links to relevant sites, book cover art, and more. File us in your Bookmarks or Hotlist!

2. Join Our Email Mailing Lists

New Product Releases
To receive automatic email with brief descriptions of all new O'Reilly products as they are released, send email to:
listproc@online.oreilly.com
Put the following information in the first line of your message (*not* in the Subject field):
subscribe oreilly-news

O'Reilly Events
If you'd also like us to send information about trade show events, special promotions, and other O'Reilly events, send email to:
listproc@online.oreilly.com
Put the following information in the first line of your message (*not* in the Subject field):
subscribe oreilly-events

3. Get Examples from Our Books via FTP

There are two ways to access an archive of example files from our books:

Regular FTP
- ftp to:
  ftp.oreilly.com
  (login: anonymous
  password: your email address)
- Point your web browser to:
  ftp://ftp.oreilly.com/

FTPMAIL
- Send an email message to:
  ftpmail@online.oreilly.com
  (Write "help" in the message body)

4. Contact Us via Email

order@oreilly.com
To place a book or software order online. Good for North American and international customers.

subscriptions@oreilly.com
To place an order for any of our newsletters or periodicals.

books@oreilly.com
General questions about any of our books.

software@oreilly.com
For general questions and product information about our software. Check out O'Reilly Software Online at **http://software.oreilly.com/** for software and technical support information. Registered O'Reilly software users send your questions to: **website-support@oreilly.com**

cs@oreilly.com
For answers to problems regarding your order or our products.

booktech@oreilly.com
For book content technical questions or corrections.

proposals@oreilly.com
To submit new book or software proposals to our editors and product managers.

international@oreilly.com
For information about our international distributors or translation queries. For a list of our distributors outside of North America check out:
http://www.oreilly.com/www/order/country.html

O'Reilly & Associates, Inc.
101 Morris Street, Sebastopol, CA 95472 USA
TEL   707-829-0515 or 800-998-9938
         (6am to 5pm PST)
FAX   707-829-0104

International Distributors

UK, EUROPE, MIDDLE EAST AND AFRICA (EXCEPT FRANCE, GERMANY, AUSTRIA, SWITZERLAND, LUXEMBOURG, LIECHTENSTEIN, AND EASTERN EUROPE)

INQUIRIES
O'Reilly UK Limited
4 Castle Street
Farnham
Surrey, GU9 7HS
United Kingdom
Telephone: 44-1252-711776
Fax: 44-1252-734211
Email: josette@oreilly.com

ORDERS
Wiley Distribution Services Ltd.
1 Oldlands Way
Bognor Regis
West Sussex PO22 9SA
United Kingdom
Telephone: 44-1243-779777
Fax: 44-1243-820250
Email: cs-books@wiley.co.uk

FRANCE

ORDERS
GEODIF
61, Bd Saint-Germain
75240 Paris Cedex 05, France
Tel: 33-1-44-41-46-16 (French books)
Tel: 33-1-44-41-11-87 (English books)
Fax: 33-1-44-41-11-44
Email: distribution@eyrolles.com

INQUIRIES
Éditions O'Reilly
18 rue Séguier
75006 Paris, France
Tel: 33-1-40-51-52-30
Fax: 33-1-40-51-52-31
Email: france@editions-oreilly.fr

GERMANY, SWITZERLAND, AUSTRIA, EASTERN EUROPE, LUXEMBOURG, AND LIECHTENSTEIN

INQUIRIES & ORDERS
O'Reilly Verlag
Balthasarstr. 81
D-50670 Köln
Germany
Telephone: 49-221-973160-91
Fax: 49-221-973160-8
Email: anfragen@oreilly.de (inquiries)
Email: order@oreilly.de (orders)

CANADA (FRENCH LANGUAGE BOOKS)

Les Éditions Flammarion ltée
375, Avenue Laurier Ouest
Montréal (Québec) H2V 2K3
Tel: 00-1-514-277-8807
Fax: 00-1-514-278-2085
Email: info@flammarion.qc.ca

HONG KONG

City Discount Subscription Service, Ltd.
Unit D, 3rd Floor, Yan's Tower
27 Wong Chuk Hang Road
Aberdeen, Hong Kong
Tel: 852-2580-3539
Fax: 852-2580-6463
Email: citydis@ppn.com.hk

KOREA

Hanbit Media, Inc.
Sonyoung Bldg. 202
Yeksam-dong 736-36
Kangnam-ku
Seoul, Korea
Tel: 822-554-9610
Fax: 822-556-0363
Email: hant93@chollian.dacom.co.kr

PHILIPPINES

Mutual Books, Inc.
429-D Shaw Boulevard
Mandaluyong City, Metro
Manila, Philippines
Tel: 632-725-7538
Fax: 632-721-3056
Email: mbikikog@mnl.sequel.net

TAIWAN

O'Reilly Taiwan
No. 3, Lane 131
Hang-Chow South Road
Section 1, Taipei, Taiwan
Tel: 886-2-23968990
Fax: 886-2-23968916
Email: taiwan@oreilly.com

CHINA

O'Reilly Beijing
Room 2410
160, FuXingMenNeiDaJie
XiCheng District
Beijing, China PR 100031
Tel: 86-10-66412305
Fax: 86-10-86631007
Email: beijing@oreilly.com

INDIA

Computer Bookshop (India) Pvt. Ltd.
190 Dr. D.N. Road, Fort
Bombay 400 001 India
Tel: 91-22-207-0989
Fax: 91-22-262-3551
Email: cbsbom@giasbm01.vsnl.net.in

JAPAN

O'Reilly Japan, Inc.
Kiyoshige Building 2F
12-Bancho, Sanei-cho
Shinjuku-ku
Tokyo 160-0008 Japan
Tel: 81-3-3356-5227
Fax: 81-3-3356-5261
Email: japan@oreilly.com

ALL OTHER ASIAN COUNTRIES

O'Reilly & Associates, Inc.
101 Morris Street
Sebastopol, CA 95472 USA
Tel: 707-829-0515
Fax: 707-829-0104
Email: order@oreilly.com

AUSTRALIA

WoodsLane Pty., Ltd.
7/5 Vuko Place
Warriewood NSW 2102
Australia
Tel: 61-2-9970-5111
Fax: 61-2-9970-5002
Email: info@woodslane.com.au

NEW ZEALAND

Woodslane New Zealand, Ltd.
21 Cooks Street (P.O. Box 575)
Waganui, New Zealand
Tel: 64-6-347-6543
Fax: 64-6-345-4840
Email: info@woodslane.com.au

LATIN AMERICA

McGraw-Hill Interamericana
Editores, S.A. de C.V.
Cedro No. 512
Col. Atlampa
06450, Mexico, D.F.
Tel: 52-5-547-6777
Fax: 52-5-547-3336
Email: mcgraw-hill@infosel.net.mx

O'REILLY®

TO ORDER: **800-998-9938** • **order@oreilly.com** • **http://www.oreilly.com/**
OUR PRODUCTS ARE AVAILABLE AT A BOOKSTORE OR SOFTWARE STORE NEAR YOU.
FOR INFORMATION: **800-998-9938** • **707-829-0515** • **info@oreilly.com**

O'REILLY®

O'Reilly & Associates, Inc.
101 Morris Street
Sebastopol, CA 95472-9902
1-800-998-9938

Visit us online at:
www.oreilly.com
order@oreilly.com

O'REILLY WOULD LIKE TO HEAR FROM YOU

Which book did this card come from?

_____

Where did you buy this book?
- ❏ Bookstore   ❏ Computer Store
- ❏ Direct from O'Reilly   ❏ Class/seminar
- ❏ Bundled with hardware/software
- ❏ Other _____

What operating system do you use?
- ❏ UNIX   ❏ Macintosh
- ❏ Windows NT   ❏ PC(Windows/DOS)
- ❏ Other _____

What is your job description?
- ❏ System Administrator   ❏ Programmer
- ❏ Network Administrator   ❏ Educator/Teacher
- ❏ Web Developer
- ❏ Other _____

❏ Please send me O'Reilly's catalog, containing
a complete listing of O'Reilly books and
software.

Name _____   Company/Organization _____

Address _____

City _____   State _____   Zip/Postal Code _____   Country _____

Telephone _____   Internet or other email address (specify network) _____

Nineteenth century wood engraving
of a bear from the O'Reilly &
Associates Nutshell Handbook®
Using & Managing UUCP.

BUSINESS REPLY MAIL

FIRST CLASS MAIL   PERMIT NO. 80   SEBASTOPOL, CA

Postage will be paid by addressee

O'Reilly & Associates, Inc.

101 Morris Street
Sebastopol, CA 95472-9902